A SPOOK'S PROGRESS

A SPOOK'S PROGRESS

FROM MAKING WAR TO MAKING PEACE

MARITZ SPAARWATER

Published by Zebra Press
an imprint of Random House Struik (Pty) Ltd
Reg. No. 1966/003153/07
Wembley Square, First Floor, Solan Road, Gardens, Cape Town 8001
PO Box 1144, Cape Town 8000, South Africa

www.zebrapress.co.za

First published 2012

1 3 5 7 9 10 8 6 4 2

Publication © Zebra Press 2012
Text © Maritz Spaarwater 2012

Cover photographs: old South African flag © Rodger Shagam/africanpix.com;
P.W. Botha © Raymond Preston/Sunday Times; helicopter © Garth Calitz;
F.W. de Klerk and Nelson Mandela © Juda Ngwenya/Reuters/Gallo Images

PUBLISHER: Marlene Fryer
MANAGING EDITOR: Robert Plummer
EDITOR: Bronwen Leak
PROOFREADER: Jane Housdon
COVER AND TEXT DESIGNER: Jacques Kaiser
COVER CONCEPT: Michael Muller
TYPESETTER: Monique van den Berg
INDEXER: Sanet le Roux

Set in 10.5 on 14 pt Minion

Paarl Media, Jan van Riebeeck Drive, Paarl, South Africa

ISBN 978 1 77022 437 7 (print)
ISBN 978 1 77022 438 4 (ePub)
ISBN 978 1 77022 439 1 (PDF)

To Anna, Suzanne, Bosman, Cobus and Lisa, who for so many years were so incompletely aware of what their husband and father was doing, and without whom the writing of this book would not have been worthwhile;

And to Everaad, Mika, Mich and Christiaan, who might someday herein find a clearer image of their grandfather;

And to Sue, who shared ten years of my life.

Contents

Acknowledgements

I am grateful to former colleagues in the South African Defence Force and the National Intelligence Service, and to friends and members of my family who encouraged, cajoled and browbeat me to write this book and generously shared with me their recollections of some of the events I describe in it;

And to my wife, Anna, who had to live with my total absorption in the writing, when for more than a year I had neither the spare time nor the spare attention to share much of either with her;

And to the good people of Zebra Press at Random House Struik, Marlene Fryer, Bronwen Leak and Robert Plummer, for their friendly and professional guidance in taking this book to fruition.

MARITZ SPAARWATER
ONRUS RIVER
2012

The Tree

Two hunters were ruminating around a campfire. The younger of the two asked the *oubaas* what he would do if he were to be charged by a lion:

'I would shoot it, of course,' said the old man.

'But what if you did not have a gun?'

'I would run away as fast as I could,' came the reply.

'What if you were not fast enough?'

'I would look for a stone and hit the lion over the head with it.'

'And if you couldn't find a stone?'

'I would pray as hard as I could.'

'But what if the lion did not know you were praying and kept charging?'

'I would climb into a tree and stay there until it went away.'

'And if you couldn't find a tree?'

The old man thought long and hard, sucking on his pipe with his eyes shut from the effort. After a long pause he eventually opened his eyes and said, slowly and deliberately in a low, firm voice: 'There has to be a tree.'

(Attributed to the late General Hendrik van den Bergh, former head of the Security Branch of the South African Police and of the Bureau for State Security.)

Preface

The intelligence profession places extraordinary demands on those who live and work in it. One's personal and professional lives are indivisible in this world where living and working are one. For the true professional, dedication is absolute; the dividing line between sleeping and waking hours often only notional. The compelling necessity of the principle of 'the need to know', also among colleagues, prevents free discussion of one's work, its pleasures and frustrations, its successes and failures, and its moral and ethical dilemmas. It is essentially a lonely business. Those closest to someone in this line of work must accept and respect these circumstances, or see their relationships crumble.

The incidence of psychological and social problems, with their sometimes devastating impact on family life, is said by experts to be markedly higher in the security community than in society at large. Through the Truth and Reconciliation Commission (TRC) and a spate of criminal prosecutions in the courts, we have been numbed by revelations of the horrifying dehumanisation of the individual that in extreme cases can occur in such an environment. And this profession is closely related to the military, only without the violence, usually. In the South African Defence Force (SADF) it was standing procedure that any soldier who had been involved in three 'contacts' – firefights – on a tour of duty would be relieved and returned home for rest and recuperation. This often did not happen, but it was the rule.

Eugene de Kock, 'celebrated' as 'prime evil' in the media, was over some years, I have been told, involved in 300 contacts while in the highly active and stressful South African Police (SAP) counterinsurgency unit, Koevoet, in South West Africa. This is probably exaggerated, but even if it were only thirty without an opportunity to recover, one can only imagine what it must have done to his psyche. I have been reliably told that De Kock's commanding officer (CO) in Koevoet started to complain that he had, through indiscipline, become unmanageable. De Kock was returned to Pretoria and, lo and behold, appointed to command the police special operations unit infamously known as Vlakplaas. I have never been able to fathom the management culture of the SAP, whether Force or Service, then or now.

There is no stereotype of what makes a good intelligence officer or agent (spy). They come as much in a mixture of ordinary human traits as any other human being, the worst frailties and foibles hopefully being weeded out in stringent psychometric testing and security vetting procedures. However, some peculiarities do seem to manifest more than others in an intelligence worker. Among these is an enquiring mind with a suspicious bent, but with the balance to not base all judgements of people and situations on this mindset. Too much scepticism can turn into paranoia, giving rise to the loss of objectivity through fanciful conclusions based on conspiracy theories. Although balanced scepticism is necessary for a good intelligence analyst, constant vigilance against cynicism and a dumbing-down of reason and independent thought is an essential. The greatest danger is perhaps the common tendency of stereotyped 'group-think' in a close-knit and mutually supportive group of dedicated people fired by the same ideals. There is one trait, however, that is indispensable in an intelligence operator: an aggressive, can-do attitude. The tree has always to be found.

The insularity of the intelligence community tends to breed an exceptional brotherhood of solidarity and personal loyalties, which also carries inherent dangers if not contained by strong ethical imperatives. This brotherhood is confirmed rather than contradicted by cases of treachery that occur from time to time in security and intelligence communities throughout the world. The treason of South African Navy (SAN) Commodore Dieter Gerhardt, who was exposed in 1982 as a Soviet spy, caused immense shock, anguish, anger and demoralisation, however transient, in the SADF, in the Navy in particular.

The intelligence brotherhood also extends across international borders, where cordial institutional relations, personal friendships and mutual respect between individuals and agencies of even adversarial countries exist. This often leads to the unobtrusive and amicable settlement of disputes between states without the public posturing and politicking that sometimes accompany the handling of such disputes through more conventional, overt diplomatic channels. There are many examples of where the brotherhood of the intelligence community has served South Africa well in its often delicate relations with important players in the international arena.

What is perhaps the outstanding element of a career in intelligence, and the most challenging given the stresses it generates, is that it daily brings one into direct contact with the realities of one's subject matter: the security of the state and the forces tending to disturb its stability and general well-being. On the strategic level, the demand is to give decision-makers the best possible overview of those realities as they manifest and develop, including the probable outcomes of such trends, and to do so as objectively and fearlessly as humanly possible. Gut feelings and ideological predilections are the preserve of the political consumers of intelligence and have no place in the processes of producing it.

Stereotypical mindsets, personal convictions, views on ideals to be pursued and the natural optimism of dedicated people, are equal imposters in the search for the 'truth'. There are perennial differences of opinion as to the extent to which intelligence producers should advise on how their intelligence be put to use by way of policy decisions. Where intelligence agencies have the obligation to inform the government on both adverse and favourable developments, it is often impossible to separate such warnings from suggesting what to do about them, especially in the form of anticipation and prediction from a rational, factual basis of what identified trends would most probably lead to. The South African National Security Management System, with considerable success, tried to solve this conundrum by separating its intelligence and executive planning functions. However, the system was sometimes confounded by different conclusions as to what the objective intelligence picture actually was or signified. These were often strongly influenced by the subjective and ideological considerations of the representatives of participating government departments and agencies.

The last three decades of the twentieth century constitute the most significant transformative period in the political history of modern South Africa since the arrival of Jan van Riebeeck at the Cape in 1652. Over this period I had the immense privilege of witnessing events unfold from a sometimes contracted and sometimes expanded periphery, first from the military perspective of making war, and thereafter on the imperatives of making peace from an intelligence perspective.

From the late 1970s, the National Intelligence Service (NIS) was gaining influence, proclaiming that the fundamental security threat to South Africa was internal political conflict and that a negotiated political settlement between South Africans of the country's travails would be the only peaceful road to a solution. The SADF was quite properly determined to fulfil its primary function of providing the coercive force to maintain the integrity of the country's borders and assist in ensuring internal order for as long as necessary to provide time and space for political solutions, the necessity of which they were as convinced of as anyone else. Although there were also strong voices proclaiming that the SADF could make war for ever and a day, the top command structures were consistently resolute in the view that political settlement could be the only ultimate objective. The terms to be sought in such a settlement were, of course, subject to strong differences of opinion.

As will appear further on, after many years in military intelligence I became convinced that the assessments of NIS on the objective realities of South Africa were nearer the truth than those of my then employers, and I moved to that organisation in 1981. It is an eternal indictment on the lack of courage and imagination of the political leadership of the time that they never gave clear direction to resolve these internal divisions.

I'm not sure what really motivates the writing down of these fragmentary and episodic stories. It is certainly at least partly because of the enormous regard, developed over many years of shared fun and frustration and risk and danger, even sorrow, in which I hold so many colleagues at home and abroad, with whom I did not so much work as share a life, and to whom I wish in some way to pay tribute. Perhaps it is the regard I have for my much misunderstood and often misrepresented and maligned profession itself, which makes me want to explain a bit. Importantly, it is in part due to a desire to distance myself and my profession from the immorality and lawlessness that it is now evident prevailed in parts of the system of which we were all members and which, therefore, reflects on us all.

It is also due to a wish to tell a few stories that some people may find interesting and may contribute towards a better understanding of certain episodes of our recent history. I am sometimes disturbed by the distortion of some events and circumstances to which I wish to add some historical perspective where I can. I would certainly also want my children to understand that we were by and large honourable men and women doing our best under demanding circumstances to serve an honourable cause by legitimate means.

I attempt to give some idea of mindsets influenced by political and security events that led me and others like me, in my profession and elsewhere, to develop doubts about aspects of what had in some respects become stereotyped views and reactions regarding the South African condition and how to address the issues involved. This intellectual and moral – even spiritual –

reorientation among crucial decision-makers at all levels that took place over time in the security services and at the political level, eventually opened avenues to new thinking that released the country from the terrible historical bind it had become entangled in over centuries. I have tried to identify seminal events that influenced me and changed my thought processes.

In writing this I have not had access to any classified documents. I tell only of events and incidents in which I was personally involved and which can no longer be regarded as in any way sensitive regarding national interests or the security of the state. In a few cases I refer to related aspects that I was reliably informed of by others, and identify them as such. All of this, of course, happened against the general background tapestry of public events. In refreshing my memory, I have here and there consulted with trusted colleagues who were involved with me and who have either kept notes, which I seldom did, or have better memories than mine. I thank and acknowledge them all but mostly do not mention their names as in the true professional tradition they would prefer me not to.

I lay no claim to any historicity, although I know that every event of importance I describe was properly recorded and documented at the time. Some of them are so old that records would, as standard procedure, by now have long been destroyed. As this is not intended to be a scientific account, I see no need to have the narrative flow disturbed by footnotes. In the text and in a bibliography at the end I acknowledge general sources I have consulted, mostly without specific attribution. Where I have been uncertain of the correctness of my recollections, I have either omitted them or stated my uncertainty.

If I have made mistakes that may discomfort anyone, I sincerely apologise, but not for where the truth as I see it may be a bit disturbing to some people here and there. After all, the distinction between fact and fiction is often subjective and can become a bit blurred, especially in the wonderful profession of which I have been privileged to be a part. And who can tell how nebulous recall can become with the passing of time? I have written this book as an impressionistic rather than historical account, and I recommend that it be read in the same referential frame of mind. I have also embellished the telling of some stories a bit to lighten them up where I thought they were worthy of telling but a little dull. In doing so, I have not deviated from the truth, leaving them fully believable as to the facts. I have taken particular care to ensure that I do not say anything that could even remotely compromise the security of the state, or unnecessarily hurt or embarrass people close to me. Where such a possibility arose, I preferred to say nothing.

Neither my person nor my life story warrant a biography of any kind, auto or otherwise, and I never intended writing one. It just happened, in spite of my always having regarded the writing of autobiographies by nondescript people the height of arrogance. I can point to no great achievements or spectacular failures in my varied careers that would particularly interest anyone. But when the stories I wanted to tell demanded some chronological order, I could find no structural peg other than the biographical one to hang them on.

From the outset I have been hesitant to spend so much time with my life all over again, and looking at myself from close up was at times exceedingly boring. But it also brought me to new insights about the roads I have travelled. And, after all, 'a life unexamined is a life not worth living' (Socrates). On the other hand, 'a life over-examined is not worth writing about' (Unknown).* I have tried hard not to err on the latter score, and sincerely hope that I have not regarded myself too seriously.

---

* For both of these quotations I am grateful to Willie Esterhuyse, *Die God van Genesis* (Christian Media Publications, 2010), pp. 69 and 70.

BEGINNING I

Early Life

I

Genetically Predisposed

After my final retirement from formal employment I embarked on a search for my roots. I compiled a family genealogy, in the course of which I came across many questions about my forebears that had become unanswerable by the passage of time. I want to leave as few of these as possible for my children to endlessly and frustratingly wonder and speculate about when I'm gone, as I have been doing. Most importantly, I wish to try to avoid as far as possible their misinterpreting what they do come to know factually.

One such subject of family conjecture is the story of my maternal grandfather, Koos Maritz. Oupa Maritz taught us to handle a .22 rifle; to shoot, cook and eat birds; to chop off a chicken's head and pluck it for the table; to receive slices of biltong from the blade of his trusty, honed-slim and always razor-sharp Joseph Rogers; to 'slaughter', as he called it, papaya and watermelon under the trees in the garden, and other such essential skills. He was a determining influence in my early years, and I loved him dearly.

From searching the records, it emerged that he had been in the British concentration camp at Volksrust for part of the Anglo-Boer War with his wife, our grandmother, a sure sign that he had surrendered, hands-upped, laid down arms, or been taken prisoner in some other way. He seems for some reason, such as perhaps having signed Lord Kitchener's Oath of Neutrality or the Oath of Allegiance to the British Crown (neither of which I could establish), to have been in fairly good standing with the British, as he would otherwise have been sent to one of the prisoner-of-war camps on foreign soil. But neither could he have at face value joined the British as an active traitor to the Boer cause, because then he and his wife would not have landed up in the camp. There is, however, also the caveat that the British sometimes placed 'joiners' in camps to protect them from the vengeance of the still-fighting Boers, or to keep an ear to the ground in the camps and report on untoward developments there.

But Oupa never said a word about his fighting on commando in the war, which he and our grandmother consistently referred to as the Second War of Liberation, or the English War. My siblings and I still marvel at his sitting immovably for endless hours on a chair in the garden smoking his pipe and seemingly just staring into faraway nothingness. The only inkling about their experiences of the war, apart from their dire circumstances in the camps, I ever got was when my grandmother once told me as a child that Oupa's good buddy, lying next to him behind cover in some firefight, was hit by a dumdum bullet that shattered his head to bits and, practical woman that she was, how she had struggled to get the mess cleaned off Oupa's clothes.

Ouma had, as a little girl, sat on an ox-wagon stranded in a ford somewhere in the Free State and witnessed a raiding party from Lesotho kill almost her entire family. The incident was authenticated by a contemporary letter that has regrettably gone missing. They took the wagon but spared her, her mother and sister, after which her mother walked them through the bush for two days and two nights to reach safety in the town of Harrismith. I more than once eavesdropped on her (with my brother, I think) while she was at her lengthy, spoken-aloud prayers, on her knees at her bedside before retiring for the night. Her end refrain was invariably: 'And Father, please forgive the kaffirs and the English, for they knew not what they were doing.'

The story of my paternal grandfather, the second traceable Pieter Spaarwater in South Africa, is different. I never knew him as he died in 1929, ten years before I was born. Apparently in anticipation of the war then strongly brewing between the Zuid-Afrikaansche Republiek (ZAR, or Transvaal Republic) and the British, he emigrated from the Cape Colony to the ZAR in 1896 shortly after the failed Jameson Raid. He joined the Geheime Politie (Secret Police) of the ZAR and was sworn in as a Geheime Speurder (Secret Detective) in late 1899, just before the start of the war. Primary sources confirm that he was in fact a spy operating mainly in the Eastern Transvaal, where a series of battles took place, and in the British colony of Natal bordering on the ZAR, which was the initial springboard for General Buller's Imperial British Forces into the Transvaal. He stayed in the field until the bitter end and was decorated for bravery.

I discovered this information only after retiring from a career spanning eighteen years in the SADF, mainly in military intelligence where I was involved in a war of another era, and another fourteen years in the NIS and related pursuits, having even once chased after a war almost a century after Oupa Spaarwater had done so. At university I first made a hash of trying to emulate my medical doctor father, the third Pieter Spaarwater in the country, but later found my niche in the military and intelligence worlds. A generational genetic skip, it seems.

2

Growing Up

The following is a personal journey through recollections that I have come to identify as either pleasurable or demonic from my early childhood. I believe that by ignoring or denying the demons that we all have, they only grow and grab hold of one's psyche. I believe in accepting and confronting them, and trying to establish what part they played or may still be playing in making me what I am. Surely the knowledge of self, the core of what you really are, requires also taking account of the miserable in your life experience to enable you to proceed past what you think you are and beyond the expectations of others, especially those of your parents.

I attended primary school in the quaint little Eastern Transvaal gold-mining town of Pilgrims' Rest where I was born. We were 150 pupils in the school in its heyday, in parallel-medium classes. My deep love for my mother tongue, Afrikaans, was engendered at home by my mother, who was great at reading us fascinating stories and poems mostly of a patriotic nature from classical Afrikaans literature. The Afrikaans language was then still in the early stages of its development towards the fully expressive, academic, scientific, technological and literary language it is today. But the Afrikaans teacher at school was a bit of an ogre and had little influence on me. I got my lifelong love of the English language from a wonderful woman and inspirational teacher, Mrs Dora Hofmeyer. I don't recall ever having had a maths teacher, which I suppose I must have, but who would have been decidedly inept at teaching me.

Some of my mates outside of school were poor and rough Afrikaans-speaking miners' kids, but, as a function of the social stratification in the town, my friends were mostly sons and daughters of mine officials and managers, who were almost invariably English-speaking. I never had any particular preference for friends from either social stratum. Fun was where it was to be found. I don't recall any 'ordinary' miners ever being invited to our house, but social life among the 'elite' was vibrant.

When word spread that I liked reading, I was showered with books from my English friends (or rather, their parents, I think), especially when in Standard 6 I was bedridden at home for an extended period as a result of a serious kidney disease. From *Boys' Own, Secret Seven, William, Hardy Boys, Biggles, Classic Comics*, cowboy books and the like, I progressed to *Laughter on the Stairs, The Snow Goose* and *Little Lord Fauntleroy*, and from there on to two books that have captivated me for life: *The Water and the Sound* by Gillian Tindall, my first novel, and Shakespeare's *Hamlet*.

Catching tadpoles in the creek, roaming the lovely hillsides with my dearly beloved Bruno, a kelpie sheepdog, and going to school on horseback from where we once lived five miles out of town, are enduring memories. There were the usual excellent sports amenities provided by the mines – well-kept tennis courts, bowling greens, a rugby field, a 'rec' hall with pool and table-tennis tables, and an Olympic-sized cemented swimming pool with two adjacent ones progressively smaller and shallower for children. There was a beautiful little nine-hole golf course with different tees making it into eighteen holes. Accessible free of charge or at a pittance (one shilling and a tickey for a round of golf), this catered magnificently to the needs of sports-loving boys, as most of us were, especially over school holidays when we were all home from boarding at high school.

What happened in school I can't really tell, having had scant interest in that sort of stuff, except for Mrs Hofmeyer's classes and the deputy headmaster, Theo Scheepers, reading to us from classic Afrikaans action pulp fiction like *Rooi Jan* or *Die Swart Luiperd* in the last period on Fridays.

One of the special pleasures I had over weekends were the long rides I took along the banks of the Blyde River, sometimes unsaddling and swimming in the river or just lying in the lush grass gazing up into the trees, with Japie also enjoying the break happily grazing around me, never wandering far off and coming trotting back at my whistling. Two of my friends during high school holidays were the Kitchener brothers, Arthur and Nigel, from a posh Johannesburg school. Nigel and I played tennis, and Arthur sometimes went riding with me, borrowing a horse from the mine stables. With another friend from Pretoria Boys' High, Peter Mabbet, I played tennis and pool, and swam. Father Kitchener was the mine secretary and quickly got the nickname of 'Lord'. I don't know whether there was any family connection with the abhorrent Lord Kitchener of 'scorched-earth' infamy from the Anglo-Boer War days.

Early one morning I took Arthur along riding to an outlying government forestry station about seven miles up the mountain at Morgenzon on the road to Lydenburg. We arrived at the resident forester, Oom Piet van Tonder's house unannounced at around 6 a.m. The coffee was already brewing with a bowl of *beskuit* standing ready, and Arthur, usually a taciturn fellow, was surprisingly outspoken in his praise for the warm hospitality of the humble, salt-of-the-earth Boer and his wife, even at that time of day. They could well have been the first (and only?) Afrikaners of this type he ever met.

I was quite naughty while at prep school (as later), once firing a shot from inside the house down the passage through an open door at the end into the mountainside with my father's lovely First World War 'broom handle' 7.65-mm Mauser pistol, which delivered to me a huge fright and a hiding. I did the same years later with the same pistol, this time through a closed window, when I should have known better, but then I was too big for a hiding. I kept and bred pigeons for purposes of exchange with like-minded friends. And there was also Thysie, a really cocky little red and black bantam cock with only one eye who rode with me on the handlebar of my tricycle, when he wasn't chasing my sister's cats or the hens. Through his good offices I also bred some chicks.

As district surgeon my father often received bodies and body parts from the police for forensic examination, and kept some of the skulls on shelves in the dentistry room that was part of his surgery. Unable to resist those lovely dentistry tongs, I once extracted all the teeth from one of those skulls. Things got a bit gruesome when on another occasion a whole skeleton – we called it Napoleon Bonesapart – arrived in a sack for examination, with pieces of flesh still clinging to it here and there. A friend, Gerrie Smit, and I decided to clean and reassemble it. To this end we cooked off the meat in a huge three-legged pot in the backyard in which washing was boiled and occasionally lard to make soap. Surprisingly, I only got a severe scolding for this and not a hiding, but it sank our reassembly project. I think my father took these exploits as a sign of my aptitude for medicine, but it was Gerrie who would later become the doctor.

A source of terror in town was George Greaver, an old-style cobbler with a shrivelled, claw-like left hand. My father said something about arfrightenus, which sounded about right, but my mother let the real cat out of the bag when she said it was from strangling naughty children, and that I would qualify if I didn't stop. From then on we moved over to the other side of the road when walking past his shop. As he grew older, George surprisingly became a nice man as his daughters Maude, Katie and Marjorie successively worked in our house and looked after us children. I grew to love them and by association to lose my fear of their father.

There was also Waskit Mongwe, a Shangaan who looked after me from a very young age. I was a scrawny little runt not much interested in eating, according to family lore, and he used to feed me and poke my cheeks with his finger to dislodge the food I tended to store there rather than chewing and swallowing it. In a tiff with my brother he once proclaimed: 'Pietertjie, I'm not your kaffir, I'm Maritz's kaffir.' We sometimes used to eat *pap en vleis* with our hands from the servants' 'kaffir' pot in front of their quarters in the backyard, where Waskit once, when I was small, scolded me quite severely for farting during such a meal. He named his son after me. In later life I went searching for Maritz Mongwe in the Bushbuckridge area of the Lowveld, where his father had come from, but without success. I was told, however, that he was a successful builder somewhere in the region. I loved Waskit dearly and was devastated when he died when I was still quite young, apparently from kidney failure for which, according to my brother, he chose to be treated by a *sangoma* rather than the doctor in whose house he worked.

And then there was the politics. At the time there were only two political parties of note in the country, the United Party (the Sappe) and the National Party (the Nats). There were also only two serious makes of car for the plebs, Chevrolet and Ford, apart from the Cadillacs and Rolls Royces of the Rand-lords. Politics and cars gelled in our town, the Nats driving Chevs and the Sappe Fords (I believe it was the other way around in some places) – the make of car as certain a statement of affiliation as a rosette on the chest. The main area of political contention at the time (the mid-1940s) was between the SAP 'imperialists' who had fought for the 'empire' in the Second World War, and the Nat 'republicans' who had stayed out of it. It could become quite rough.

The Torch Commando, a pro-war and largely SAP-aligned organisation, was founded by the Royal Air Force fighter-ace, South African 'Sailor' Malan. One evening they held a rally on the rugby field below the main road and a few of us – I think my brother was also one – went to throw stones at them in the dark from the street. The following day my mother spoke with disgust of her hairdresser having had to have my father dress a wound to her head. They agreed it must have been those awful boys from Brown's Hill, where the poor white people lived some way out of town. I have always thought my father, who was from a SAP background (his father, a friend and loyalist of Louis Botha, had been a founding member of the party), would have joined up for the war were it not for his medical practice, and my mother saying no.

Our parents gave us almost everything money could buy, including exposing us to the finer things in life. Weekends at the Carlton Hotel in Johannesburg for the La Scala Opera of Milan's presentations like *Rigoletto*, *Aïda*, *Lucia di Lammermoor* and others at His Majesty's Theatre, with stars like Beniamino Gigli, his daughter Rina, and Tito Gobbi, among other artists of world renown; symphony concerts and concerts by world stars Elisabeth Schwarzkopf, Heinrich Schlussnuss and Jan Peerce in Pretoria's City Hall; and pantomimes with international stars like Terry Thomas in the Plaza Theatre in Pretoria.

Locally, we once heard the wonderful Afrikaans lyrical tenor Dirk Lourens in the town hall of nearby Graskop, and were entertained by the trick artist Doc Wilson and his travelling show in Pilgrims' Rest. During his perform-ance in the health committee hall, Doc once called me onto the stage from the ranks of kids sitting on the floor in front to assist him in demonstrating how he could drink upwards. I was to give him something to drink from a small glass while he stood on his head. Unfortunately, I didn't understand him too well – he had a funny accent – and twice drank the potion myself, with him each time remonstrating with me from upside down, of which I understood even less. Doc's trick worked on our third go, but by then I had stolen the show.

Wonderful Christmas holidays were usually spent at the Bay View Hotel in Hermanus, and we had regular weekends or longer periods in the nearby Kruger National Park, to which my father had free access as district sur-geon for the area. As a child I got to know the legendary game ranger Harry Wolhuter. One night around a campfire in the then still primitive and unfenced Pretorius Kop rest camp we listened to his fascinating tales, some quite tall, I thought, such as his large yellow dog, Bull, returning home from a nocturnal outing in the bush with lion hair between his teeth. But this in no way detracts from the countless remarkable and undoubtedly real experiences this great man of the bush told us about and recounted in his memoirs.

The most astonishing perhaps, to which there were a number of wit-nesses, was being sprung from his horse by a lion which dragged him by the shoulder for some distance in setting up his meal. I vividly recall his telling of how, with his rifle still in its scabbard on his saddle and while being dragged and smothered in blood, he managed to get out his hunting knife and felt the lion's ribcage to find the best place to stab him in the heart. He did so and the lion dropped him. He then climbed into a tree, where he tied himself securely with his belt, fearing that he might fall down from loss of blood. The lion spent the night audibly dying nearby. His helpers, who were present when the lion struck but had 'dispersed' when it happened, returned the next morning and found him in the tree. They then took him for medical care in time to save his life.

My father got to know Wolhuter well through their association in the huge campaigns in the 1940s and 1950s to eradicate malaria and the pox throughout the Transvaal Lowveld, including the Kruger Park. I sensed that he disliked Wolhuter, although he never said anything. I only much later found the probable cause: Wolhuter had fought for the British in the Anglo-Boer War in the infamous Steinacker's Horse regiment deployed in the Transvaal Lowveld to patrol the Mozambique border and prevent the Portuguese from assisting the Boers. They used brutal methods, looted from the locals, both black and white, and wreaked general mayhem in the area. There is no historical record or even the slightest suggestion that Wolhuter was ever involved in any of this, he having acted mainly as a guide.

Steinacker was an Austrian soldier of fortune who offered his services to the British. He had some unspecified military background and was not much liked but found useful by the British. In Wolhuter's telling, the diminutive Steinacker struck a quite ludicrous figure as he loved dressing up in elaborate Habsburg dress uniforms, feathered helmet and all, in the sweltering heat of the Lowveld. He and his unit came to be generally loathed by both black and white people in the region for his ruthless methods.

Our home had plenty of books and good music, things our parents hardly had as children, coming as they did from the abject poverty that was rife among Afrikaners after the war. Both intelligent and diligent, they raised themselves out of this condition by their own bootstraps, my father becoming a doctor and my mother a teacher. They were determined to give their children better than they had had, a little materially over-indulgent, perhaps, probably engendering in us a bit of hedonism as well. But my mother was also a quite strict disciplinarian and we certainly were not spoilt children in the usual sense.

With Oupa's instruction in various disciplines, the dentistry, anatomical reconstruction, pistol shooting and poultry husbandry, the dark menace of George Greaver, Waskit's teachings on table manners and social graces, a significant stage debut, grand opera and my horse and dog, one might say I enjoyed a quite eclectic education in my early formative years.

The only thing that marred this almost idyllic existence was the incessant squabbling between our parents. As if programmed, these altercations invariably came to a head every evening over the dinner table, initiated more often than not by some nasty remark from my father about the food, or by some provocation from my mother. I thought it was a way for my rather unassertive father (except in his profession, by all accounts), usually emboldened by a G&T or three beforehand, to show us by verbal assault that he could stand up to my small but aggressively overassertive mother. We three children to this day recall this ritual with horror. It was psychological abuse of the worst kind of a captive audience of young children. As the middle child, I think it was perhaps easier for me to cope than it was for my multi-talented elder brother or compassionate younger sister. I spun my own protective cocoon and melted into the background. It essentially made of me a psychologically self-sufficient loner for life, although I did later develop some decidedly gregarious tastes as well.

It seemed to me that our parents spent their lives trying to deny their impoverished origins. They were inclined to romanticise things rather than face reality. For the same reason, they were somewhat given to pretension and snobbery. They also romanticised their children, and I was never acceptable merely for what I was. I don't know whether my brother or sister experienced this, but it sometimes caused me acute embarrassment, for instance when my father introduced me to people as 'Advocate' when I was not, or told someone in my presence that I was a fourth-year medical student when I was in my second abortive first year. Or, when I achieved senior rank in the SADF, out of the blue telling friends that I had been appointed as bodyguard to Prime Minister John Vorster, which he seemed to regard as some sort of pinnacle, but which could not have been further from the truth.

Rather than just regarding these utterances simply as blatant lies, which they were, I suppose in this postmodern age one should try to 'understand'. Without any background in psychology, I regard these strange manifestations as expressions of an incompletely integrated personality, resulting in mood swings, and something of a Jekyll and Hyde syndrome. Although sometimes quite cruel, my father could also be very sweet and wittily charming. I am wholly incompetent to pronounce on the possibility of bipolar disorder, but such thoughts have occurred to me.

In spite of having every reason to be extremely proud of their own efforts at heaving themselves out of their received condition, and of their personal achievements, which at the time were rare among Afrikaners, they were unable to transcend their background and adjust to their newfound status and relative affluence with balance and grace. I developed a lifelong aversion to such unrealistic denial, and to this day resent that I was forced to run away, as I saw it, instead of facing some shameful personal music back at school in Pretoria, about which more later. I charitably regard them as having had the best of intentions, but having been decidedly inept at parenting the whole of a child.

My father also had a penchant for making derogatory remarks about me. Although never to my face, they were sometimes gleefully related to me by my brother and even my mother. By way of example: I'm so quiet because I'm so stupid; I'm a two-faced bastard (when I was in early high school); and much else, some of which were so disturbing that to this day I balk at recounting them. I sensed that this might also have had to do with the fact that I bear the Maritz name, for which he harboured an only slightly disguised disdain, without to my knowledge ever saying anything directly. Since coming across my grandfathers' differing war records, I've had little doubt that that could have been a factor in his attitude towards me, and part of the needle between my parents.

I don't recall their ever speaking about the war or the politics of the time. When I was first decorated in the SADF, my father, in my mother's presence, gave me his father's decorations awarded after the war, saying approximately: 'Now this was a *real* man.' As part of this complex of avoidance of reality, they also prevented me from seeing my dearly beloved Oupa Maritz's corpse or attending his funeral while I was in my uncle's house in Middelburg, Transvaal when he died there. Neither did they tell me when my beloved dog died while I was at home, instructing the gardener to bury it surreptitiously so that I wouldn't see it. I knew that Bruno had been suffering from epileptic seizures, but never had the courage to ask what had happened to him, as their handling of the subject made it taboo.

Emanating no doubt from her former material deprivation, my mother demonstrated on many occasions a tendency to believe that money could buy love and respect. Leaving aside many examples from my early youth, at university and in a quandary as to the wisdom of carrying on with my spluttering medical studies, I wrote a letter to my father confiding in him that my aptitudes and predilections were not in the natural sciences but rather in humanities. I tried to express confidence in him and imprudently wrote, among other things, that I did not want to involve my mother as she 'would only complicate matters'. The next I heard was a letter from her severely scolding me along the lines of 'is this the thanks I get for buying you a scooter', which she had indeed done shortly before, a well-used Lambretta. She used one of her favourite expressions, *stank vir dank*, literally 'stench for thanks', and railed for five pages about my disgusting thanklessness, solemnly promising never to buy me anything ever again, a vow she regularly broke over the following years, perhaps to redeem her love's labour's lost. Not a word in the five pages on my existential dilemma.

But she was otherwise an immensely caring and nurturing mother to her children, with always our best interests at heart, as she saw it. She was strict, especially uncompromising as far as our education was concerned – home-work before all else – and inculcated in us a lifelong love of books and good music. My underperformance at school was a painful disappointment to her, with some redemption later on, but she had by then taught me the sorrow of a mother's tears.

Apart from the aforementioned letter to my father, I had never before nor since had any inclination to bare my soul to him, either in writing or orally – we simply never had that sort of relationship. I have little doubt that he deliberately broke the confidentiality of my letter by giving it to my mother to bring to her attention that I trusted him more than I did her. I got a reply from him shortly after my mother's letter, urging me to carry on with medical studies as this was 'the only really worthy career in the world, and think about what wonderful status it would give you in society' – his words, more or less verbatim. He also wrote that he would not pay for any other studies of mine, although he did later relent and help a little, conceding to my mother's cajoling. He merely fell back on his romanticised view of the profession by which he had yanked himself out of poverty. There was not a single word of rational consideration of my situation, which I had explained to him at some length.

The irony of parents in marital strife staying together 'for the sake of the children' was painfully brought home to me at an early age. I know I would much rather have coped with a separation. But my parents could never bring themselves to such a rational outcome, and I do not think they stayed together for their children's sake, but this was their comfort blanket. Their own deep-seated insecurities led to their becoming incapable of doing without each other. They stayed together for fifty-one mutually destructive years of married life until death parted them.

My two uncles, Dr Ryk Becker and Dr Koos Maritz, successively worked with my father in his practice and gained intimate knowledge of our domestic circumstances, even on occasion being called on to mediate between our parents. These two, and especially Oom Ryk's wife, my mother's youngest sister and our favourite aunt, Ellen Becker, or Ansien, as we called her, had a hugely positive influence on my development as an individual. Instead of the impression I always got at home of my inadequacies being the basis of my parents' approach to me, these three exuded an attitude of respect for and confidence in me, sometimes outspokenly so, even at times when I was experiencing bad lows. Ansien especially, wonderful woman that she was, was always non-judgemental and an immensely positive influence in my life. As a family, we were totally devastated when she died suddenly of a heart attack at a relatively young age.

I once from a distance overheard Oom Ryk say to someone that 'it was surprising how [I] had turned out so well, given [my] background'. It was an enormous fillip for me to hear that I 'had turned out well' from a man I respected and liked so much. And these well-balanced, cheerily positive people had come from a similarly deprived background to that of my parents. I will never be too grateful to them for having given me a positive self-image and feeling of own worth when other influences tended to break me down. Their approval has stayed with me throughout my life and I can only wonder at what would have remained of any positive ego I may have had, had it not been for these three wonderful people. Now all deceased, I still love them with all my heart.

We children immensely appreciate the advantage we had of being born into relative privilege and what our parents provided us with, materially and spiritually. Although deeply resentful, I never lost my love for them and still long for them to this day. I cared for them as best I could in the unavoidable absence of my brother and sister when my mother had a stroke in her late seventies that paralysed her on one side, which at her age meant total paralysis.

From this she took four excruciatingly degrading years to die at the age of eighty in a frail-care unit in Pretoria.

I spoke to a family friend, a renowned Pretoria specialist physician who had initially treated her for the stroke, about gently ending her terrible suffering, but he shut me down. His personal ethics weighed heavier than the abject misery of a suffering human being without any prospect of betterment. I seriously considered going it alone, but thought of my brother and sister, whom I was sure would never agree, and I had neither the nerve nor the means. I have since been a firm believer in legalising voluntary euthanasia and will be issuing such instructions on my own behalf. My father died a few months before her from the effects of the anaesthetic after a successful hip-replacement operation. I loved and detested him as long as he lived.

I suppose most children harbour some resentment towards their parents, often justifiably so. I hope mine don't labour too much under such a burden. It isn't a comfortable place to be.

3

Boarding School

It was with relief that I left home in 1952 for boarding school at the Afrikaanse Hoër Seunskool in Pretoria, where my brother, together with a cousin, the fourth Pieter Spaarwater in the country, had already been for the previous two or three years. I was followed one or two years later by my sister, Ina-Marie (or Amie), who attended the Afrikaanse Hoër Meisieskool across the road. I am convinced that my parents breathed a sigh of relief at this spatial separation from their responsibilities towards us, although my mother professed the opposite. If she were to be believed, why then were we not sent to one of the perfectly good high schools, all with boarding facilities, in nearby Sabie, Lydenburg or Nelspruit, they being just over the mountains in opposite directions and easily within reach for weekends at home? But the Pretoria schools were prestigious Afrikaner institutions; the closer ones humdrum, socially suspect and, I think, too near.

My brother and sister both profess to have hated every minute of boarding school. Although quite harsh in those days, I thrived on the lifestyle. As regards my experiences there in general, I can do no better than refer to the eerily exact descriptions of John van de Ruit in his book *Spud*, right down to our adolescent fantasies of our delectable middle-aged lady music teacher, as a parallel to his art teacher. But I don't think Mrs Eckels was given to providing private life-coaching to senior boys after hours. I find it amazing how Van de Ruit's imperialist-inspired Michaelhouse in the Natal province, sometimes branded the Last Outpost of the British Empire, and the Christian National Education Afrikaanse Hoër Seunskool in the conservative Afrikaner city of Pretoria, can sociologically be such carbon copies of each other. The answer, of course, is simple: boys will be boys, universally.

Living and learning(?) just across the street from the famed Loftus Versfeld rugby ground, at the time still accessible free of charge by underground stormwater drain, was to rugby-mad me the ultimate attraction. We used to run around that hallowed ground passing rugby balls virtually every afternoon. Role models were then-current Springboks Salty du Rand, Jaap Bekker, Fonnie du Toit, Hannes Brewis, Ernst Dinkelmann, Daan Retief and the like. I hadn't an academic care in the world, as nicely evinced by my abjectly failing Standard 9 at the end of 1955.

But failing was the least of my – and my poor parents' – worries that year. Apart from rugby, we were also mad about cars. A dream I had one night as a very young boy, and which I remember vividly to this day, was of driving a car that magically propelled itself with me only steering and pressing pedals, having seen this done but not quite knowing why. I lay awake for most of the rest of that night marvelling at the very idea that such a thing was possible, and that it was so easy for me to drive. Cars have captivated me to this day.

In that self-same Standard 9 academic *annus horribilis*, far removed from my parents' cars, which I had sometimes driven with their permission and in their presence and sometimes 'borrowed' without either, some school friends and I started borrowing cars of others off the streets and taking them for joyrides. Under the tutelage of a technically minded one of us, we became adept at starting cars with silver cigarette paper, few at the time having any security measures like steering locks or alarms. It was enormously exciting and challenging, especially when returning the cars, as we mostly tried to do, to the exact place or as near as possible to where we had found them, out of consideration for the poor owners who might be inconvenienced by the disappearance of their transport.

But these exploits came to an end with a shattering bang when one evening in Pretorius Street in Arcadia, Pretoria, right in front of the Andrew McColm Hospital, a pink Ford Zephyr 6 driven by a nun swerved in front of me and I drove a thus-borrowed Opel Kapitän into a streetlight standard on the sidewalk, waking up in hospital under police guard. Louis suggested we make a break for it, but we decided against this when, apart from his battered face and my double vision and dislocated hip, we recognised our police guard as one Constable Karel (Tom) van Vollenhoven, the then-current star rugby Springbok wing in the test series against the British Lions in South Africa that year. We were rather disdainful of the police, but now we knew we were beaten. I became painfully, in more ways than one, aware of the difference between borrowing and stealing. Policemen, or for that matter Springbok rugby players, weren't normally deployed in cases of borrowing.

We were spared prosecution and criminal records by our fathers buying the owner of the written-off car a new one to avoid his pressing charges and, I suspect, by the intercession with the police of a prominent criminal law judge of the Supreme Court, a distant relative on my mother's side whom my father knew well. My father was also on friendly terms with the school headmaster; Louis's was an important donor to the school and had served on the school board; while the third suspect Philip's dad was a teacher at the school. While lying in traction at home, I got a friendly letter from the headmaster, Dr Gert Potgieter, assuring me I'd be welcome to return to the school and hostel as soon as I had recovered, as I was sure to have learnt my lesson. I am convinced that my utter boredom, even spiritual destitution, when the rugby season came to an end after the middle of that year, contributed to my failing Standard 9 and becoming involved in this exciting extra-curricular activity. I think there may be some truth to the notion that rugby is a religion of sorts for some in our country.

I have remained conscious of what would have happened to children our age in similar circumstances who did not have influential parents. The event was something of an epiphany for me, as it brought home the pain and desperate concern the disastrous slippery slope to perdition I was on was causing my parents. My father had a heart-to-heart talk with me: he asked me whether I had criminal tendencies. I said, 'No'. He said, 'Good'. And that was that.

I came out of the incident ashamed but determined to return to face that shame back at school. I had not the slightest inclination to go back to brag about it, but rather in deep contrition and determined to rehabilitate myself in the eyes of my non-criminal peers. But I think my father expected bravado from me. Against my wishes, he decided that a change of environment would be a good thing and enrolled me as a boarder at Lydenburg High School, thirty-seven miles from home, for my second Standard 9 year. In the event I thoroughly enjoyed Lydenburg, especially as it was co-educational, a new experience for me. I did fairly well, even though my first priorities were captaining the first rugby team, playing first-team tennis and representing the school and region in athletics. I even became a prefect on the students' council. For the most part I steered clear of serious disciplinary problems, except for once visiting my lovely newly acquired girlfriend, Hettie Coetzee, in town after hours and getting caught out. I suffered some acceptable consequences, such as less freedom of movement for a while and some diminution of status, the housemaster keeping his word to not inform my parents.

And yes, I did in fact pass matric, in 1957, with fair to middling results. I got a distinction in English and almost in Afrikaans and history, in spite of my dear teacher of the latter once writing a note on one of my assignment papers: 'You write lovely essays but you know nothing about history.' I was delighted at this generous compliment. My marks for maths and science must remain a family sensitivity for now, save to say that the standards authorities of the time must have been culpably lenient to have given me pass marks for both. On the strength of these excellent markers of aptitude and interest, and my father's inimitable judgement and romanticism, I later drifted into the study of medicine.

Most importantly, perhaps, at Lydenburg, for the first time in my life, I got to mingle and live on a daily basis with children from underprivileged backgrounds; some indeed very poor from rural 'poor white' settlements and other less-privileged circumstances, which nevertheless produced some outstanding pupils, academically and morally. The names of people like Jaco Swart, Ben van Heerden, Piet Smith, Louis Changuion and others come to mind, people with no kick-start in life but with natural talent and the determination to make the most of it. I have immense respect and admiration for them. My outlook on life generally has benefited from this experience, as it enabled me to see what the other half was like. Over two years of positive introspection, these people helped me to take hold of myself, although I don't think they realised it. I still feel that by not going back to my previous school in Pretoria to present myself in a different light, I never got the closure I should have. But my father had been right on the choice of school.

I made a most valued friend for life in Louis Changuion, son of a highly regarded motor mechanic in town. An outstanding provincial middle-distance athlete, Louis later became a professor of history and a prolific writer on especially the Anglo-Boer War. Once, after a shower, I grabbed him by the dick and ran down the passage dragging him staggering behind screeching all the way like a stuck pig. As I was quite ruthless in executing my silly impulse, I suspect it must have contributed to the length of the appendage concerned. This puerile little incident was utterly devoid of even the slightest trace of homo-eroticism (there never was any between us), but we had other bindings that exist to this day, in spite of sometimes not seeing or speaking to each other for many years on end. With a third friend, Koos Nell, we were close at school and together attended the Army Gymnasium and the University of Pretoria, also known as Tukkies, the latter in different disciplines. It was truly a sad loss when Koos, a dentist, whom I had not seen for a very long time, died of cancer in late 2010.

In the early evening of my eighteenth birthday, 4 October in my matric year of 1957, I lay on my back on the front lawn of the hostel watching the first man-made earth satellite, the Soviet 'Sputnik', launched that day, traversing the clear, starry sky. I wondered whether the sky might really be my limit, as Mr Lötz, my marvellous English teacher, had suggested to me earlier that very day when encouraging me to do language studies and journalism after school. When I told him I was going to do medicine, he was aghast. He phoned my father, of all people, to plead with him to help me reconsider. My father never told me about this call; I only heard about it years later from my mother.

4

First Nibble at the Military

On finishing school I wasn't sure what should follow, but thought of ways of staying away from medical or any other studies for as long as possible. I felt like a gap year and some adventure, so I volunteered for a year's military training in 1958 at the Army Gymnasium ('Gym') at Voortrekkerhoogte outside Pretoria, which my parents found patriotically acceptable. I had no such lofty motives, but it sounded like fun and could have the added advantage of exempting me from later being drafted for compulsory national service for a year or two, which was then very much in the offing.

The Gym was structured in combined arms battalion format with an infantry company, an armoured squadron, an artillery battery and a signals squadron. I asked for and got a mustering in the infantry. The first half of the year proceeded for the most part as I had expected with all that PT, parade-ground drilling and other sophisticated forms of inhuman movement science. There was also interesting basic weapons training in marksmanship, including fire and movement, with .303 Lee-Metfords, mortars (the six-inch and the nifty two-inch varieties), the handy 'Energa' rifle grenade, hand grenades, the 'bazooka' anti-tank rocket launcher, the Bren .303 light-machine gun (a wonderful light-weight and user-friendly weapon), the dangerous-to-the-user-and-bystanders Sten sub-machine gun and field-craft.

The only trouble was that these weapons were of Second World War vintage and somewhat antiquated, with other equipment such as vehicles, boots and webbing to match, which did little to prepare us for what was then considered modern warfare. The Lee-Metford was heavy with limited magazine capacity and weak muzzle velocity; the six-inch mortar was dreadfully heavy, especially the notoriously difficult-to-handle base-plate, which Koos Nell had to lug in a team with me carrying the easier-to-handle tube. Koos sometimes got left so far behind over the hills and valleys of the training area that there was no way of getting the mortar into action when the order came. I was rightfully reprimanded for breaking up the team and rendering the weapon useless, but Koos was really poor at this job, sometimes giving rise to much hilarity. Another problem was the slippery Second World War hobnailed boots, designed for mushy European conditions and ill-suited to the hard grasslands of the training areas in the hills around Pretoria and at Potchefstroom, where we had our 'manoeuvres'.

The SADF was at that stage still, to a large extent, stuck in the old imperial mould of being set up to provide only elements to British Imperial Forces, and was neither structured nor equipped to act on its own as an independent fighting force. The supposition was that South Africa would always be fighting on the side of the British. South Africa's participation in the United Nations (UN) forces during the Korean War in the early 1950s was a case in point. We provided mostly fighter pilots and some technical personnel, all of whom by their performance left a great impression in the overall effort to prevent a communist takeover of South Korea, foreshadowing what was to confront the SADF again some three decades later in southern Africa. The Korean War provided impetus to the modernisation of the SADF, among other things through the acquisition on favourable terms of modern fighter aircraft, the North American F-86 Sabre jet, and experience gained. But comprehensive modernisation of the SADF only really took off towards the middle of the 1960s.

After the first six months at the Gym things became decidedly boring. Having signed on for a year, I even very reluctantly but desperately asked my father to buy me out, but he refused, obviously thinking that I was just being gutless. Keeping idle troops out of mischief in quiet times is a universal problem of military management. Doing only repetitive refresher training and much parade-ground work, including preparing for slow-marching at the funeral of Prime Minister J.G. Strijdom who died that year, bored us to death. I got two weeks' pack drill for, on a dare, taking a Jeep for a joyride around the base. My previous experience was not required as vehicles' keys were at the time still routinely left in them in the vehicle park.

One Saturday afternoon, my great friend Jannie McLachlan, known for life by his friends of the time as Charlie, and I felt like a swim. Charlie was a nuggety little man who got his nickname when, on arrival at the Gym, he was issued with a far too large uniform, including boots, which he put on the wrong feet and looked the picture of Charlie Chaplin. We became firm friends. Military bases at the time did not have swimming pools and the one at the outside sports grounds was too far and we needed a pass to go there, which was not in prospect. So we plugged all the outlets of a large bathroom, flooded the place and had our swim, for what it was worth. On disciplinary report the following Monday morning, the young duty captain asked Charlie for his name, and then asked me for mine. When I answered 'Spaarwater' (literally 'save water') he hesitated quizzically for a moment, and then his studied, stern demeanour disintegrated and he burst out laughing. We were only reprimanded. We never found out who split on us, but the resulting deluge had been there for all to see. Charlie later became a long-serving Sheriff of the Court in Hermanus.

Further pack drills for various reasons followed, but only reprimands for mass assaults some weekends on the 'ducktails' at the Hamburger Hut in the centre of Pretoria, which sometimes spilled over onto the streets and the nearby Church Square, with the police only 'keeping an eye' on the goings-on. The real problem with pack drills, which of themselves were not too bad, was that they sometimes took place outside of working hours and the corporals ordered to administer them were usually in a foul mood at having their private time messed up.

At the Gym I also acquired another highly valued, lifelong friend in Carel Trichardt, and later also his lovely and loveable wife, Petru Wessels. Through the good offices of these two wonderful actors and friends, my wife and I were introduced to the fascination of backstage in the wonderful world of theatre in the vibrant times of the Performing Arts Council of the Transvaal in Pretoria in the 1960s.

The end of the year arrived, fortuitously without criminal records or disqualification from ever again serving in the military. Much fun had been had and growing up done.

5

University, and Another World

I decided not to start at the bottom of a military career, however enticing it seemed at the time, but to try to make something 'better' of myself in life. In a misguided attempt to study medicine, I had two wonderful years of *jolling* at university, with a bit of everything thrown in: parties, rugby, tennis and squash; a university motorcar time trial and a gymkhana, the one with my mother's Simca Aronde and the other with my later mother-in-law's Morris Minor; finding a future wife, Anna Bosman; much sketching of cars, mainly concept Alfa Romeos and Ferraris during zoology lectures, while said future wife took notes and made sketches for me. (She was, however, annoyingly inconsiderate in insisting on attending her own lectures during my other classes. However, I did pass zoology on a promotion, i.e. without having to write the year-end exam, testifying to the good job she had done.)

I am still convinced that I would have made a good doctor if only it weren't for all that studying, especially of things I neither understood nor saw the point of. What on earth, for instance, have phloem and xylem cells in plants to do with sick people? And the rate of acceleration of objects in physics? I was nonplussed by much of it, but I accepted the relevance of chemistry and zoology, enjoying and passing both on the second go. I also worked on my bedside manner, but with equally scant achievement. It became glaringly obvious that this state of affairs could not last. After three gap years it was about time for something constructive to happen in my life.

My father was not prepared to pay for any studies other than medicine, until my mother some time later managed to wangle some money out of him to help a little. I did not think there was much prospect of a reasonable career in languages, so I switched to law and extramural studies at Tukkies. I had a succession of jobs in the civil service and later entered into articles of clerkship with a firm of attorneys in Pretoria, which was to have been the beginning of a wonderful career. My first principal as an articled clerk, Leon Smuts, not long after I had started there, agreed with me that the R20 he was paying me per month was too little – I explained to him that I had to pay my own way. He said he would think about it and come back to me. The next day he said he agreed with me and offered me R21. At the time, many articled clerks still had to pay for the privilege of being a dogsbody, often with little or no legal training thrown in.

I got a job in the Deeds Office where I got to know many attorneys. One of them was from the prestigious old firm of MacRobert, De Villiers and Hitge, and he offered me a job and an articled clerkship with a starting salary almost on a par with what I had been earning as a 'Clerical Assistant Grade II' in the civil service, about R40 per month, I seem to recall. Towards the end of my articles after five years, in 1968, I had by general consensus among fellow articled clerks reached the exalted status of being thought to be the highest paid clerk in Pretoria at R250 per month.

With my wife's (the zoology artist) R300 per month as an education librarian and my mother's old Volkswagen Beetle – her second, spectacular disavowal of her previous determination never to buy me anything ever again as long as she lived (she had by then already given me a gold Omega Seamaster for my twenty-first birthday), we had a quite comfortable existence for two years until our first child was born. Amazing how such a little thing can almost impenetrably tighten purse strings overnight. That little bundle of joy, Suzanne, turned into a multi-gifted, slightly bigger one.

While at MacRobert's I also met friends for life in fellow articled clerk André Groenewaldt and his sweet and lovely wife Isabel. Although we hardly saw each other over many years when André left Pretoria to establish a flourishing legal practice in Malmesbury in the Cape, later moving to Stellenbosch, and although we are temperamentally somewhat different – he is a phlegmatically reflective, unshakeably composed man, unlike me – we have remained close in a highly valued friendship.

Everything really only started for me some time in 1967 with a telephone call from one Blackie Swart of the Security Branch of the SAP, inviting me for coffee at the Gloria Café in Pretorius Street, central Pretoria, to discuss an important matter. I was in my last year of articles with the attorneys and my final year of study for the B.Iuris degree. I was on the threshold of what was sure to be an illustrious and lucrative career in law. I was also convinced of the necessity and indeed the historical inevitability of Verwoerdian, or 'grand' apartheid. It was the God-given destiny of the Afrikaner to implement this design and give to the world the solution to the vexed question of organising society to provide for the needs and aspirations of all ethnic and racial groups, without threatening the freedom and well-being of others.

The petty absurdity of things like separate park benches and lifts and post office queues was a necessary phase in progressing towards the grand objective. It would hurt no one and was accepted by millions of black people who realised what tremendous good would come to them from such insignificant and temporary inconveniences. This would come to an end as soon as everyone was happily settled in their own homelands, secure against threat from other ethnic groups with differing interests and cultures, economically self-sufficient and free of the myriad uncomfortable restrictions placed on them in White South Africa, which would also in time be removed.

And this would not take long. Blaar Coetzee, a prominent spokesperson for the Verwoerd cabinet on this issue at the time, as well as successive ministers of government departments such as Native Affairs, Bantu Administration and Development, Cooperation and Development and Plural Affairs, was assuring us that the influx of blacks to the cities would be reversed by 1978, signalling the fulfilment of the grand design. By then the homelands would have developed their own economic attractions so as to draw their citizens back from the cities. Moreover, the Afrikaans churches were staunchly and outspokenly in support of this process, which, they said, fully conformed to what Scripture demanded of us, especially as a way of keeping the ungodly, evil communists from our door.

At the time, I was entering the Establishment through the Nasionale Jeugbond (Youth League of the National Party), and thereafter the Rapportryers, as a halfway house in my progression to the Afrikaner Broederbond (AB), of that I was sure. It was no surprise to me that the security police wanted to talk to me. They must have known that I would eminently serve the System in future. As usual, their judgement was sound, I thought.

At the Gloria, Blackie confirmed to me my view of myself, life and the world in general. He had by discreet enquiry established that 'my heart was in the right place', in spite of my working for an English firm. I had also had qualms about that, until I learnt that a seemingly English senior partner was in fact 'one of us'. Moreover, Old Man MacRobert, of Scotch descent, then about ninety years old and at the office daily (he was known as the sleeping partner), told me of his adventures with his greatest buddy, a namesake but no relation of mine called Nic Maritz, while fighting together for the Boers against the British in what he, like my grandparents, called the Second War of Liberation (the Anglo-Boer War). I was further reassured when on joining I learnt that F.W. de Klerk, an up-and-coming young National Party (NP) politician who was later to become president of the country, had recently left the firm on completion of his articles of clerkship.

Blackie explained to me just how active the communists were in the legal profession and asked whether I would be prepared to assist in countering this threat by helping him gather information. A partner in the firm was handling certain sensitive defence-related contracts which, if revealed to the communists, could seriously compromise the security of the state. Two other partners were 'listed' communists. Of course I would help; I'd rather die than not do so. I confirmed the nature of the defence contracts: detailed plans and specifications of the national air defence system acquired from the electronic company Plessey in the United Kingdom, then being installed in South Africa. It was centred in Devon in the Eastern Transvaal, with slave stations along the borders of the country. It was obvious that if this information should land up in the wrong hands, it could indeed seriously compromise the security of the state.

Security measures around these files were non-existent and I carried a large number of them out in batches after hours, gave them to Blackie to copy, and put them back in their filing cabinet before the start of the next work day. Only years later did I confirm the presence of the two very real communists in the office; at the time any effort to do so would have seemed too much like doubting Blackie's word. What I did know was that the partner handling the defence contracts, a son of the Old Man, was not one of them, but a crusty old patriot in the very best sense of the word, albeit with a shocking insensitivity to security considerations. But those were sanguine times.

Blackie was an impressive old-style cop who I suspect would not have made it in the later, more complicated era of special operations and political machinations. He explained to me beforehand the ethical dilemma of carrying information out of a professional firm, but pointed out how all of us had at times to weigh the greater good that was to be achieved by committing a lesser evil to protect our value system and the very fabric of our society against a heinous threat, such as we then faced. To Blackie this did not mean that ends always justified means, but that life in fact boiled down to an unending series of often very difficult choices between lesser and greater evils. My many years since in both the military and in intelligence, and in life in general, have amply confirmed this truth.

I am quite certain that Blackie would never have broken his undertaking to me that what I told and gave him would never be used, deliberately or inadvertently, for any purpose other than the security of the state, and that the good name of my employers would never be compromised. He simply wasn't that sort of man. I never saw him again after 1967 and never even knew whether he had given me his real name. Some years later I read that a retired colonel of the Security Branch of that name had died of natural causes. It was also only later, after much experience and considerable tribulation in the field, that I realised how good an agent handler Blackie had been and how fundamental, contrary to popular belief, moral values and ethical conduct were to that discipline. The basis of successful agent handling (or 'controlling') will almost always be trust between two human beings, as many doubters of this axiom have found to their cost. The trick, of course, is to recognise the cases where such norms don't apply and have to be replaced by the dark arts of coercion, blackmail, money and pandering to man's baser instincts and predilections in general.

I was hooked for life by the Blackie episode. I knew I could not spend my life as an attorney in an office inundated with other people's problems, drafting and signing endless documents, hanging about courts and deeds offices, debiting fees and so on after having sampled first-hand this other, exciting world. It also offered a direct role in the preservation of apartheid and the protection of Western values and Christian civilisation against the onslaught of the Antichrist. To be so unequivocally on the side of the righteous in the fight against the evil of communism and its assorted cohorts, was invigorating and inspiring. The excitement that such a career promised was irresistible. The legal profession had all of a sudden become a distinctly less attractive prospect.

At about the same time as the Blackie incident, I was confidentially told that I had been proposed (you couldn't apply) but turned down for membership of the AB on the grounds that I was too liberal. A loss of innocence to some extent, I suppose, it engendered in me an abiding resentment of those Afrikaners who arrogate to themselves the right – the divine right, apparently, absent of any perceptible democratic, legal or other process to confer it – to prescribe how and what a 'true Afrikaner' is. I was relieved when Prime Minister John Vorster in 1969 in Parliament, in rejecting this holier-than-thou prescriptiveness, berated Albert Hertzog of the Herstigte Nasionale Party (Reconstituted National Party) and his rightist supporters as 'self-appointed guardians on the ramparts of Zion'. But it soon became apparent that this was merely intended to assign this role to another part of Afrikanerdom, namely that represented by Vorster's own National Party.

At university in the 1960s, I had read *Woord en Daad* (*Word and Deed*), a philosophical and practical theology publication of the Gereformeerde Kerk (Reformed Church, the 'Doppers'), theologically the most conservative Afrikaans church, but ideologically often the most progressive. Under the guidance of Professor Hennie Coetzee of the Potchefstroom University for Christian Higher Education, they were already then writing what was in some quarters regarded as blasphemy, sacrilege or treason, to some all three. I understood *Woord en Daad* to be saying two things clearly between the lines: apartheid was not biblically founded, contrary to what was insistently claimed by its leading theological and political protagonists, and that in practice it was morally wrong and ethically unacceptable. It also insisted that public policy had to pass the test of neighbourly love and justice.

I wondered why these writings did not have any apparent dire repercussions in the Afrikaner establishment. After all, those troublesome priests, Beyers Naudé and Albert Geyser at Tukkies, had been ostracised by their respective denominations and the Afrikaner establishment for what to me seemed lesser transgressions. I was at the time seriously considering converting from the Dutch Reformed Church (DRC) to the Doppers until I dared mention it to my arch-DRC mother, who abhorred the idea – I think she may have relented had I wanted to become something exotic like a Jew or a Muslim or a Buddhist, but another Afrikaans church was unthinkable. I also for the first time discovered my own doubts about religious belief in general, and that I was no longer as interested in such theological and ideological niceties as I had once been. But I was nevertheless both impressed and troubled by *Woord en Daad*.

Although still repeated in public from time to time, assurances of a turn of the tide of black migration to urban areas by 1978 had become threadbare in the face of official statistics indicating an opposite trend. But, they said, there was still plenty of time for turning around what was, after all, in the context of the grand design, a relative triviality. This migration was in any case, for the time being, still in the best interests of the country. The economy was booming and generated a big demand for the labour provided by the migrants. The authorities had ample legislative muscle and policing capacity to ensure that the situation did not get out of hand, while the economy kept humming. Although the migrant workers were forbidden to bring their wives and families to the cities, this was not really of any great concern as they remained in their traditional homelands, enjoying the succour of their extended families there. The social iniquities in the cities, generated by the massive convergence of single males, weren't the doing of the authorities, but the result of individual choice and the personal responsibility of the people concerned, they said.

The Afrikaner was also becoming a mighty factor in the economy. Were not the likes of Federale Volksbeleggings, Sanlam, General Mining and Rembrandt on the verge of taking over there as well? The future was beckoning; all we had to do was ensure there would be enough time to implement the social and political blueprints of the brilliant Doctors Hendrik Verwoerd (the psychologist), Nico Diederichs (the economist) and Geoff Cronje (the sociologist) for the ordering of society so that all would get their due and all would be well. This would be plain sailing as the world at large was coming around to our views and could not do without our reserves of strategic minerals or our strategic geographical position on one of the crucial sea lanes of the world, neither of which they'd be able to secure by themselves without huge expense and political fallout. South Africa's strongly anti-communist and effective government, backed by the most feared military capability south of the Sahara, was a well-placed and reliable surrogate. While the Soviet Union (USSR) was our threat, the Cold War was thus our salvation. We were at the apotheosis of hegemonic Afrikaner power and proudly self-confident. And Nelson Mandela and the other communists were safely in jail, forever.

Having attended the Rivonia trial in 1964 and listened to Nelson Mandela's closing statement from the dock, I thought at the time that it was a grave mistake to have sentenced him only to life imprisonment while the death sentence was available. Professor Nic van der Merwe of the Tukkies law faculty often warned against bad law and bad decisions of courts. 'Reality avenges itself,' he used to say.

6

War

By 1968 war had been declared against the South African state by the African National Congress (ANC) and the South African Communist Party (SACP). Umkhonto we Sizwe (or MK and translated as 'Spear of the Nation'), the armed wing of the ANC, had been established in 1961. The USSR was as intent as ever on expanding its influence and hegemony throughout southern Africa as part of its strategy for world domination. Control of the continent's minerals and the Cape sea lanes was as important to them as it was to the Western powers. Although Mandela and others were in prison, many of their comrades were free, planning and plotting and being trained, mainly in the USSR and East Germany, but also in African states and within South Africa itself. War was in the air and many schemes for the overthrow of the apartheid regime were being hatched around the world.

In 1960, after the Sharpeville incident where large numbers of protesting black people were killed and wounded by the police, the ANC and the Pan Africanist Congress (PAC) were banned from political activity. The UN General Assembly instituted the first limited, non-mandatory economic and diplomatic sanctions against the country in 1962. In 1963 the UN Security Council instituted the first voluntary arms embargo against South Africa, and in 1968 the Carnegie Peace Institute in the United States of America published a study on how South Africa might be invaded militarily, replete with proposals for economic sanctions, naval blockades and the confiscation of South African fixed and liquid assets held overseas. Although these plans were widely derided by objective commentators as unrealistic given South Africa's capacity to resist, the battle had been joined. In November 1977 the UN Security Council adopted a comprehensive, mandatory resolution forbidding the providing of any arms of war to South Africa.

The modernisation of the SADF, which had started in the early 1960s under Lieutenant General S.A. Engelbrecht as Chief of the SADF (then known as Chief of Staff), had been proceeding apace. It was carried forward by successive ministers of defence such as Frans Erasmus, who deconstructed imperialist institutional mindsets, which was psychologically important in ridding the military establishment of the mentality of hanging on to British apron strings for its fighting capacity, and the able Jim Fouché, who was later to become president of the country. Commandants General (as the Chief of the SADF was then designated), such as General Rudolph Hiemstra of the South African Air Force (SAAF) and Admiral Hugo Biermann of the Navy, were also energetic in their pursuit of the project of renewal.

This process culminated in the enormously effective and innovative pairing of minister of defence (and later President) P.W. Botha and Chief of the SADF General Magnus Malan. Between them they transformed the relatively small SADF into a balanced, modern fighting force able to make war on its own, independent of assistance from outside. This development came to significant fruition in the war in South West Africa and Angola from the late 1960s onward. The country owes Botha and Malan a huge debt of gratitude for creating an effective instrument for preventing the country from being overrun, through South West Africa, by communist forces in the 1970s and 1980s.

They also established ARMSCOR, the armaments manufacturing and procurement agency for the SADF, which played a crucial role in its modernisation and in making the armed forces largely independent of the usual overt, pre-sanctions external supply lines, which had been cut off. By innovation and technical excellence in producing own armaments, ARMSCOR gained not only universal respect but also lucrative export markets the world over. Systems such as the G5 and G6 artillery, infantry fighting vehicles like the Ratel, Centurion tanks modernised to Olifant specifications, and electronic innovations to extend the life and efficacy of the French-sourced but obsolescent Mirage III and F1 fighters and fighter-bombers, were state of the art and attracted much demand, even from some surprising overseas quarters. The locally produced Samil (South African Military) logistics vehicle, based on the German Magirus Deutz and powered by locally produced Atlantis Diesel Engines, also commissioned by the SADF/ARMSCOR, provided for all the needs in this more mundane but indispensable regard. Where technology and material could not be developed locally, they were obtained by innovative methods from sources and through highly sensitive partnerships with overseas countries and industries. But that is a fascinating story all on its own.

The SADF was in a state of high excitement at the prospect of at last getting the chance to fight a real and tangible war, where issues would be uncomplicated and the objective simple and clear: to win. We were completely confident of attaining this objective with the cooperation and support of our 'buffer' neighbours, Rhodesia and the Portuguese in their colonies of Angola and Mozambique, as well as of our 'friends in the West'. I could not bear the thought of not being part of this excitement and adventure, apart even from the moral certitude of what patriotic duty demanded of one. Those tiresome Doppers of *Woord en Daad* would have to wait. There were now more urgent and less complicated matters at hand than the morality of apartheid and its biblical justification or not.

The searing anti-war poetry of Siegfried Sassoon from 1917 commenting on the horrors of the First World War – the Great War, the war to end all wars, his 'great patriotic adventure' – was apposite to a widespread attitude prevailing in South Africa at the time among soldiers as well as (white) civilians in general, although here without the irony. He records the terrible slaughter of that conflict in poems with stirring titles such as 'They lead the last attack on anti-Christ', 'Stand to and man the fire-step!' and 'Fall in! Now get a move on!' I was raring to do exactly that. I admired the poems, but did not think much of the poet's patriotism in his ironic themes.

BEGINNING II

Military Intelligence

7

The SADF

On 8 May 1968, immediately after completing my law studies and articles, I joined the then Directorate of Military Intelligence (DMI) as a civilian. As modernisation of the military progressed and the SADF expanded, this directorate was first elevated to a Directorate General (DGMI) and then later to Staff Division II, Chief of Staff Intelligence (CSI). I had to wait for a uniform to be issued to me as I had to go through some training first and be appointed to a military post. After all, you couldn't wear a uniform before you were at least able to identify insignia of rank, knew how to wear your beret and how to salute – imagine the dire military consequences if you should get any of these wrong. Having attended the Army Gym ten years before, I knew all these things, but exceptions were frowned upon and I had to wait for the training, appointment and uniform. Then a Part II Order (I think) was issued, by which we were informed that us rookies were to wear uniform after all, prematurely or not, and would receive an allowance for the purpose. The uniform allowance arrived without much delay, almost simultaneously with a further order rescinding the first (but not the allowance) and again requiring us to wear 'civvies', as we were, after all, where the spies were. I was eventually appointed to the exalted rank of lieutenant in September of that year, but still in civvies.

Thus I became aware very early in my career that there might be some substance to the facetious little epithets sometimes attached to the military, such as that military intelligence was a contradiction in terms, and that the army was like a circus, only with more tents and clowns. I bought a lovely Finnish Sako .308 hunting rifle with my uniform allowance. I don't think the auditors bothered too much about accountability, especially as we were some years later again ordered to wear uniform, and again issued with an allowance. Although typifying the old army description of 'great-coats on, great-coats off' to depict changing orders, this latter has at least been consistently in force to the present day. The wearing of a uniform was one of the great boons of military life for me, not having to make the daily decision of what to wear or to keep my wardrobe up with the times, in fact not having to keep any wardrobe at all. And the quality of tailoring and materials of uniforms for all purposes had been steadily improving, in time becoming quite excellent.

One of the things that impressed me with the military was the wide variety of career options it offered. I have never been able to identify a single profession or trade in which the military did not provide career opportunities, apart from combat soldiering as such. As a newly qualified attorney, I was worried that I would be put into military legal services to apply the Rules of Military Discipline for endless years, which would have driven me to distraction. I therefore did not put my application through the general recruitment offices of the SADF, but rather directly to DMI. Somewhat to my surprise, I passed the security clearance process without a hitch. I think a recommendation from my previously mentioned school friend, Louis Changuion, who worked there at the time, might have helped – I had given his name as a referee on my application form. I knew they could not have been too rigorous in tracing my somewhat chequered background.

I had been at DMI for a few days when the phone in my shared office rang and it was for me, which surprised me as I didn't think any outsider or even the switchboard knew I was there. It was a Lieutenant Vermeulen of the military police wanting to speak to me urgently. It appeared that since leaving the Gym ten years earlier as a reservist, I had neglected to advise the authorities of my many changes of address. The lieutenant was right; I had been grossly negligent and this was a serious offence. I almost heard him smack his lips at the prospect of further steps to be taken when he asked me where I worked because he had to come and see me immediately. When I told him, there was a long pause and I thought I distinctly heard a deep sob at the other end. Almost ten years of diligent tracking of this draft-dodger down the drain.

At DMI I started off in Research (political/security/military) while being assessed as to my best placement. I underwent comprehensive research and operational training courses, the latter presented by the best educator I ever came across, Major Dirk Greyling. A former teacher with a master's degree in education, his course covered the moral and philosophical aspects of intelligence work as thoroughly as it did technique and tradecraft, integrating the full spectrum of the discipline and ingraining its essentials on one's consciousness. He was an amazing educational psychologist and, together with another excellent teacher, Captain Tolletjie Botha, both of them energetic and innovative, they made this course a truly unforgettable experience. Nothing I did afterwards, be it quite extensive academic study or full military training up to the highest level, really matched the personal enrichment I got from this course. Perhaps the *tabula rasa* syndrome applied – I was an excited child bounding up the stairs for his first school day with a spanking clean slate clutched under his arm and between his ears.

I was placed in Production (collection of information) under the tutelage, guidance and command of Major Greyling, and was assigned to an experienced mentor in agent handling, Captain André Barnard, who found me to be a bit too free-thinking for the job, I was given to understand. Barnard later left to become a political science lecturer at the University of South Africa (UNISA) for some years, but returned to the fold in the form of the NIS in about 1982, where we worked together again for a further number of years in a division of political research. Greyling later got his doctorate *cum laude* part-time while in a highly demanding military job, and left the SADF prematurely at the rank of brigadier general to take up an *ad hominem* Chair in Education offered to him by UNISA. His was a sorry loss to military intelligence in particular and to the SADF in general.

One of my first tasks at DMI was to listen to and transcribe tapes of daily radio broadcasts from Lusaka and Dar es Salaam by the ANC's Radio Freedom and the PAC's Radio Free Africa respectively. The rhetoric was filled with incessant exhortations to the 'people of South Africa' (or Azania, as the country was dubbed by the PAC) to rise to war and liberation. Graphic descriptions abounded of how the Boers would be annihilated and their property burnt, their women raped, and their children disembowelled and their heads bashed against trees, which we had in any case learnt from Voortrekker history was 'their' wont. Violent incursions into the white-controlled countries of southern Africa by, among others, the South West Africa People's Organisation (SWAPO) and its military wing, the People's Liberation Army of Namibia (PLAN) into South West Africa, led to the first deployment in 1966 of SADF combat units along the borders of that country with Angola.

I was assigned as desk officer to our declared resident in Paris to handle communication between him and headquarters (HQ) at the time of the severe student uprisings in France and elsewhere in Europe in 1968. It entailed, among other things, the encrypting and decrypting of high volumes of two-way traffic, mostly by way of one-time code pads. I also became involved in projects to provide arms and other equipment as well as training support to some friendly forces in Africa, in one instance the delivery of a DC4 Skymaster aircraft with equipment and armaments, and three T6 Harvard fighters from

SAAF stock, obsolete but perfectly maintained and fit for the purpose. The SAAF also trained a small group of freelance French fighter pilots on the Harvards, only later learning that one of them was under a death sentence for some atrocity or other committed during France's war in Algeria.

I thrived on this new environment and the stimulating nature of the work. What struck me most of all from the outset were the impressive people I met and worked with. There was a receptiveness to alternative ideas and opinions, contrary to the image the outside world had of the armed forces, and to what I had expected. But when the exchanging of ideas stopped and the last word spoken by whomever was in charge, it became an order to be adhered to by all, sometimes to my intense irritation and frustration if my views had not prevailed.

8

Academic Interlude

I had without much motivation stumbled piecemeal through the B.Iuris degree extramurally at Tukkies and simultaneously the attorneys' admission and conveyancing exams, taking a year longer than scheduled for the former. I had thought of it simply as a vehicle to something that I hoped would offer a liveable job opportunity, and also took two year-courses each in economics and political science to fill the five years I had to spend in articles. As already recounted, this aspiration faded even before I qualified as an attorney, and was accompanied by the realisation that I would never be motivated by money. I liked reading law, but not practising it. This led to my entering the military and a fulfilling career that would last a lifetime. At DMI I became absorbed in something other than sport and partying for the first time in my life: my job. I had over time been reading a bit on military history, especially the Anglo-Boer War, but now became captivated by the full spectrum of the science and art of war. I was transformed overnight from a dilettante to a workaholic. Crucially, I came into contact with Brigadier Fritz Loots and the aforementioned Major Dirk Greyling.

Loots was Director of Military Intelligence and a Second World War veteran with, as far as I can recall, no tertiary education apart from military training. But he had a passion for soldiers to better themselves through study, in which he was fully supported by my first immediate commanding officer, Greyling. Both had a wonderful way with people, especially the young. At the time, the University of the Witwatersrand (Wits) in Johannesburg, that irredeemable leftist den of iniquity in official thinking, was offering an honours course in international relations with subjects including contemporary history, strategic studies, international organisation and international law. I was alerted to this offering by a long-standing friend, Deon Fourie, then a lecturer and later a professor in strategic studies at UNISA. The very thought of this course entranced me and for the first time in my life I was excited at the prospect of academic study. However, there was a seemingly insurmountable practical problem: seminars were held from four o'clock in the afternoon at Wits, which meant that I would have to leave Pretoria not much after 2:30 p.m. four afternoons a week to attend. Cost was another factor, but Wits generously awarded me a small bursary, which made all the difference.

I did not have much hope that the powers that be would approve of an intelligence officer, of all people, attending Wits, of all places, apart even from the practicalities involved. But Greyling was supportive and arranged for me to see Brigadier Loots. A few days later I was instructed to report to Loots's office. As I arrived, he was rushing out to an unforeseen urgent meeting somewhere else in the building, apologised to me and asked that I wait for him in his office – he wouldn't be long. While there I noticed his cap with the gold braid and red band hanging on a hat-stand next to a small mirror on the wall. It fascinated me. Surely such an appurtenance was worth striving for and working for, but how long would it take a lieutenant to get there?

For the first and only time Brigadier Loots misled me: he took very long. It felt like hours and he was decidedly thoughtless to leave me alone for so long with that cap, on which I became fixated. The rest was diabolically predictable. He walked into the office the very moment I put the cap on my head in front of the mirror. He laughed heartily and said: 'Just a little patience, just a little patience.'

The upshot was that he approved my application to attend the course at Wits, on condition that all work assigned to me got done. He even offered to speak to the relevant people about the possibility of some financial assistance, but for technical budgeting reasons this could not be done. I sometimes wondered whether my blatant demonstration of ambition for the red band might have given him an impression of probable success. If he had, he would have been right. I enjoyed the course immensely and did well. I also kept up my end of the bargain and often came in to the office at around 5 a.m. to catch up on work. After all, a wise man once said that work was only work if you'd rather be doing something else.

At Wits I came under the tutelage of two inspirational lecturers: Ben Cockram, Jan Smuts Professor of International Relations, and John Dugard, a professor of international law, both eminent in their fields. Dugard later became dean of the law faculty at Wits and an ad hoc judge on the International Court of Justice in The Hague, Netherlands. Cockram was a former British diplomat (I suspect also of the British Secret Intelligence Service – SIS, or MI6) and once told of his fascinating experience in the USA in the early 1930s observing and reporting on joint exercises in crowd mobilisation and control in Chicago between gangster organisations and the Nazi Sturmabteilung (SA, or Brown Shirts). Both Cantabrigians, Cockram and Dugard encouraged me to apply to Cambridge University for admission to advanced studies in international law. I did so successfully, certainly due in no small measure to their generous testimonials and, I suspect, even perhaps a bit of networking on my behalf.

I borrowed money from an uncle and my mother-in-law, and at the end of September 1970 we left for England and a great new adventure. Major General Loots, to which rank he had shortly before been promoted, fully supported me in this further endeavour, assuring me that I would have a job at DMI when I got back if I wanted it. Both he and his wife came all the way from Pretoria to Jan Smuts Airport in Kempton Park the evening we left to wish me, my wife and our three small children well and see us off. It was a stunning gesture by a major general towards an insignificant little lieutenant under his command and a telling measure of the man.

We entered Churchill College in October 1970 and I was awarded an LLB in international law in June 1972, fair to middling effort rendering fair to middling results. I am eternally thankful to General Loots, Professor Dugard, Professor Cockram and my financial sponsors, 'skoonma' Emma Bosman Senior and my uncle Oom Koos, Dr Koos Maritz, for this priceless opportunity. The names of the outstanding teachers of international law at Cambridge, Elihu Lauterpacht, Derek Bowett (both later knighted) and the diminutive but intellectually towering Kurt Lipstein, together with Dugard and Cockram – as well as Nic van der Merwe, Pierre Olivier, Retief van Rooyen and Charles Nieuwoudt at Tukkies – will forever have pride of place in my personal pantheon of gods of learning. Many years later they were to be joined by my wonderful teachers at Stellenbosch University.

An epilogue to this Cambridge degree occurred twenty years later, in 1993, when I got a letter from the university informing me that my LLB had been 'redesignated' an LLM. Knowing of this Oxbridge usage and in light of my Calvinist upbringing which taught, among other things, that one never got anything of value in life without slaving for it, I somewhat mischievously wrote to the university enquiring on what grounds this was done. I got a snotty little letter (as mine had been) saying in effect that that was the way they did things there, but that I probably wouldn't understand. They were right, but neither would I, of course, look a gift horse in the mouth –

my Calvinist morality wasn't that compelling. I later received a gracious formal letter informing me that the LLB had been done away with and only the LLM remained. Rightly so, I thought, as the structure and content of the LLB were those of a specialised taught master's rather than a bachelor's degree.

As someone in his early thirties with a family, traditional student fun was not in my scheme of things. Very important elements of value in my time at Cambridge were the fringe benefits of meeting people from faculties other than that of law, and having contact with eminent international lawyers and others passing through.

The American Telford Taylor, a one-time chief prosecutor in the 1945–46 Nuremberg trials of Nazi leaders on charges of war crimes, delivered a series of three lectures on those momentous events. I had occasion around a tea table to exchange a few words with him about the vexed legal question of retroactive legislation, especially in this case where it was unilaterally imposed by a somewhat incongruous 'allied community', including as it did the Soviet Union, and carrying the severest penalties. He again emphasised, as in his lectures, that the horrendous nature of the Nazi rampage and the outrage it engendered among almost all nations on earth, created a universal consensus that the perpetrators had to be punished. The banning of aggressive war was probably the most momentous outcome. The Nuremberg prosecutions also provided for a new framework and institutions for administering and enforcing international law. Among the results were the establishment in 1945 of the International Court of Justice, successor to the former Permanent Court of Arbitration in The Hague, and over time a range of international instruments, including on genocide and the protection of minorities. The old Hague and Geneva Red Cross conventions (1864–1907) were reviewed and strengthened, resulting in the new Geneva Convention of 1949. The world's outrage at the Nazi scourge demanded this process. There was no question that the brutality of that regime could go unpunished.

But I'm not sure about the legal perspective, based as it was on the same outrage of the international community that put Libya and Cuba on the UN Human Rights Council, even to chair it. The same international community remained silent on the horrific genocide in Rwanda. Is this outrage transient and selective, dependent on the mood of the time? And against South Africa, with a human rights and human development record far superior to that of many member states of the UN? In 1971 I took the opportunity to attend some sessions of the International Court of Justice then considering the question of South Africa's mandate over South West Africa, which to me seemed to confirm this moral selectivity.

The coincidence of the racist horrors of the Nazi regime in Germany and the surge in the drive for decolonisation to shed the dominance of the colonialist powers from the late 1950s onward, meant that South Africa's domestic policies invited the full brunt of international opprobrium. Together with the ambition for global hegemony of the Soviet Union, South Africa eventually paid the price of ostracism from the international community.

Another man I came across at a college master's 'at home' (cocktail party) introduced himself to me as Tony Hewish. A pleasant and soft-spoken man, he expressed an interest in South Africa and we talked mostly about South African inanities like rugby and wine. He was quite well informed about the country, but we steered clear of politics. I later learnt that I had had this pleasant little chat with Professor Sir Anthony Hewish, the head of the Cambridge Department of Radio Astronomy, and the principal discoverer of pulsar stars. A year or two after our encounter, he was a co-recipient of the Nobel Prize for Physics.

One of the academic highlights of my time at Cambridge was attending seminars given by the eminent historian and head of the history department, Professor Harry Hinsley. He was highly regarded internationally as an expert on the Second World War, but had made his perhaps more telling yet understated mark as a member of the cryptography centre (later known as Government Communications Headquarters) situated at Bletchley Park in Cheltenham, England, during the war. He had played a significant role in the decoding of the sophisticated German 'Enigma' machine code, which had long been regarded as unbreakable, and had assisted physically in retrieving Enigma machines for analysis from captured German weather-boats in the English Channel and North Sea.

As I was not enrolled for any course in his department, I asked his permission to attend. A friendly man, he had no objection and asked me a few questions to establish my particular interests. He was quite intrigued by the fact that I had been in military intelligence, and had a bit of experience in cryptography. His seminars did not touch on this arcane art, but rather covered selections from the history of Europe in the twentieth century, in particular the two world wars. I was enormously impressed by this great man, and was saddened when in 1998 I read that Professor Sir Francis Harry Hinsley, OBE, had died.

This ancient institution of learning also had some less palatable aspects to it. The leftist West German student activist, Rudi Dutschke, who had been shot in the head in 1968 during the student riots in Europe, also enrolled at Cambridge in 1970. His presence raised questions in the House of Commons as to whether, in light of his alleged reduced mental capacity, he was at Cambridge for academic purposes or to practise his agitprop expertise. Serious protest resulted against his being allowed into England at all, and he was eventually forced to leave the country when his student visa was revoked. New protests, this time from the Left, erupted against this constraint on freedom of expression and association by the Conservative government of Prime Minister Edward Heath and Education Secretary Margaret Thatcher.

In this atmosphere it was announced that the anti-apartheid activist who had been key in instigating the 1969–70 sports boycott of South Africa, former South African Peter Hain, was to hold a public meeting one evening in the Old Schools in Cambridge, the main lecture building of the law faculty. A friendly, right-wing Canadian fellow-student, who had told me about the rough gap year he had spent as a lumberjack in Canada before doing his undergraduate studies, suggested we go to the meeting together. He also said he felt that something should be done about Hain, with which I heartily agreed. I was always wary of being compromised by people of his political bent, who tended to automatically regard any South African as 'one of us', but agreed to go, not considering what 'doing something' might mean.

He collected me from my flat and as we approached his car I noticed some other people inside who didn't look much like students to me. Before getting in he said he wanted to show me something in the boot. It contained about a dozen brand-new pickhandles. I explained to him that as a South African I could not possibly get involved in any political event concerning my country that might turn violent, although I would dearly have liked to meet Mr Hain somewhere in a dark alley out of the public eye, and declined to go along. We were not aware that by then the police had already at the last moment forbidden the meeting to proceed as they 'had certain informations (*sic*) that Mr Hain's safety might be at risk'. For a while I worried that my near-participation might have featured in their 'informations' and affect my visa, but nothing came of it.

While at Cambridge, I was also able to pay a memorable visit to Professor Frits Kalshoven of the law faculty of the University of Leiden in the Netherlands, who had been an officer in the Royal Dutch Navy before entering academia. Our mutual military backgrounds made it easy to find common ground on a personal level. Together we exalted in the exploits of our illustrious common Dutch forebears, Admirals Piet Hein, Michiel de Ruyter and Maarten Tromp, who had hammered the Spanish and English fleets in the sixteenth and seventeenth centuries respectively. We did not dwell on trying to find more recent cause for common patriotism, but he did, without prompt from me, raise the exploits of Boer War generals Christiaan de Wet and Koos de la Rey. He was intrigued by my analogy of De la Rey and De Wet as counterparts to Second World War field marshals Erich von Manstein and Erwin Rommel, as two similar pairings of the brilliant supreme strategist and equally brilliant supreme tactician, of course in totally different settings and on totally different scales.

We did eventually come to the purpose of my visit. Kalshoven was gaining renown as an international humanitarian lawyer. I had chosen the following as the title for a long essay I had to do, thinking it looked impressively learned: 'The legal protection of non-combatants in situations approaching but short of war (status mixtus).' Kalshoven had written a book on related aspects and was enamoured of the subject I had chosen. I was not, and neither was my supervisor at Cambridge, Derek Bowett, who lectured in the laws of war. He suggested that I speak to Kalshoven about it. Good riddance, I thought he thought.

I don't really remember what Kalshoven and I discussed academically, but it was a pleasure speaking to him and a tremendous experience walking around the older parts of that ancient institution in the hallowed footsteps of so many great men. These included the 'father of international law', the late sixteenth- and early seventeenth-century Dutch academic and statesman, Hugo de Groot (Grotius), who founded the discipline with his seminal *De Jure Belli ac Pacis* (*On the Laws of War and Peace*), published in 1625. Bowett later did somewhat reluctantly accept my essay as sufficient for the purpose. Kalshoven became pre-eminent in the field of international humanitarian law, gathering numerous awards from the International Committee of the Red Cross and many other human rights organisations worldwide.

Other outstanding highlights were visits I was able to pay to John Ericsson, a renowned professor of strategic studies at Edinburgh University and an expert on the Soviet military with a reputation as the only Westerner to have got drunk with non-commissioned officers of the Red Army at their barracks in the Soviet Union, and to the authoritative French Général d'Armée André Beaufre in Paris, renowned military commander and strategist, and ground-breaking theoretician of the concept of 'total strategy', a concept and term he was the first to insert as a rational method into the lexicon of strategic studies worldwide. In his works and teachings, Beaufre emphasised the necessity of the involvement of the total capacity of the state in waging war. Having fought in the French army in Indochina and Algeria, he commanded the French forces in the joint British/French/Israeli invasion of Egypt in 1956 to safe-guard free passage through the Suez Canal, which President Nasser of Egypt had threatened to blockade. In 1958 he became Chief of General Staff, Allied Forces Europe of the North Atlantic Treaty Organisation (NATO).

Beaufre's ideas have infused and enriched training and theorising in mili-tary establishments the world over, including the SADF. He lived in a flat in the centre of Paris, not far from the residence of the French president, the Élysée Palace. Battle and unit standards from his long and illustrious career jutted inwards from both sides of the entrance passage leading to his old-world library, making for a unique experience of the palpable presence of modern French military history. He died in 1975 while on a lecturing visit to Belgrade, Yugoslavia.

These enlightening visits were facilitated by my remarkable friend Deon Fourie, who had arranged the appointments and asked me along. Probably the foremost military historian and teacher of the discipline of strategic stud-ies in South Africa, Fourie was a professor of strategic studies in the political science department at UNISA; a former CO of the Pretoria Regiment, an armoured citizen force unit; an influential voice in state and especially military heraldry; and later a brigadier general in the South African Army Citizen Force. Of unshakeable integrity, his immense erudition on matters mili-tary – together with a delightful sense of humour – made these visits highly instructive and pleasurable, and ensured that our (his, really) discussions with the abovementioned two world authorities in their fields were not merely one-way.

Although not without considerable hardship, our travels also brought some amusement. On a night train to Edinburgh to see Ericsson, we had neglected to book a sleeper and spent the night standing and sitting, some-times lying, around the onboard pub, with only a bottle of Rémy Martin between us to feed and warm us. We also paid a visit to Berlin where we attended, among other attractions, a performance of Verdi's *Aïda* and an unforgettable concert of medieval music in the oak-lined Eichengalerie of the Charlottenburg Palace in West Berlin. We also properly paid our soldierly respects to the fallen at the Soviet War Memorial and military cemetery in East Berlin. One night, after attending the opera, I think, we missed the last U-Bahn (underground train) and had to walk back to our lodgings in temperatures of $-16\,^{\circ}$C, with a wind-chill effect at times of $-30\,^{\circ}$C, according to the newspaper the following morning. But we bravely overcame our adversity by sheltering as often as we could in just about every one of the numerous pubs along the way.

While in East Berlin, at our enquiry, our young lady student guide assured us everything was fine in the (East) German Democratic Republic, but wistfully added that she would like to be able to travel. She tensed up, even panicked somewhat, it seemed, at our question of whether she thought Erich Honecker, of whom a photo hung on the wall of the bus terminal, would succeed the ageing Walter Ulbricht as head of state, which was then being speculated on in the West, and said she couldn't talk about such things. It was quite sad to experience such a mindset in an intelligent young girl in the oppressive circumstances of a totalitarian communist state. This priceless 'grand' tour was perhaps the most educational experience of my stay in England.

Much later, in 2009, I was awarded a BPhil in Translation by the University of Stellenbosch. This was, at last, the one academic sojourn I took purely for my own gratification, well after I had retired from formal employment and already in my late sixties. Sitting in seminars listening to learned and enthusiastic experts – and some impressive students – on translating into and out of the Afrikaans and English languages, my lifelong love affair with both came to pleasurable fulfilment. I owe a huge debt of gratitude to my excellent and sympathetic teachers there: Ilse Feinauer, Elsa Silke, Elaine Ridge, Edwin Hees and Rudolph Gouws, for this enormously enriching experience.

I had from the beginning of my academic endeavours often thought that I should have done language studies, as Mr Lötz at Lydenburg and others had urged me to do. But I also remember my first principal as an articled clerk in Pretoria, Leon Smuts, once saying to me that had he known when starting out what he then knew, he would not have done law, and that that would have been a mistake. What marvellous experiences would I have forfeited had I not followed the path I did? How does one ever find out retrospectively what one should have done differently, and whether that would have been a mistake or not? After all, the vaunted 20/20 hindsight never really comes along.

The foregoing hyperbolic name-dropping stems from a heartfelt desire to pay tribute before a wider audience, however limited, to these and other magnificent men and women who have so profoundly contributed to making me what I am, which is not to imply that any of them would necessarily be particularly thrilled at the outcome. But neither would I go as far as the inimitable satirist Ben Trovato when he said in the *Sunday Times*: 'My teachers made me what I am today, the bastards.' Only stylistic constraints prevent me from being even more effusive in my praise-singing. In particular, I remain eternally grateful to those two remarkable career soldiers, Fritz Loots and Dirk Greyling, who inspired and directed me onto this path.

9

Back in the Fold, Briefly

On returning to South Africa from England, I rejoined military intelligence in January 1973, the DMI now having been upgraded to the DGMI, and Major General Hein du Toit having succeeded General Loots as director general. Du Toit was a historian, a former state archivist and an authoritative voice in state heraldry. He also held an LLB and later became CSI as a lieutenant general. He retired from the military towards the mid-1970s and was appointed professor of strategic studies at the Rand Afrikaans University in Johannesburg. He was a strong-minded and erudite intellectual who I suspect did not always see eye to eye with the rest of the top brass of the SADF. Although a somewhat distant personality, I developed great respect for him personally and for the qualities he brought to the organisation.

I was appointed to the rank of captain and proudly but somewhat disappointingly simultaneously promoted to temporary major, depriving me of ever wearing those nice three stars on my shoulders. (These had the added attraction of in low light being easily confused with the rank insignia of a colonel, sometimes momentarily massaging the *folie de grandeur* of the wearer.) I was placed in security research on parts of Africa and the Middle East for a while and then transferred to the oversight division of Research and Editing, where I had the pleasure of again working under the direct command of Dirk Greyling, who had by then attained the rank of colonel. During that year I attended some intelligence and two qualifying courses, Battle Handling and Tactics (Platoon Commanders) at the Infantry School in Oudtshoorn, and Battle Group (Company) Commanders at the Army College in Pretoria, both demanding but interesting and good fun.

In that year I also had the opportunity to serve for three months with an SADF signals intelligence (SIGINT) radio-interception unit based at Chirundu near Lake Kariba on the Zambezi River border between Rhodesia and Zambia. I was appointed the CO for a tour of duty with this unit. The radio operators, mostly national servicemen, sat day and night in shifts listening to and recording primarily Zambian military radio traffic for anything that might affect the security situation in Namibia and South Africa. This entailed intercepting reports by Zambian army call-signs to each other and to their HQ on movements of SWAPO elements on their way to crossing the border into South West Africa from Zambia, mainly via Angola or Botswana.

In such a static situation, radio operators get to know their counterparts on the other side well, speaking to and often swearing at one another ('ops chat'), as but one of the many different battlegrounds in war. They learn to identify particular operators, even by their tapping style when using Morse code. Changes of operators can sometimes be important battle indicators, for instance when more experienced ones and those of higher rank come on air. I was impressed by how crucial this can be when briefed on a visit to Israeli military intelligence in late 1973, shortly after their harrowing experience of being caught off guard by their Arab invaders in the Yom Kippur War of that year.

All interceptions were immediately signalled back to CSI in Pretoria, and then transcribed and forwarded in hard copy as well. Operators also had to record all ops chat in their reports, and I had on several occasions to reprimand some of them for their too unbridled use of foul language. In one instance, a young Portuguese-speaking national serviceman who was also fluent in Afrikaans and English had addressed his Zambian counterpart as 'You fucking cunt. I'm not your fucking comrade'. I ordered him to rewrite the report in more civilised language. He came up with an exact, literal translation into Afrikaans from the English, which looked and sounded even worse. I was now very angry with him, but he insisted that he had complied with my instructions. Surely Afrikaans was a more civilised language than English?

In another incident, a Zambian radio operator apologetically reported to his HQ in Lusaka that a certain report, identified by the usual string of reference numbers, date-time groups, etc. should have been sent in code but inadvertently wasn't. 'Here it is now in code,' he added to the delight of our cryptographers, in the context a coup comparable to the breaking of the German Enigma code by the British (and a Polish mathematical genius). A short while later, a message came for this call-sign that the colonel was coming down from Lusaka to speak to the operator, one Richard, as he had become known to our operators, and who was usually under the influence of some inebriating agent. Richard was ordered to remain on station to be available to the colonel when he arrived. After a while the reply went back: 'Richard has fucked off into the bush and taken the radio with him.' We never heard what fate may have befallen poor Richard, but he did not appear on air again.

At Chirundu we had opportunities to mix with some locals, play soccer and socialise, and get to know the local British South Africa Police (BSAP), mostly Special Branch, quite well. We had as neighbours an SAP Counter Insurgency Unit commanded by Colonel Theuns O'Connell, with whom we enjoyed good relations, sometimes lending and borrowing things like sugar and toilet paper, and providing them with information that could be useful to them in their patrols along the border. The relationship was pleasantly neighbourly. They also had film projection facilities, something we did not, to which we had a standing invitation.

I once accompanied a platoon of theirs on one of their regular patrols down the Zambezi to Cheworeworeng and Mana Pools, surely among the most stunning pieces of bushveld there are – and the most frightening, considering the abundance of cover for ambushes along the way. These young policemen and their only slightly older leaders were very brave indeed. Early evening braais at our base on the high ground directly above the steep drop down into the valley towards the river, often against a stupendous African sunset, watching large herds of elephant and other wildlife come down for drinks as we simultaneously engaged in the same restful pursuit, was as idyllic an experience as one could wish for.

One of the national service signals troops, Corporal 'Chappy' Chapman, rigged a loudspeaker system over which he played the one 78-speed vinyl record he had brought along with an old gramophone over and over again, for the unsolicited entertainment of the whole camp. It was a record of Cat Stevens, with 'Morning has broken' on one side. After a while I forbade his incessant playing of it, except with my specific permission. Chappy, the charmingly chancy boy that he was, approached me for such permission as often as he had previously been playing the record.

An incident indelibly ingrained Chappy, Cat Stevens and 'Morning has broken' in my consciousness. Early one evening, just as Cat was reaching the crescendo of 'Morning has bro …' he was interrupted by a shattering blast not far from the camp. I went with our police to have a look. A soft-skinned BSAP vehicle transporting some Rhodesian policemen had hit a landmine on a nearby road. The occupants of the vehicle had no chance at all and the carnage was horrific.

I still sometimes wonder what was on the other side of Chappy's record.

10

The Law, Again

Part of my life story is that the bad things crossing my path have often been self-inflicted, while the good things have often been thrust upon me by the doings of others and good fortune. After just one year back in the army, I was in considerable financial straits, having to repay study loans and now keep four children. I took the wrenching decision to go back into legal practice to seek hopefully quick redemption. Towards the middle of 1975, I joined a firm of attorneys in Bronkhorstspruit in a partnership agreement providing for my temporary release from the firm on reduced income should I, as a reserve officer in the SADF, be called up for active service. When it happened and I was already deployed almost unreachably in 2 Military Area in Ovamboland in northern South West Africa, my partners advised my wife back home that they were no longer prepared to release me and that she would no longer be receiving my income from the firm.

Apart from my partners' later backstabbing, this brief sojourn into the legal field was a valuable reality check in other respects. To prepare for joining the practice, I first did a stint as a state prosecutor in Pretoria to polish up on criminal law and procedure, with which I had gained only cursory acquaintance during my articled training. As with all rookies, I was initially assigned to the 'petty courts', where mostly traffic and influx-control offences were heard. The latter was colloquially called *onwettig slaap* ('illegal sleeping'), for which prisoners arrested in a 'white-by-night' area were tried. At the time, legislation forbade black people to overnight in designated white areas. When calling cases, court orderlies and prosecutors came to calling the charges merely as '*onwettig slaap*', which for brevity's sake was usually accepted by the magistrates. I don't even recall what the relevant parts of the influx-control legislation were that created this offence. Routinely all accused would plead guilty and get the standard R10 fine or ten days' incarceration.

And woe betide the poor misguided soul who would dare to plead not guilty! How on earth would we ever get through the huge court rolls if this should become standard practice? It was simply untenable and brought forth general opprobrium upon the head of the hapless accused – from the prosecutors, the court orderlies and sometimes even the public galleries of family and friends, who often would have been waiting for hours or even days just to get the matter done with so that they could return home. Such cases had to be postponed, sometimes for long remands, with the accused usually refused bail and kept in salutary confinement. Even attorneys, except for those with no other work, were generally loath to defend people so obdurately confounding the system. Someone once jokingly congratulated me on having broken a record: eighty of these cases, if memory serves, finalised in a day, the man said.

Now with only three years to the magic date of 1978 when the influx of migrants to the cities would supposedly be reversed, it became blindingly obvious that the apartheid system as it stood could not be sustained. Hardly a politician still preached that Verwoerdian gospel in public. Few things contributed more to the loss of confidence in the NP government – and in the country's future – than this big lie. It must have also contributed to the disillusionment with the Afrikaans churches later on. People simply could not stomach the churches' switch from consistent support for the apartheid policies as the will of God, to the notion that He must have changed His mind midstream. For a recently born-again agnostic like me, without much truck with religion but steeped in Afrikaner culture and history, the role of the Afrikaans churches over time was exposed as politically manipulative and theologically fraudulent. Could it be that the Covenant handed down by the putative Moses, Sarel Cilliers, from the Mount Sinai that the Battle of Blood River had become in Afrikaner lore, was also fraudulent? Foundations were beginning to shudder as in an earthquake.

Another valuable experience came my way in the traffic court. Mr Grobler had committed the heinous offence of changing traffic lanes in one-way Pretorius Street in the centre of Pretoria without indicating his intention to do so, thereby almost causing an accident. An alert traffic cop had observed this, as he testified in court. There were matters of fact and law to be established, as the defendant pleaded not guilty. I relished this opportunity to cross-examine someone, for which I had been itching. I was brilliant at it and knew I had him when he said to the magistrate: 'I'm sorry, sir, but I'm now quite confused with all these questions.' 'Oom' Braam Pretorius was a retired magistrate of great repute who had been recalled temporarily to help out in the petty courts, and stayed forever. He was a sweet humanitarian with a delightful sense of humour, on and off the bench. He took off his glasses and quizzically looked first at me and then at the accused, and said: 'Don't worry, Mr Grobler. That makes two of us.' When the court adjourned he invited me to his chambers and, after first asking my permission, had only one piece of advice to offer: 'Always keep things as simple as possible.' I don't remember what the verdict was.

I was soon moved to the (higher) regional court where I was once cross-examining a suspect through an interpreter. The accused, a black man accused of housebreaking and robbery, was intelligent, slick in his responses and quite a challenge. The interpreter was one of the long-winded ones I'd sometimes encountered, who diligently engaged in long discussions with the accused to make sure that he fully understood the questions and to extract full answers to them. At last the accused contradicted himself and I referred to various things he had said before which did not accord with what he was now saying, pointing out that both versions could not be true, and asking for his response. As I knew would happen, a very long discussion between interpreter and accused followed. Eventually came the response: 'Your Honour, I was surprised myself.' I got a conviction in that case, but have often marvelled at how people sometimes say things that seem to surprise themselves as well as others, in and out of court – myself included.

Most importantly, perhaps, in Bronkhorstspruit I finally learnt that I could not have a fulfilling career as an attorney. I was simply not motivated by the idea of making money, which was then certainly a prospect there, where an eruption of industrial development was taking place. Moreover, I have no financial sense or interest in matters monetary, which I think are prerequisites for being a good attorney. I hasten to add that I have some lifelong attorney friends who have done very well in legal practice, but whom I know to be motivated by an ethic of service and care. I seriously considered doing the few additional exams I needed to be admitted to the Bar as an advocate, which, being more concerned with pure law, would have suited my temperament better. I would have specialised in criminal law, with instructing attorneys responsible for my fees, and thus had no need to concern myself with financial matters. But I had already found my niche in the military and intelligence worlds.

II

Demise of an Empire

After anti-colonialist insurgencies had steadily been gaining in intensity in Angola and Mozambique, and to a lesser extent in Guinea-Bissau, since the early 1960s, Portugal's African empire finally crumbled in 1974, when the mother country was hit by the 'Carnation Revolution'. It came to be called thus when peaceful demonstrators stuck carnations into the muzzles of the rifles of soldiers trying to control the crowds on the streets of Lisbon. Soon the soldiers themselves followed suit, the flower markets in Lisbon at the time overflowing with carnations. The wars in these 'overseas provinces', as they were called by the metropolitan government, had become untenably expensive in the face of economic and social hardship at home, leading to increasing political instability. The left-leaning Armed Forces Movement of middle-ranking army officers launched a bloodless coup against the autocratic government of Prime Minister Marcelo Caetano, triggered by his attempt to fire the head of the armed forces, General António de Spinola. De Spinola had published a book in 1973 in which he argued that the country's colonial wars could no longer be sustained. He became president of Portugal after the coup, but had himself to flee the country shortly afterwards in the face of a rightist counter-coup attempt. This led to a series of unstable provisional governments, finally destroying any residual authority Portugal might still have had in its colonies.

With the demise of the Portuguese presence in their African possessions, the various liberation movements in Angola in 1975 jointly signed the so-called Alvor Agreement with the metropolitan power. Chief among these were the Soviet-backed, communist Popular Movement for the Liberation of Angola (MPLA) under the leadership of Agostinho Neto in the central regions; the anti-communist National Union for the Total Independence of Angola (UNITA) under Jonas Savimbi in the south; and the National Front for the Liberation of Angola (FNLA) under Holden Roberto in the north. The agreement granted the country independence and established a joint transitional government, pending the holding of free democratic elections. Neto's MPLA, in control of the capital Luanda, procrastinated and eventually, on the pretext of instability in the country, failed to hold elections and installed a government on its own. UNITA returned to the bush and commenced an insurgency campaign against the usurped government in Luanda. A vicious civil war engulfed the country.

Refugees started pouring over the border into South West Africa in all manner of vehicle and on foot. In early 1976 I was distressed at the sight of an elderly white couple walking across the border, both dressed in black and wearing black hats. The man carried two large suitcases on which they sat down, perspiring heavily and covered in dust, exhausted, confused and fearful. I had a heart-rending vision of the total spiritual destitution of Hemingway's *Old Man at the Bridge*.

For the next ten years, UNITA was to be a thorn in the side of the MPLA government, later with considerable military and other support from South Africa. They were also backed covertly by some Western powers, mainly the USA. Savimbi established his HQ at Jamba in the south-east of the country. From the outset, the MPLA and its military arm, the People's Armed Forces for the Liberation of Angola (FAPLA), was supported by Cuba as surrogate of the USSR, which provided huge material, leadership, planning and command support. The Soviets also provided instructors and pilots from other communist sources, notably East Germany.

The other overseas province of Portugal in the region, Mozambique, under President Samora Machel of the communist-backed resistance movement the Front for the Liberation of Mozambique (FRELIMO), became independent of the metropolitan in 1975, but was still being harassed by the anti-communist Mozambican National Resistance (RENAMO) supported by South Africa, until the signing of the non-aggression pact, the Nkomati Accord, between the two countries in 1984.

After the Unilateral Declaration of Independence by Prime Minister Ian Smith in 1965, Rhodesia, under international sanctions, became something of a client state of South Africa, with little alternate access to the outside world or sources of finance, fuel, armaments and political support. As almost always happens in such cases, Rhodesians came to resent this situation. One evening in a pub in 1973, a young lieutenant at the King George VI Barracks in Salisbury told my second in command at Chirundu, Lieutenant Nico Smith: 'Of course, you realise we don't like you [South Africans] but tolerate you only because we need you.' I sensed that this was a fairly general sentiment among Rhodesians at the time.

The South African government under Prime Minister John Vorster had embarked on a foreign policy characterised as 'outward moving' in an attempt at *rapprochement* with black African states, who were the main drivers of sustained attempts to isolate South Africa. The country's relations with Ian Smith's Rhodesia were counterproductive to this objective. Under immense pressure from Harold Wilson's British Labour government in particular, Vorster increasingly pressurised Smith to find an internationally acceptable solution, which was the last straw in forcing the Rhodesian government towards the Lancaster House settlement negotiations in 1979. As a result, the rather naïve Reverend Abel Muzorewa became interim prime minister of what was then known as Zimbabwe-Rhodesia, pending general elections. The Zimbabwe African National Union (ZANU) party with its Zimbabwe African National Liberation Army (ZANLA) under the capable but ultimately disastrous Robert Mugabe, won the election and the latter became prime minister of Zimbabwe in 1980. The new country was recognised internationally and was heavily supported by the People's Republic of China and the Democratic People's Republic of (North) Korea.

South Africa had lost its last buffer state and was now surrounded by states under communist and communist-influenced governments, and under direct assault from communist-supported forces both inside and outside the country.

12

Escape to Sanity, Again

My escape from the soul-destroying attorneys' practice in Bronkhorstspruit was due to good fortune on a grand scale. In late 1975, I got word that top-secret (I still had buddies in those quarters) preparations were under way in the SADF for an incursion into Angola in support of the UNITA movement there. It was called Operation Savannah. UNITA was now under serious conventional attack from FAPLA and its communist backers, mainly Cuban combat units – it was said about twenty brigades, consisting at times of up to 50 000 men – with virtually unlimited support from the USSR. Vital South African interests were now being directly threatened, as FAPLA and its communist backers also supported SWAPO in its drive to oust South Africa from South West Africa. The very real threat of a direct conventional military incursion into the latter galvanised the SADF into action. The vitally important water resources of the Kunene River, the underground hydroelectric plant at Ruacana on the river and the nearby dam at Calueque just across the border in Angola, were also under threat and had to be protected.

They evidently thought they could win the war without me. More likely, and even more disturbingly, they weren't thinking of me at all. I would have none of it – to miss an opportunity of a lifetime? So I approached the second in command of my citizen force unit, Colonel Shorty Brown of the 8th Armoured Division HQ, and insisted that I be drafted for active service. But he was familiar with draft *evaders*, and this was outside his field of experience. My telling argument was that it was my life; not the government's, his or the army's, but mine to do with as I pleased, the classic mindset of virtually every draft-dodger the world over.

After some browbeating from me and a long, thoughtful pause, he merely shook his head in disbelief. Exerting my right to be let into the army was difficult for him to get his head around. He handed me a standard printed letter warning me that my call-up papers would be delivered shortly and that I should arrange my affairs accordingly. I insisted that my affairs were in order and that I wanted the call-up papers immediately, afraid that Shorty and his establishment might have a rethink. After having to wait for some time, once I had the papers in hand I felt a tremendous sense of relief. I would now, in the slightly paraphrased immortal words of American general George S. Patton, not have to tell my children that I was 'shovelling shit in Bronkhorstspruit' if they should ask what I did in the war. I had left an uncongenial, extremely tedious legal practice to enter another reality, which I could not have bettered had I designed it myself. If they should read this account, I'm sure my erstwhile partners in law will feel vindicated for having constructively fired me so ignominiously, even though they were in gross breach of contract in so doing.

I rejoined the army in May 1976 as an intelligence officer in HQ 81st Armoured Brigade and was immediately deployed to South West Africa. I flew to the Grootfontein rear base for a brief stay before moving by road to Ondangwa in 2 Military Area in northern Ovamboland. I was allocated a Land Rover for this trip and an enthusiastic, talkative young national service minister of an Afrikaans church on his first full assignment after a brief training and orientation visit as a military chaplain, asked me for a lift. Along the way he told me of his disgust when on his previous visit to the operational area he had met troops who were actually keen on going out to find the enemy and kill as many of them as possible. He found this unconscionable. I explained to him as gently as I could that that was what soldiers and soldiering were all about and that such an attitude made for a good, aggressive combat soldier. Moreover, that those were the sort of soldiers who were most likely to end up in need of his services and care. He did not utter another word for the remaining couple of hours of the trip.

I was disgusted to learn that by this time our forces were already in the process of being withdrawn from Angola and Operation Savannah was being terminated, just as my chase after it was approaching success. However, I then had the great opportunity to serve as Senior Officer Intelligence in General Constand Viljoen's HQ 101 Task Force at Ondangwa for Operation Cobra, a sweep operation throughout Ovamboland to clear the area of SWAPO insurgents. I developed a huge respect for General Viljoen, an ascetic, energetic, aggressive soldier of outstanding and innovative intellect, and a sincere, thorough gentleman to the core. Here I had, among others, the unenviable task of maintaining radio contact with Colonel Jan Breytenbach, in command of Bravo Group operating in Angola. Made up of mostly battle-hardened former liberation fighters against the Portuguese in Angola but opposed to the communist MPLA, they were arguably the best infantry in the war. They were also under probably the most aggressive and effective command as well. Jan did not take too kindly to meddling generals always wanting to know what he was up to and a radio, of course, only works if it's switched on.

At the time Ondangwa was also a staging post for Operation Savannah units returning from Angola. One such, an armoured-car unit that had earned accolades in hard fighting, were on their return bivouacked within the secure area not far from the HQ building, and set about celebrating with equal gusto. At first, in view of their excellent record, we were all tolerant of their well-deserved chance to blow off steam. But after dark the cacophony got out of hand and the general instructed me to go and quieten them down, pointing out that we were still in an active operational area with things like mortars a distinct threat. He also told me to remember to take my pistol. I had to search a bit through the general celebratory carnage for the CO, a captain, but eventually found him, introduced myself and ordered him, compliments of the general, to shut up. He was immediately compliant, saluted smartly and gave me a snappy 'Yes, Major' – while lying flat on his back in the sand. To my amazement, the noise died down almost immediately. I gather he must have had a good regimental sergeant major who had overheard our 'conversation'.

I was billeted in a tent just off the apron of the operational air force base at Ondangwa. Space for incoming units within the perimeter fence was at a premium and tents were pitched very close together, with the ropes intertwined between them. It was difficult to navigate one's way through, even when sober. While sitting outside my tent early one evening a commotion approached from between the tents, which included a steady stream of heartfelt expletives. The source was a citizen force officer with the rank of commandant (lieutenant colonel), as it transpired, trying largely unsuccessfully to proceed between the tents, heroically fighting to untangle himself from the ropes, but having freed himself, falling down again at the next step. I gingerly ventured into the labyrinth to see if I could be of assistance, thinking the man might not be well. From the swearing I suspected that he was indeed somewhat unwell. About the length of a tent away I got confirmation from the approaching aroma. I estimated that he had accumulated at least a week's rust on him, apart from the dust he had gathered in his epic wrestling match with the ropes.

Having with some difficulty guided him to a clearing in front of my tent, holding him upright and dusting him off, he pushed me away, almost falling over backwards. He was the archetype of the respected and enduring figure of the lifelong citizen force officer who may have fought in the Second World War or Korea, or wished that he had, and had been searching for a role in the armed forces ever since. So often these figures had difficulty adjusting to the humdrum of peace and life in general. Sometimes, out of respect and sympathy, they became ensconced in an office at some citizen force unit, keeping themselves busy, or not, with whatever took their fancy.

The commandant had a greying walrus moustache in a scorching red face, and was obviously too old for any active duty. He straightened himself to his full height and looked me quizzically in the eye: 'What are you?' he demanded. I wasn't sure what he meant and replied with the self-evident fact that I was an officer in the SADF. 'Yes, but what *are* you?' I once again guessed at his enquiry and said I was a major, sir. 'Look, young man, what is your mustering?', now quite agitated. I said I was in Intelligence. 'Aha,' he exclaimed, waving a histrionic finger skywards, 'an intelligent officer. Every army needs one of those!'

I asked him where he was billeted and if I could perhaps assist him in getting there. He assured me he was perfectly capable of looking after himself and getting to his billet, thank you very much, and unsteadily turned around to re-enter the rope labyrinth from whence he had come. I gently turned him around to face the alley that was left uncluttered on the other side of my tent. He gave me a bear hug and staggered away into the dark. As he didn't have the usual name tag on his 'browns' (field uniform), which didn't display unit insignia either, I never found out who, or 'what', he was.

From my tent on the edge of the airfield, I was within shouting distance of both the HQ building where I worked, an old corrugated-iron community hall, and the HQ tent of the reaction force ('fireforce') on full-time standby to react instantly to any contact with the enemy, and to do regular patrolling in between. This force usually consisted of members of the parachute battalion based in Bloemfontein. I got to know one of their COs quite well, a young, enthusiastic captain who had at his request spent several terms, normally of three months at a time, in that position. His name was Loekie Grundling and he had been through several scraps with SWAPO insurgents. He sometimes made use of a command helicopter, usually an Alouette, to control firefights from the air, often accompanied by another Alouette or

Puma gunship chopper armed with a heavy machine gun or even a potent 20-mm cannon.

One of my abiding memories of this time is the whine of the choppers having their turbine engines started up and the smell of aviation fuel as the fireforce departed on patrol at first light, with the gunship soon after take-off firing two (always only two) shots with the 20 mil or a short burst with the machine gun into a nearby *oshana* (a shallow seasonal pan common in Ovamboland) to test the weapons. The occasional visits to the base by Mirage III fighter-bombers brought an exhilarating thunder of quite another order.

On a few occasions I went with Loekie in the command chopper, ostensibly as an observer – one prudently never asked permission for things if you were fairly certain of being refused. To be accused of bad judgement was far preferable to a charge of insubordination. My boss, General Viljoen, was not readily given to granting permission for capers that might entail unwarranted risk, although once he himself as a commanding general bravely, but to my mind imprudently, parachuted into the SWAPO base at Cassinga with troops in the air-assault phase of Operation Reindeer, taking unnecessary personal risks that required diverting some troops for his protection, and probably disturbing command structures on the ground, apart from the huge risk of his being killed. But I heeded his standing exhortation to soldiers to use their initiative, and so on occasion joined Loekie in the chopper. On a later sortie, the Alouette was hit by ground fire. After it had landed safely with the loss of some aluminium but no critical damage, General Viljoen asked Loekie what had gone through his mind, to which he replied: 'General, I only thought of that white bum at home.'

Some citizen force as well as regular soldiers became serial volunteers for operational service. Their motives were varied: preponderantly a desire to do their bit and a sense of adventure, sometimes for the operational allowances and quite often to escape unhappy circumstances at home. Loekie struck me as being one from the first category. Although I was much older than he was, and of higher rank, we developed a certain affinity, even friendship. Also, I think, something of a father–son relationship developed – Loekie and people like him lived daily under immense stress. Eventually Loekie left the operational area to return to his home base in Bloemfontein. Sometime later, I learnt that as a result of a pilot error concerning the drop zone in a training jump he had fallen into a dam, failed to release his harness, and drowned.

A standing exhortation in the SADF was 'Do what you can with what you have'. A good example of that was Captain Buffel van Niekerk, a member of a citizen force regiment somewhere on the East Rand and a cheerfully dynamic man who owned an earth-moving company in civilian life and had volunteered for operational service. At the time, a start had been made with the construction of a defensive 'cut line' along the northern border of South West Africa with Angola, to leave a broad strip of open sand after the clearing of all foliage. This was to facilitate patrols to pick up spoor of infiltrators. Mechanised patrolling would also be enhanced, including quick reaction to incursions across the border.

The work had been spluttering along, not sticking to the schedule. I did not know who or what was responsible for this, but one day General Viljoen expressed his irritation with this incompetence and those responsible, who raised all sorts of excuses for not getting on with the job. At the time, Buffel was employed in a desk job on base and I mentioned his background and expertise to the general. As was the latter's well-known wont, Buffel left for a first inspection of the proceedings on the cut line that very day, with instructions to deliver a report with a needs analysis the following morning. He was put in charge and I later heard that thereafter the cut line was completed efficiently and in double-quick time. General Viljoen's nickname wasn't 'Stofstrepie' (little streak of dust) for nothing. That was mostly all you ever saw of him.

One morning we stood shaving together (with cold water) in our rudimentary ablution facility and talked about the problem of often failing to follow up spoor of infiltrators fast enough. Horses and dogs were being employed, but both presented unique challenges: horses required large and cumbersome logistics, and even the best of dogs had problems of stamina in that environment. Also, their paws, even in leather bootees, succumbed very quickly to the extremely hot sand of Ovamboland. I was then in my bike phase and suggested to the general that we try off-road motorcycles, or scramblers – quads were not yet around. The general objected that they would be too noisy for the purpose. I disagreed, pointing out that they could be very effectively silenced and would also give a psychological advantage to the rider, given the speeds of which they were capable and their height, which would provide better observation.

I suggested that initially some bikers in the Springs Regiment be called up for the purpose – Springs is on the East Rand in Gauteng, at the time somewhat notorious for its rough motorbike clubs (not to call them gangs), perhaps the right stuff for what was required operationally. He instructed his operational staff to prepare an assessment and submission to higher authority requesting that such a unit be established, including calling up a contingent of biking national servicemen. These units were deployed with little delay although I didn't know from which regiment and, after devising and practising the necessary tactics and techniques for employing the new weapon, I was later told that they had proven to be effective. It was another case of doing what you could with what you had. An army of citizens in uniform does have handy fringe capacities.

We received a report one day that a Cuban had been seen at a water tower near Tsumeb, a mining town in the centre of the northern region of the country. To my utter shame I accepted this titbit at face value for inclusion in my daily intelligence briefing to the staff, the general included. I was clearly blindsided by the paranoia about Cubans that prevailed at the time, and I thought back to my prosecuting experience of people saying things that surprised even themselves. This was met with derision, mine included once I realised how stupid I had been. Tsumeb was quite far south of the border where no Cuban presence would have been at all feasible then. A local unit was instructed to send a patrol to investigate, and the report came back that the 'Cuban' was in fact a farmer by the name of Van der Merwe inspecting his wind-pump. Asked why it had been thought he was Cuban, the answer came that he had a beard. In intelligence operations the danger of stereotyping is always present. I still cringe at the memory of this incident.

At Ondangwa I got to know a remarkable desert 'flower' called the 'lily'. It was a funnel with a very long pipe stuck deep into the Ovamboland sand for use as a urinal. On more permanent bases they were sometimes connected to an underground septic tank. The writer and social commentator Dana Snyman in his column in *Die Burger* of 9 December 2011, relates a story of the '*dankietannies*', more properly the charitable ladies of the Southern Cross Fund, who at Christmas time used to visit the operational area on the border with gift parcels of small comforts for the troops, and to thank them for sacrificing their personal lives in service to the country. On one occasion a group of these *tannies* was being shown around a base by the CO when they walked past a row of lilies and asked what they were for. The bashful major could not bring himself to tell them the truth and said they were ventilation shafts for the underground control room. One *tannie* went up to a lily, bent down, put her mouth close to the funnel and said: 'Hullo you lovely boys down there. Have a Merry Christmas, and thank you for your wonderful service to the country.'

The HQ building at Ondangwa, with its corrugated-iron roof and walls, was not ideal for the scorching sun of Ovamboland. On the front edge of a stage at one end stood a red telephone. When we arrived there, we wondered what this phone was for, but never made any effort to find out. We had no use for it as all the required secure communications were available for operational purposes. Because of its colour, one of the troopies decided it had to be the direct line to the White House in Washington, in case we should develop a pressing need for some nuclear back-up. He waxed lyrical about how we would all get medals and be fêted if we were to arrange to end the war there and then. He only relented when his colleagues pointed out that they would then lose their operational allowances.

While we were clearing up the place for evacuation at the end of Operation Cobra, that phone rang for the first and only time in the weeks we were there. I was nearest and answered it, full of curious expectation. To my utter astonishment, it was my wife calling from Bronkhorstspruit! It turned out that a senior citizen force officer and friend of mine, a lawyer named Nico van Rensburg who at the time was the secretary of the Transvaal Law Society and had served with us for a while in the HQ, had on returning to Pretoria made it his mission to find out what that puzzling telephone was about. He was an old hand who knew his way around the military establishment in Pretoria, and learnt from the chief of the SADF's HQ signals unit, which maintained direct communications with the operational area, that it was indeed connected to an open direct line, and got the number. Knowing how we had all been wondering what was going on at home, he suggested to my wife that she phone me, unwittingly at the very time of her dire need to tell me of my partners' perfidy in reneging on our partnership agreement. I took some time to recover from the shock of both the medium and the message. That telephone did after all deliver nuclear fallout of a kind, it felt like to me.

13

Special Forces/ARMSCOR

In 1976 South West Africa was abuzz with wheeling and dealing and much excitement due to the multiparty Turnhalle Constitutional Conference that was under way. The conference was an effort to reach agreement on an internal settlement leading to a democratically elected indigenous government, with a view to pre-empting international demands for democratisation and for South Africa to withdraw from the territory. I regretted leaving this vibrant environment when I was returned to South Africa after the completion of Operation Cobra, still as a citizen force officer.

I applied for and got attested again in the permanent force, and was appointed to the newly established HQ Special Forces, where my old mentor, General Fritz Loots, was now in command. The HQ was established to integrate the command structures of the Reconnaissance Commandos, which until then had had to do without a big brother unit to look after their interests at chief of staff level.

At the rank of major, I initially and somewhat laughably filled three colonels' posts – those of Senior Staff Officers Intelligence, Logistics and Personnel. No one, myself included, was surprised that very little happened during my tenure, but I was glad to get to know my wonderful colleagues in Special Forces. Apart from the workload, rank matters in the military. In the absence of any other staff officers in the fledgling HQ, General Loots had to do much of the wheeling and dealing required to get a new HQ established, equipped and working, an impossible job for one man, even of high rank. A little while after I arrived there, things were eased considerably by the appointment of a retired former chief of staff of the SADF, General S.A. Engelbrecht. With a background in physics, he had played an important role in the initial modernisation of the SADF some years before, among other things in the acquisition of the standard NATO assault rifle, which in South Africa was called the R1. Only when he arrived did things get moving organisationally at HQ Special Forces.

I passed the exhaustive and exhausting psychometric and physical examinations and tests to become an operator in Special Forces, but failed the medical because of my eyesight. As the nice young doctor who did the examination put it, I had to be able to at least see the earth should I lose my spectacles jumping out of an aeroplane, otherwise who knows where I might land. My eyes did not have the tolerance for contact lenses either, but parachuting later in another context proved the doctor's qualms to have been unfounded. Because of my sound physical fitness revealed in stringent tests at the time, he also said he wasn't worried about my congenitally deformed aorta valve, which some years later had to be replaced in an emergency operation. It is one of the primary causes of sudden death, the doctors then explained to me.

Whether I would have passed the exceptionally demanding selection course will have to remain moot, as will the question of whether I would have had the guts to perform the tasks and earn the respect of the magnificent men I got to know as operators. I had every confidence then that I could have done both. However, I somehow doubt it now, perhaps as a function of advancing age and receding capacity. At the time I was already approaching my late thirties, a little old for starting the job, but in good shape and, in an inversion of the cliché from the rugby world, I was assured that 'if you're good enough, you're young enough'. I later learnt that the oldest man to qualify as an operator had been an amazing forty-nine years. I was told that he was a small, wiry fellow – both of which I am not – and had formerly been in the Portuguese Special Forces in Angola.

At their inception in the late 1960s, I had presented the then fledgling 1 Reconnaissance Commando under the command of the inimitable Commandant (Lieutenant Colonel, and later Colonel) Jan Breytenbach, a highly intelligent, effective and aggressive soldier and a principled man, with their first intelligence training course before they set off into Africa on their first, I believe, covert operation in support of friendly forces far up in Africa. Only many years later did I learn that my brother-in-law, Izak Bosman, a commercial pilot now deceased, had flown supplies in to them under extremely hazardous battle conditions. I developed a sense of affinity with these impressive people, reinforced by my later association with them.

But the last thing I want to do is to insinuate myself into the aura of excellence and honour that surrounds Special Forces. To do so would be to demean their great legacy of professionalism and exceptionally brave conduct and achievements. By the good offices and indulgence of General Loots and the wonderful friends I made there, I gained experience of such things as small group, small boat and submarine operations, and had occasion to work with the Selous Scouts in Rhodesia. I am immensely proud of having had the privilege of being associated with them. I was later invited to join the Special Forces Association of former members, but declined. I would dearly like to let the world know their names and of some of their exploits, but that could still put some of them at risk and embarrass others.

After some time at HQ Special Forces, I was transferred to an ARMSCOR unit styled the Special Equipment Division that, among other things, did target studies of militarily relevant infrastructure in some of our neighbouring countries, which was my specific tasking. For this purpose two colleagues, one an engineer of sorts and one a geographer of sorts, and I once travelled by car to Botswana. After a few days we became tired and bored with the job of photographing and annotating bridges, telephone and electricity lines, the state of roads, etc. and were no longer terribly security conscious. We were supposed to be tourists having a good time, and to live our cover we were properly stocked up with cameras, maps, binoculars and, of course, some beers and other goodies that tourists would normally have in their vehicle.

Setting out on our travels one day, the searing heat caused us to start indulging fairly early in our liquid sandwiches from the coolbox. The result was that by the time we got to the Botswana Meat Corporation in Lobatse, we were sweaty but full of bonhomie and no longer very security conscious at all. The corporation was the main abattoir and meat processing factory, which at the time was the main export product of the country. The manager, Mr X, was very friendly and extremely helpful in showing tourists around his installation, of which he was very proud. He showed and explained to us every nook and cranny, but must have wondered why we consistently asked him to stand next to this valve or that transfer box or generator or diesel storage tank, etc. to take pictures of him. It was the province of our engineer colleague, who made copious notes and sketches. Our somewhat befuddled, unprofessional conduct on that assignment is still a matter of some shame to me. By the grace of the forefathers, no doubt, no adverse consequences arose. And we did in fact take home some worthwhile information. I felt a twinge of conscience at the thought that the time might come that Mr X's pride and joy might someday have to be undone, and fervently hoped that he would then no longer be there.

Years later, when the worst of our wars in southern Africa were over and we knew that the Botswana authorities were aware of these excursions of ours, I related these episodes to a former head of the Special Branch of the Botswana Police, who was greatly amused. We once entertained him and his stunning wife to a braai at our home in Pretoria, and what delightful conversationalists and erudite a couple they were. He related how he heard his first 'Van der Merwe' joke, told by a Kenyan to a Ghanaian, at the HQ of the Organisation of African Unity in Addis Ababa, Ethiopia. Van der Merwe is the traditional figure of fun and the central character in many a benign self-deprecatory joke told mostly by Afrikaners in Afrikaans about Afrikaners, but also by Kenyans and Ghanaians, it would appear. Our guest hilariously told of a similar character called Mokotedi, if I remember rightly, in the Tswana compendium of traditional jokes.

The Special Equipment Division was also responsible for manufacturing all sorts of funnies for use by intelligence and security agencies. These included a range of documentation for a variety of purposes, among which were identity cards of some target organisations. As a little experiment a colleague and I decided to test the efficacy of ANC identity cards for gaining access to SADF installations, thereby at the same time testing the latter's security systems. Not having had any formal authority to do such a thing, permission for this scientific experiment was neither obtained nor sought. This was in 1978, when civil disobedience and general unrest in the townships of the Witwatersrand area were fairly intense under the instigation and leadership of the ANC, following the Soweto uprising of schoolchildren two years earlier. We therefore chose the HQ of the Witwatersrand Command of the SADF situated in central Johannesburg as the subject of a fair test of their readiness.

We introduced ourselves as members of ARMSCOR, with me using my military rank but in civvies, on a goodwill mission to see how the other half lived. Flashing our cards at two gated and barred security checkpoints manned by armed national servicemen, we gained access to what is the heart of any military HQ, the operations room. There we were shown around by the captain in charge, who explained to us in detail how things worked in his establishment. On the way out we showed our cards to the troopies who had let us through at each checkpoint, demanding that they study them carefully and explain their negligence. We told them that they shouldn't ever let anyone in without properly scrutinising their purported identification, least of all those with ANC identity cards, but that such people should be arrested on the spot and shot without question if they should try to get away. Fortunately for us, none of them took this advice to heart. Their relief was palpable at our severe reprimand and undertaking not to report them higher up, on condition that they never did such a stupid thing again.

In 1978 I was transferred back from HQ Special Forces to CSI, promoted to commandant (lieutenant colonel) and almost immediately again posted to South West Africa.

14

South West Africa

South West Africa, now Namibia, was a captivating place. It took about a week there to get hooked for life. The country and its capital city, Windhoek, projected an ambience I had never experienced anywhere else. The varied natural beauty and wildlife, fascinating ethnic variety, interesting people, mild climate and palpable German-based cosmopolitanism were enthralling. A sense of *gemütlichkeit* pervaded society, among both black and white people. I have not been there for more than three decades and am still as entranced as ever. I was pleased to receive word that I would be sent from CSI to Windhoek again for three weeks in 1978. It became five months. Although domestically unsettling, the country and the excitement of the profound political developments there fascinated me, and I had no objections.

When I arrived in Windhoek in 1978, Judge M.T. Steyn of the Supreme Court bench of the Orange Free State province in Bloemfontein and grandson of the venerable President M.T. Steyn of the Orange Free State Republic during the Anglo-Boer War was the administrator general of South West Africa, appointed by the South African government. A robust, powerful personality with a keen sense of humour, he regaled any audience he could find with amusing and sometimes highly irreverent stories (outside of the limelight) about South African politicians in particular. The local Joint Intelligence Coordinating Committee (JICC), of which I was a member, reported to him as and when necessary. He was always accessible and we were impressed by his swift grasp and own insights regarding the security situation in the country. He was a pleasant man, always courteous to and appreciative of his underlings. He could also be quite imperious, as in his periodic decamping to his 'Summer Palace', as he called it, a marvellous historic building from the time of the German occupation of South West Africa that was later turned into a summer residence for administrators of South West Africa and visiting dignitaries in the pleasantly mild climate of Swakopmund on the coast, a most congenial place. It was an amusing pleasure to see him holding court and lording it in great style over his retinue. As the JICC we had the pleasure of also having to go on these sojourns to keep him briefed on developments.

In early 1978, after convoluted and complex negotiations lasting some years, agreement on a settlement plan for the war over South West Africa had been reached between all parties involved in the conflict. Apart from the main protagonists, South Africa and SWAPO, these included just about every state and grouping of states with interests in the region, including Cuba, the so-called Frontline (southern African) States, the British Commonwealth, the Organisation of African Unity and, crucially, the USA and USSR, all under the auspices of the secretary general of the UN, but all also with their own critical political, economic and strategic interests at stake.

The Cold War was at its height, although it had at about that time started to become apparent that the USSR's internal situation was beginning to crumble and that they were developing doubts about their huge commitment to their allies in the South West Africa/Angola war and elsewhere. This became a determining factor in the cessation of hostilities as the Soviet economy, the main source of support to the communist forces in the region, was beginning to splutter towards an eventual implosion. The war had also become financially unsustainable for South Africa, lending urgency to the realisation that a negotiated settlement would have to be found for both South West Africa and the Republic of South Africa. The 'Plan', as the agreement became known, was formalised by the UN Security Council in September 1978 through its unanimously adopted Resolution 435. Most importantly for South Africa, it included the withdrawal of all Cuban and other external communist forces from Angola as a quid pro quo for the SADF's orderly, staged withdrawal from South West Africa, in conjunction with procedures for reaching a political settlement.

The secretary general of the UN established an observer group to ascertain the requirements for the implementation of Resolution 435 in South West Africa. This UN Transitional Assistance Group (UNTAG) initially consisted of about forty (I'm guessing) international civil servants and a military contingent as observers and advisors. As his special representative for South West Africa he appointed Martti Ahtisaari, a Finnish diplomat later to become president of Finland, to lead the group, with General Hannes Philipp of Austria to head a military component. To oversee the comprehensive transition to the agreed fully democratic transformation of Namibia to independence, the capacity of this mission was later extended enormously to include a large contingent of 1500 policemen and women from various countries, and an independent legal advisor from Denmark. General Philipp was replaced by General Prem Chand of India to head the greatly enlarged UNTAG military monitoring contingent.

I was stationed at the Bastion, the HQ of the South West African Territorial Force (SWATF) in Windhoek and did not have much to do with all these intricate goings-on, with only few excursions outside of the city, mainly to the north of the country for consultations. My core job was to keep track of the movements, attitudes and opinions of the members of the UN group by collating inputs from our units throughout the country and preparing a daily intelligence assessment for General Jannie Geldenhuys, the CO of the SWATF. This report had to be on his table by 7 a.m. every morning.

The unavoidable result was that I more or less routinely had to start work at around 2 a.m. sorting out intelligence reports of the previous day and night, and preparing the consolidated report. A vindictive little pleasure I took was having, at such hours, to contact the originator for clarification of a badly written report, which had the positive effect of improving report-writing, especially that of some serial offenders. Trying to get a typist into the office at that time was a non-starter, and so I got the added bonus of acquiring this handy skill as well. Besides, the operations room never closed and there was always coffee and a bit of chit-chat to be had, my reports often providing hilarity for the light relief of the bleary-eyed. Some of the members of the UN military contingent had some strange habits and opinions, but especially fears, one colonel from Nigeria in confidence listing his as snakes, spiders and South African soldiers.

General Geldenhuys was the archetypical intellectual soldier, with an acute mind in a hard head, and immense energy. He had written a number of books, the most telling of which was his later work on the war titled *Dié wat gewen het*. I was not much given to the heavy socialising that sometimes took place among the officers, and did not get to know him well personally. But on one or two occasions I was impressed by his capacity for carousing until the early hours and then, shaven and spotlessly dressed, presiding at an order group a mere hour or two later, as fresh as a daisy, surrounded by his somewhat wilted senior staff. I also got an impression that he, as is often the case with superiorly intelligent and strong-minded people, did not much relish the ideas of others, but preferred to do the thinking and talking, expecting his staff to fulfil only their executive functions. This approach was also, I thought, reflected in some of his senior staff appointments. I was not involved in the negotiations to end the war, but by all accounts General Geldenhuys played a crucial role in that process.

Ahtisaari impressed me as a more substantial man than was suggested by his babyish, somewhat flabby appearance. He had a firm handshake and was soft spoken, but full of confidence. He was also a most courteous man. He and his staff were travelling the country in pursuit of their task of compiling their report on planning for the full deployment of UNTAG to the UN secretary general, talking to as many people at grassroots level as they could. One of Ahtisaari's stopovers was at Ohopoho (more commonly Opuwo), the then somewhat desolate capital of the Kaokoland, the sparsely populated semi-desert tribal area of the Himba and other peoples in the north-west of the country. The Himba smeared themselves from head to foot with ochre clay to fend off insects and, I was given to believe, also evil spirits. There isn't much water in Kaokoland and the Himba tended to conserve even the little there was.

The SADF had a company base at Ohopoho, with Major Jurie Lombaard in command. Jurie was a huge man with a wild red beard, not usually allowed in the SADF but quite appropriate in those surroundings, the colour of his beard matching that of the Himbas' clay-smeared skin. His role seemed to be somewhat indeterminate, alternating between that of a military governor, local head of administration, Company CO and father of the community. He had an excellent relationship with the Himbas and was sometimes referred to as the King of Kaokoland. I was told that on Ahtisaari's visit to Ohopoho, through an interpreter he asked the local Afrikaans-speaking Himba head-man, tongue in cheek and with a twinkle in his eye, for which party the latter would be voting in the coming internal general election, then projected to take place in December 1978. The headman answered: 'I don't know. Baas Jurie hasn't said yet.' But the interpreter – I was told it was the prominent South African radio and television reporter and commentator Jan Snyman – interpreted it merely as that he had not yet decided.

A terrible tragedy almost occurred when a group of journalists accompanying the Ahtisaari group left Ohopoho ahead of the main party by air to be at the UN group's next stop in advance. On take-off the pilot apparently made an error, a wing clipped a building or a tree or another plane on the ground, I forget which, and the plane crashed to the ground. As I recall, no one died but the well-known journalist and author, Max du Preez, sustained serious head injuries. He records in one of his books, *Pale Native*, that when the Ahtisaari group departed shortly afterwards, they took him along in their aircraft, still unconscious. When he came to, he found himself lying across a row of seats with his head cradled in a man's hands. It was Ahtisaari.

It was said that Ohopoho had been true to the Afrikaans idiomatic description, phonetically closely derived from its name, of what it was like to fly an aeroplane into and out of there: '*Hou poepol, hou!*' I'm somewhat at a loss as to how to translate this into English – perhaps something like, but grossly inadequately, 'Hold on to your hats!'

As my term of duty kept being extended way beyond the intended three weeks, about two months into it my wife paid me a brief private visit over a weekend. About a month later, my immediate superior, the thoughtfully empathetic Colonel Gert van Niekerk, the Senior Staff Officer Intelligence in HQ SWATF, arranged for her and our four young children to be flown to Windhoek for a week on a Flossie, the C-130 Hercules aircraft that shuttled between Waterkloof Air Force Base in Pretoria and the Eros Airport in Windhoek, and a few other ports of call. He then instructed me to go on an inspection tour of intelligence units scattered throughout the north-western parts of the country, taking my family along in his official Ford F250 4×4 bakkie with its 400-litre auxiliary petrol tank and enough space for the kids on mattresses under the canopy on the back. We even got the use for a day or two of a house that was at the disposal of the SWATF in the quaint little town of Henties Bay on the Atlantic coast, a haven for fishermen, with holiday accommodation with walls sometimes constructed of tarred canvas and even cardboard, a golf course with sand fairways and grass only on the greens, and an excruciatingly cold Atlantic Ocean. I have never been more generously compensated for hardship I had not suffered.

There was much fun to be had in Windhoek by way of nice pubs and restaurants, and socialising with the cosmopolitan UN group and the many international journalists. There were also some good facilities at the Wanderers Sport Club, such as squash courts. And the place was crawling with spies from all over the world, some identified, and others doubtlessly not. The city saw a fascinating congruence of the national interests of just about every significant country in the world. I became particularly friendly with a married couple of foreign journalists from a European country, well-informed and attractive people, especially the rather voluptuous wife. She was a tall and vivacious, interestingly intellectual, erudite woman, with a surprising and seemingly sympathetic grasp of the political situation in South Africa, even of the personal backgrounds of some of the main political players there. A more substantial person than her husband, it was a pleasure talking to her in more senses than one.

One morning they phoned to invite me for dinner that evening at their rented home in Klein Windhoek, a residential suburb of the city, which I readily accepted. Around midday a man I did not know sidled up to me on the street in the centre of town and called me by my first name, but did not introduce himself. He told me he was from NIS and warned me to be careful of what I said or did during my dinner date that evening, especially in the main bedroom, and walked off. The whole encounter took about as long as the telling of it. Real-time intelligence, if ever there was.

I told the chairman of the JICC, a senior man from NIS, Pieter Swanepoel, of this encounter and he informed me that it was more or less confirmed that my prospective hosts were working for the Soviet KGB intelligence agency, and were 'receiving attention'. On my description of the man who had spoken to me, he immediately said something like: 'Oh, that's so-and-so, the best technical man in the business.' I was pleasantly surprised by this unusually caring gesture by a member of the 'opposition' at the time. He later became a colleague at NIS, where I got to know him well.

I was grateful for the warning and had a convivial dinner with stimulating conversation that evening. Later on, the man excused himself, apologising that he had to see someone at the airport, but would I please stay and have another glass of wine with his wife because, he said, she enjoyed my company so much. I was really sorry to remember suddenly that I had to go back to work. I'd never before or since been that close to a honey trap, as far as I know. I had felt quite secure up until then – after all, I had been warned, hadn't I? I was really scared, but again resented my Calvinist upbringing just a little bit. I understood that the couple regularly hosted senior officers of the SADF/SWATF and UNTAG at their home.

The negotiating of the Resolution 435 agreement was a truly Herculean effort by dedicated and extremely hard-working teams on all sides that mattered. The role of Dr Chester Crocker, assistant secretary of state for Africa in the Reagan administration and leader of the American mediating team, was particularly demanding and thankless. In an article in the prestigious academic publication *Foreign Affairs* some years before, he and a co-author had initiated the approach of 'constructive engagement' with South Africa in addressing the southern African situation. In it they argued that the confrontational attitude towards South Africa of the majority of UN members was counter-productive, and that a more rational effort was required to safeguard American and Western interests in contention with the USSR for influence in the region. Crocker now faced cross purposes on the South African side between the diplomats and soldiers, where some influential generals seemed at times to be more concerned about the interests of their surrogate Jonas Savimbi and UNITA than for South African policy, in negotiating a way towards extricating the country from the situation surrounding South West Africa, which had become untenable.

But Crocker was also in the invidious position of having to contend with a similar situation between his own State Department and the American security establishment, particularly in the persons of the affable rightist William Casey, the director of the Central Intelligence Agency (CIA), and the chairman of the National Security Council, Admiral John Poindexter. Moreover, there was opposition from right-wing Republican elements in the American Congress, who basically insisted that no concessions of any kind should be made to the communists, with influential civil society organisations and think-tanks in the USA like the Republican-connected Heritage Foundation, also tending to support such a hard-line approach. These elements in the USA were assiduously cultivated by Lieutenant General Wessie van der Westhuizen, the CSI of the SADF, who paid numerous visits to that country, some formally, others not, in an effort to persuade them that South Africa deserved more assistance from the US in opposing the spread of communism, rather than the 'backstabbing' by Crocker and his ever-present sidekick Robert Cabelli, whom I assumed to be from the CIA.

Crocker was chiefly concerned with protecting the interests of the USA in preventing the USSR from establishing a commanding presence in southern Africa. This was also the primary aim of South Africa, while trying to maintain the fortunes of Savimbi's anti-communist UNITA in the contention for power in Angola. This was regarded by some, perhaps not entirely unjustifiably, as part of a larger scheme in certain quarters to preserve the apartheid system by setting such stringent conditions for a negotiated settlement that compromise would not be possible. There were still elements within the SADF who believed that they could make war indefinitely, while playing off the various opposing interests against one another to their own advantage. For Crocker to reconcile the common anti-Soviet interest with the need to avoid being accused of compromising with this latter objective, he had to face a road full of pitfalls on both sides of the Atlantic. With hindsight, it is a wonder that he managed to juggle all the balls and remain in the job, considering that his conservative opposition in the USA had the ear, some say the support, of President Ronald Reagan.

But Crocker's tenacity trumped even his outstanding intellect, and in the later stages of the process he probably couldn't have done it without the full support of his boss, secretary of state George Schultz. Furthermore, he fortunately had level-headed and dedicated South African counterparts and honourable gladiatorial opponents in excellent people like General Jannie Geldenhuys, Minister Pik Botha, diplomats Neil van Heerden and Derek Auret, as well as various other government officials, including Niel Barnard, director general (DG) of NIS. Shedding the albatross of South West Africa without humiliation and with a proud military record intact, and in the process achieving the internationally backed withdrawal of all external communist forces from Angola, was a brilliant achievement and a huge relief for South Africa, not least for the treasury.

But the undivided opprobrium of the world now turned squarely on the Republic of South Africa. I was transferred back to CSI in Pretoria in late 1978.

15

CSI Revisited

When I rejoined CSI, Lieutenant General Hein du Toit had been replaced by Major General Ivan Lemmer as CSI, who in turn was replaced shortly thereafter by Lieutenant General P.W. (Wessie) van der Westhuizen. I was again placed in Research and Editing, with the main task of overseeing the production of intelligence and situation reports (intreps and sitreps) on the military situation for higher authority, and assisting with the preparation of the annual strategic military threat assessment.

The accumulation of talent and capability at CSI was impressive. Van der Westhuizen was a former teacher and former CO of both the Military Academy at Saldanha and the Army College in Voortrekkerhoogte. A dynamic and immensely hard-working man, he was an inspirational, demanding CO who was good to and much liked by his subordinates. I knew him from the old DMI days and shared this respect and liking for him, but was saddened by an unfortunate encounter we had when I later left CSI for NIS. He was fluent in French after an undisclosed term of service in France and, after a stint as ambassador to Chile at the end of his military career, also in Spanish, I have been led to believe.

Major (later Major General) Neels van Tonder was a mathematics graduate and qualified teacher of the subject. He was also a private pilot of light aircraft and built his own two-seater aerobatic kit aeroplane, with which he once almost killed me by assaulting my stomach in a 'friendly' flip he treated me to while we were on a course together at the Infantry School in Oudtshoorn. He was an outstanding organiser, a forceful personality and a great mind; he was also adept at managing some of his superiors from below, sometimes to the chagrin of his peers. As a declared resident of DMI in Paris during the 1960s, he quickly became fluent in French and gained the respect of the French intelligence services. In cooperation with them, he established politically invaluable contacts for South Africa with certain French-speaking West African states, notably Ivory Coast and Gabon, with more or less open-door access to both Presidents Houphuët-Boigny and Omar Bongo respectively.

There were a number of other very impressive people at CSI when I returned. Names that come to mind include Major (later Major General) 'Pine'

Pienaar, also a mathematician and qualified teacher of the subject, and an outstanding cryptographer and code-breaker who won wide respect for his exceptional skills; SAN Captain (later Rear-Admiral) James Sleigh, for whom I developed great respect; Major (later Major General) Jan Erasmus, a graduate in the social sciences, also a former teacher and long-standing friend; SAAF Captain André Bekker, who died at a young age when he crashed at an air show; and SAAF Commandant Max van Dijkhorst, who sported a scarred face and heavy limp from buzzing his girlfriend's father's farm and landing up in the chicken run, aeroplane and all, as he told it. I don't recall what aircraft it was, as Max was also an enthusiastic glider pilot.

There was the bright, young SAAF Captain Callie Steyn, who worked at CSI because he had been disqualified from flying after sustaining slight brain damage in a car crash. This was after he had made a remarkable number of successful crash-landings, in Harvards, without serious injury. He vowed that he would never in his life jump from an aeroplane with a parachute while it was still flying – he didn't say anything about after it had stopped flying. The last time I saw him he was a colonel serving in the office of the Chief of the SADF, and still on the up, I was told. And there was the remarkable Major (later Major General) Chris Thirion, who later fell foul of political machinations that sadly ended his career, but more about that later. On one occasion in Windhoek, Thirion and I made a valiant effort to save a young damsel in distress from the claws of a predatory fellow officer, only to find to our embarrassment that the damsel did not want to be saved.

Nothing else at CSI had changed much since I left, except that it had expanded considerably and the pace was even more hectic than before. One thing that had not changed was the disdain that politicians and even some in the upper echelons of the SADF held for the intelligence component in planning processes, some in CSI itself. The intellectualism of General Du Toit had perhaps even exacerbated this tendency since appointments at top levels almost always favoured officers with operational muster, the so-called fighting soldiers, something I often found puzzling.

One senior officer once expounded at some length on how he hated reading and what a waste of time it was, priding himself on not having read a single book in his entire life! Of course this is an extreme case and one should not generalise, but it does demonstrate the mindset of some in the higher ranks. General Du Toit probably did not fit too comfortably into such an environment, and I don't think he was ever very popular among his peers on the Command Council, the top operational management body in the SADF, of which all chiefs of staff were members.

To illustrate the contempt of some top officers for the role of intelligence, I was once involved in the mad rush to prepare the final version of the annual national strategic military threat assessment. At the time I was the production coordinator of this assessment, which had to be completed by the usual impossible deadline. As the SADF's strategic intelligence agency, CSI was required to gather input from all four arms of the SADF (Army, Air Force, Navy and Military Medical Services). It was a laborious and stressful job, reconciling competing budgetary demands and managing overblown egos. And woe betide CSI if it should find, for example, that the landward conventional military threat may have receded somewhat during a particular year; we must have our new tanks, for God's sake! Endless days and long nights of relentless argument was the standard procedure, in which reference to objective reality often counted for little in the face of contention for a position in the pecking order. Of course, there were also many principled differences of opinion.

When it was complete, I had to deliver this substantial bundle of documents by hand to the Chief of Staff Operations (CSO) at SADF HQ, to enable him to determine operational needs for the year to come in view of the threat assessment. When I handed the documents to the CSO, literally with the other hand he gave me his complete operational plan of aspects such as force design, required force levels and their procurement, development and preparation, deployments, strategic adjustments and readjustments, etc. for which the intelligence assessment was supposed to be the foundation document. I was livid and immediately reported this to CSI General Van der Westhuizen. I told him I was not prepared to accept such flagrant disregard for intelligence and proper procedure, especially after the huge, exhausting effort it required of everyone involved in producing the assessments. I requested that should this approach continue, I be relieved of responsibility for the process.

He was highly upset at the CSO. It was also a question of turf between them and, as had happened frequently before, yet another machination by that generally obnoxious CSO. He was of equal rank and position to the CSI, and disdainfully expressed his personal opinion whenever he could that he did not need the CSI or anyone else to prescribe to him his operational needs and claims on budget allocations. Van der Westhuizen said he would take the matter up with the Chief of the SADF, General Magnus Malan. I later learnt that he had done so, but understandably I did not get any feedback.

I had much opportunity for self-actualisation while at CSI, and had the privilege of quite a few overseas visits to friendly counterparts on different continents for reciprocal briefings on common interests. I was also especially fortunate in 1979 to be able to attend the Navy Staff Course at the Navy Staff College in Muizenberg, Cape Town. Although I was formally in the army, CSI personnel were allocated between the three operational staff courses of the army, air force and navy, to diversify their experience. The course was orientated primarily towards senior management level, with a component on this discipline presented by the Graduate School of Business of the University of Cape Town.

The navy had a culture intangibly different from that of other arms of the SADF, with a charming air harking back to a strong British naval heritage of supposedly gentlemanly decorum. This, however, tended sometimes to come a bit undone at evening 'choir practice', when at the ring of a ship's bell all were summoned for some gentlemanly conviviality. But I got to know the sailors as fully equal in dedication and motivation to any soldier. It was a demanding and stimulating course of high quality, also because the terrain was somewhat new to me. I cherish the memories of friends made and experiences shared there.

We had quite a few guest lecturers on the course, one of whom was the CO of South Africa's principal shipyard in its main naval base at Simon's Town, Commodore Dieter Gerhardt. He also showed us around the shipyard on a course visit. In 1982 he was arrested for probably (no details ever having been released) spying for the Soviet Union's KGB (or their military intelligence, the GRU). It was a devastating psychological blow to the SADF, in particular to the navy. The wider implication was that our navy, in spite of sanctions against the country, still enjoyed mutually fruitful cooperation with NATO, in particular regarding the continued availability of the Simon's Town shipyard facilities to Western navies, and the shipping tracking station at nearby Silvermine. Given that the Cape sea route occupied an important place in the strategic thinking and planning of the big powers on both sides in the Cold War, the damage to the interests of the Western powers was probably far greater than for South Africa and its navy. Again, no details of this have to my knowledge ever become publicly available.

The incident illustrated the practical and psychological devastation that treason can bring about. Most military establishments the world over from time to time suffer such trauma, and it will inevitably occur again. Treachery is worse than a battlefield defeat, as such losses can always be redeemed through the next battle. Losses suffered through treachery are irredeemable. There is no such thing as absolute security, especially not personal security. There is no way of preventing people from carrying what they have in their heads out to the enemy, apart from their dedication to and faith in the cause they serve. Gerhardt had lost his for financial gain, however much he apparently tried to sugar it over with an ideological veneer.

Back at CSI I noticed two trends that were new to me since having been there before: a tendency to be more outspoken in criticism of politicians in general and the government in particular, and an almost visceral contempt for NIS, especially since the beginning of 1980 when the young Dr Niel Barnard was appointed its DG.

Although sometimes a bit irresponsibly harsh, I thought, I welcomed the greater preparedness to openly discuss and criticise government attitudes and actions or inactions as they affected security matters, especially the lack of progress in making and implementing policies designed to alleviate the plight of the impoverished black masses. The mantra pervading throughout was that the country was in dire need of fundamental political reform and that the military could only ensure time and space for this to take place. Once in a meeting presided over by the general second in command of CSI, Major General Lang Faan van Rensburg, in the midst of a fairly heated argument around the pathetic plight of the millions of black people, I said that if I were black in our country, I would be tempted to join MK. Others in CSI shared such sentiments. I was asked to see the general in his office afterwards, who only cautioned me to keep in mind that 'all of us are not yet on the same wavelength'. The military also tried to galvanise some indolent civil service departments into reaching their set targets or even just to make progress in alleviating the worst of the social iniquities in the daily existence of black people, but without much success.

General Van Rensburg was a very tall, thin string bean of a man. He was also an affable man with an impish sense of humour. He had a habit in meetings in our conference room of rocking back in his chair to the extent that the front legs lifted until he was leaning back against the wall behind him. Once the chair slipped and he fell over backwards on to the floor with his long, gangly legs flailing in the air, the legs of his pants falling down over his knees. This had long been anticipated and there were tortured attempts around the table to stifle guffaws. Everyone rushed to assist in getting him and his chair back on their legs. Having dusted himself off and settled in his chair once more, decorum regained, he said something like: *'Julle het my toestemming om te lag, kêrels.'* (You have my permission to laugh, guys.) It brought the house down.

The disdain for NIS arose from the fact that it seemed to have been gaining influence with President P.W. Botha, which the powers at CSI had come to regard as their particular preserve. Since the mid-1970s, NIS, under the research leadership of Mike Louw and later with the support of Niel Barnard, had been writing in formal documentation and personal briefings submitted to the government at the highest levels that, in spite of the incontestable fact of the communist threat internally and from across our borders in the Soviet Union's quest to establish its hegemony in southern Africa, the overriding security threat to South Africa lay inside the country in the dehumanising destitution and hopelessness of the vast majority of its citizens. Such circumstances created an ideal breeding ground for discontent and insurrection, readymade for exploitation by communist or any other influences. The SADF maintained a militarily sound forward defensive strategy, but that would not resolve this basic cause of instability. The point was also made that we could go on making war for another ten or twenty years, but that a settlement would in the end have to be negotiated anyway, if anyone would then still be interested in inheriting a devastated country.

This engendered tremendous animosity towards NIS and especially towards Louw and Barnard. The advent of Barnard as DG in 1980 greatly increased NIS's influence in the effect it had on government thinking. Barnard, a brilliant young political science professor at the University of the Orange Free State and a powerful personality, had apparently been recommended to Botha for the job by Minister Alwyn Schlebusch, the leader of the NP in the Free State and a Botha confidant, and approved no doubt through the inner workings of the AB, in which Barnard was understood to be regarded as an up-and-coming star. It was a most fortunate appointment and increased the influence of NIS with Botha and the government.

Between Barnard and Louw, NIS was intellectualised and transformed from a former executive-minded and often ideologically driven activist organisation, into a think-tank that tried as near as possible to establish the truth and fearlessly report it to their principal clients, the president and cabinet. Van der Westhuizen and others at CSI resented this intrusion of NIS on their traditional patch, and resisted it wherever they could. However, some more objective thinkers at senior levels in CSI recognised this line of argument, which also conformed to the approach of the High Command of the SADF.

16

Thoughts on the Military

Organisation and culture

Excessive power and ruthless politicking by the military are often generalised, mostly engendered by ignorance of how military establishments function, to apply to all such establishments the world over, sometimes justifiably so and in authoritarian states always so. Dictatorships are invariably installed and sustained by the coercive power of military force, but the stereotype does not apply to mature democracies. In the latter, militaries are instruments of coercive force only as ultimate guarantors of territorial integrity and sovereignty against the outside world, and to assist in ensuring domestic stability and social development at the behest of their elected political masters. As a function of this basic mandate, the military also plays an often crucial role in support of foreign policy objectives.

If a military force is in synchronicity with the government, ideologically and politically neutral and loyal only to the state and its constitution, the supportive role of the military is assured. This also implies support for the basic values of the government of the day, with religion often an important component. If these intertwined loyalties are not present, the potential for instability and the repositioning of the military in an anti-democratic role becomes real.

To further ensure against the misuse of their powers and to limit expenditure by the fiscus, military forces in democracies often only have a small core permanent establishment, with conscripts and volunteers providing human resources as and when needed. 'Citizens in uniform', springing as they do from the population at large and as such also voters and taxpayers, are not as easily mustered for improper purposes as large standing forces, which depend on the military for their livelihood. In such citizen armies, limited permanent force command structures and units keep administrative and logistical infrastructure functional, train soldiers and procure and maintain equipment in peacetime. South Africa had such a military philosophy and structure.

When I joined the SADF, there was no doubt in my mind that we had a mature democracy in this sense; our military was at one with the government and state, and fully capable of fulfilling its functions. It fully supported the apartheid policies of the political authorities, but not, as proven later, to the extent that it would revolt to ensure apartheid's preservation. In the larger context, the SADF was also in full compliance with the government's anti-communist ideology and policies, and dedicated itself to resisting the USSR and its surrogates in their avowed purpose of spreading communist influence in southern Africa and globally, with South Africa clearly the ultimate prize in the region. The communists' intensive propaganda, as well as more thought-ful studies and utterances by their own and other socialist and Marxist academics, including some within South Africa itself, left no room for doubt about their agenda. This was consistently cloaked in lofty sanctimony of the highest moral justification: to destroy the abhorrent system of denial of human rights to the masses of citizens of South Africa. Nary a word, of course, about the total subjugation to the state of the individual citizen of the USSR and other communist states, or about the widespread denial of basic human rights in many African states, quite often characterised by mass murder on a frightening scale.

Total onslaught and total strategy

I was fully conscious of the incomplete nature of our 'democracy', but was confident that government policy was heading toward the eradication of its many anomalies and shortcomings, while the present power structure would stifle the 'total onslaught' against our country – total onslaught as formulated and documented by the ANC for the first time at its Morogoro Conference in Tanzania in 1969. Their struggle, they resolved, would in future be conducted with strategy and tactics based on the following four 'pillars': armed struggle, internal mass mobilisation, a viable political (subversive) underground, and the diplomatic and economic isolation of South Africa from the international community.

When the government took the self-evident, logical decision to develop a 'total strategy' to counter every facet of this total onslaught by our enemies – they would have been culpably derelict in their duty if they hadn't done so – their communication of the issue was so ham-handed that the message that it had originated as a response to the ANC simply never got through. The government were gleefully ridiculed in the hostile part of the media as clutching at the straws of self-manufactured threats. The result was that an overwhelming propaganda advantage went to the other side, with South

African counterstrategies being dismissed out of hand as merely further instruments of oppression. Even today, few people are aware that the concept of total onslaught originated with the ANC at Morogoro.

The SADF as peace-monger

The notion that the ultimate aim of the military was to achieve peace in our country and region was dogma in the SADF. The area of contention was how and on what conditions this was to be achieved. The determination to resist the imposition of a Soviet-style centralist democracy with its record of ruthless suppression of individual human rights and freedoms, murder on a grand scale, command economies leading to eventual meltdown, and its atheism, was always paramount in the collective thinking. But, as stated above, concern over the gross inequities black people in South Africa were subjected to in their daily lives and the dire negative implications this had for state security, was also growing. I've been told that when General Constand Viljoen was Chief of the SADF, he once instructed some senior students from the Rhodesian military on a staff course in South Africa to prepare a consensus opinion on what had gone wrong in that country. Their unanimous answer was that political decisions had been delayed for too long and were overtaken by events.

Apart from Niel Barnard and NIS, generals like Magnus Malan who were close to Botha and who had his ear, shared the hearts-and-minds approach to the low-intensity counterinsurgency war that was being fought inside the country. Botha did initiate the demise of apartheid by revoking or amending some cornerstone legislation, such as the Prohibition of Mixed Marriages Act and the influx control (pass) laws, and by declaring the homelands policy dead, accepting that South Africa would in future be one nation comprising all of its citizens. The Tricameral Constitution of 1983 confirmed and institutionalised the concept of joint government by the different races, but was ultimately disastrous as it retained white control and denied participation to black South Africans. Civil action to alleviate living conditions of black people was now being prioritised, but there was resentment and derision in the SADF at the failure of other civil service departments to deliver on their responsibilities in this regard, as delegated to them through the generally effective National Security Management System, which was ridiculously maligned as a sinister 'taking over of the country by the military'.

Disconnect of resolve

The tardiness of civilian state departments often led to the SADF undesirably becoming involved in projects outside its normal purview, such as the successful upgrade in the 1970s of Alexandra township north of Johannesburg. As a start, streets were tarred and street lighting installed with the assistance of the SADF, as a function of the so-called 'oil spot' approach. This entailed the fanning out of reconstruction and development work from a central starting point. Other government departments who were to contribute to this effort, such as Health and Public Works, regularly fell short of their assigned targets. Concomitantly, the mindset that only the SADF could get things done gained currency, also within the cabinet. The effort made in Alexandra by the SADF alerted activists of anti-government organisations to the damage this sort of progress could do to their cause, with the result that violent protest erupted, ending the initiative.

Obviously this disconnect of resolve led to tension between some departments and the energised SADF. But the fault line in military thinking on the ultimate solution to be sought through negotiation in general seemed to be that such a solution had to be achieved on terms fully acceptable to the present power structure of the country. The SADF would be able to continue making war to ensure this outcome, however long it might take, while recognising that war alone would not bring solutions. But I don't think the notion of a black majority government in a true democracy was ever attractive to them as a possible solution.

Ultimately, however, the SADF under General George Meiring, to its historical credit, was crucial to the peaceful and stable transition to democracy in 1994 by professing fealty to the new government of Nelson Mandela and making it clear that it would brook no anti-democratic action that might jeopardise the transition. Rumours at the time of a threatened military coup by the SADF, apart from bravado in pubs, around braai fires and in meetings held by some of the disgruntled taking place here and there behind closed doors, cannot but be regarded as so much claptrap. There was no such possibility.

Afrikaner gestation

The realism of the top leadership of the SADF gelled with the brooding gestation in Afrikaner thinking on the doubtful prospects for the ultimate success of apartheid policies, also implying an increasing distrust of the politicians with their pat solutions, which fewer and fewer people were taking seriously. During the 1970s, for example, noted Afrikaans authors, in spite of the threat of censorship and books being banned, wrote incisively in ways that raised the ire of the authorities, who were very much under the heel of the most conservative political and religious persuasions in the power establishment of the time.

Books by internationally recognised and much translated authors André P. Brink (*Kennis van die aand*) and Etienne Leroux (*Magersfontein, O Magersfontein!*) were banned amid serious protest from intellectual Afrikaner quarters. I read both and was puzzled and amused, if not somewhat disappointed, at not having found anything that threatened my tender soul or my patriotism and commitment to the security of my country, unless peeing in the road (a character in *Magersfontein*) or somewhat puerile fornication (*Kennis van die aand*) could have that effect. *Magersfontein*, with its theme of the inexorably rising tide with the colonel(!) sounding the alarm, was brilliant political satire. I was hugely impressed by this book, and a few years later found a thematic parallel in J.M. Coetzee's *Waiting for the Barbarians*, which was equally impressive and disturbing, especially with its context of a border war. Except that Coetzee never had the barbarians coming across the border, but rather residing within ourselves, I surmise (as one always has to do with Coetzee).

Even some ministers of the traditional Afrikaans churches seemed to be veering towards suggesting that the biblical justification for apartheid might no longer be what it used to be according to God's Afrikaans disciples on earth. But a long, tortuous road through years of endless church commissions and synods to gain recognition by top church hierarchies still lay ahead. Theologians Beyers Naudé and Albert Geyser had already in the sixties started this trend, with dire consequences for them, and some of the views consistently put forward over the years by the Doppers of *Woord en Daad* were still in evidence. I realised at the time that I was personally becoming increasingly alienated from the traditionalist power structures of the Afrikaner community and government, including their religiosity, whether real or feigned, as it often seemed to me to be.

I found these sentiments of mine disturbing, as I had once myself been sincere in my Christian beliefs and active on church councils. My apostasy was engendered by personal experience of reality and the endless anomalies of the human condition, especially the obscene, unremitting tragedy of millions upon millions of diseased and starving children. Why, oh why, should God/

god visit his/her wrath at the sins of mankind on these innocents who never even had a chance to sin? And, why, oh why, should a mortar bomb horrendously shatter two eighteen-year-old bodies and leave others standing in close proximity unscathed, apart from small shrapnel wounds and hearing impairment for a few days? Innumerable books and theses and dogmas and myths have been written on the subject and declared by their producers to be the absolute truth, promising redemption, without the slightest shred of confirmation, except by imagination and delusion. Yet the anomalies and tragedies persist and accumulate. I may even have been influenced by my reading of the tortuous Desiderius Erasmus and Kenneth Kaunda on humanism. There are simply too many things I don't understand.

This mindshift in Afrikaner circles unavoidably also had an effect on military thinking and approaches to the insurgency movements developing in the region, with many in these circles being members of the Broederbond. Although there was still the conviction among some in the military and in politics that the hearts and minds would follow if you first got them by their elusive balls, it was by now clear that nothing could be achieved in a system based on racial discrimination. The hearts and minds of Afrikaner intellectualism were being prised from apartheid ideology.

Frantz Fanon showed up the dangers of the alienation of the masses from formal authority, and I became convinced that apartheid would have to go in its entirety if we were to get the majority of the population to participate in the building of a new country.

Protecting a value system

How far does one go in defending a value system, without acting in ways that themselves tend to negate rather than preserve those values? On the other hand, by being hesitant, by how much is the risk of the destruction of that value system increased? How far do you allow protest and mass action to go before it crosses the line of constitutional and democratic acceptability, while underground insurgency action is proceeding apace? Does one allow the revolutionary deluge to swamp that dividing line before one acts or only after, with the risk that it may then be too late? When do you reach the point where international and internal opprobrium are outweighed by the need for harsh counterinsurgency methods?

These are some of the practical and moral dilemmas the South African security establishment had to grapple with from the 1970s onwards. The 1976 schoolchildren's protest in Soweto illustrated the dilemma. The breaching of that dividing line by large numbers of protestors and the heightened vituperation poured on the authorities struggling to stem the deluge, made the task extremely difficult and rising to near impossible towards the middle of the 1980s. For a government that still considered itself bound by the standards of civilised Christian and democratic contentions, however often honoured only in the breach thereof, the writing was on the wall. I felt for the brave policemen and later national service boy-soldiers, often very young, who were expected to enforce these standards on the tumultuous, terrifying streets.

The insurgents had not the slightest moral qualm in this regard. They acted with disdain for the law and ethical standards of conduct, which must realistically be understood to have sprung from their utter frustration at having for centuries been merely dictated to by governments without consultation, with the imposition of Afrikaans as the language of instruction in some subjects at school the last straw. The outflow of young people from the country and the training in foreign countries of these disillusioned youths in political action and insurgency techniques, including violent terrorism like sabotage and murder, was the spur to the large-scale civil unrest in the mid-1980s. It irrevocably changed the nature and scope of our security situation.

The security forces were stretched to breaking point, despite successive draconian states of emergency declared by the government in 1985 and expanded in 1986. The slogan 'no education before liberation' also caused serious concern with some more far-sighted senior ANC leaders like Thabo Mbeki and Nelson Mandela. The iniquitous results are evident to this day in the seemingly insurmountable disciplinary problems at many schools, leading to the poor academic performance of large numbers of them. Soweto 1976 was a watershed of historical consequence for South Africa. Black South Africans were now more determined than ever to escape from their Egypt and, more importantly, in Soweto 1976, they gained an expectation of success.

JSS submission

In the mid-1980s I was delegated to represent NIS on the Joint Security Staff (JSS), then jointly chaired by Major General Bert Wandrag of the SAP and Major General Jan van Loggerenberg of the SAAF. It was clear from the outset that the expanded state of emergency declared in June 1986 was bound to fail as any kind of permanent solution, although it did quell the worst of the unrest through, among other measures, large-scale detentions. In June 1986

I drafted a submission on the situation and requested permission from the DG of NIS to submit it to the JSS for consideration. He refused permission to do so as an official NIS submission, but gave me to understand that if I wished I could submit it as a personal input for discussion.

The main points I made were broadly that there were no more easy options available to the government; that imaginative political initiatives had to be taken; that the liberation organisations, excluding the SACP, be unbanned and all political prisoners released; and that a strict prohibition on all violent political agitation and actions that could lead to violence be ruthlessly enforced. I was later persuaded by Mike Louw that the continued banning of the SACP would make a complete non-starter of any possible negotiation initiative as just about every top leader of the ANC was then still a member of that party, however nominally in some cases. I submitted the document to the joint chairpersons for consideration for the agenda, which never happened, and they never said a word about it to me. I did, however, sense a certain chill in their attitudes towards me personally, which until then had been quite hearty.

The SADF in Angola

The SADF remained resolute in its determination to establish conditions conducive to political settlement, but the dominant aim was always to win militarily, wherever and whenever required. There is little doubt that without our effective military resistance to our enemies' armed assaults, starting with South West Africa, our chances of achieving negotiated settlements there and in South Africa would have been limited. This resistance by the SADF and the SAP in Angola and South West Africa significantly increased the cost to the USSR of its machinations in southern Africa. What they had initially thought would be a walk in the park, became a festering ulcer haemorrhaging manpower, money, material and prestige at an alarming rate, with concrete results falling far short of their expectations.

The SADF's involvement must have been a factor, together with their own domestic ills and other international issues, in the USSR's decision to first scale down and then end its military and financial support to its surrogates' war effort in Angola. Pressure from the Western powers, especially from the USA and Britain under Ronald Reagan and Margaret Thatcher respectively, who were concerned that the Soviets might gain a permanent foothold in the region, also had an important effect, and gave temporary succour to South

Africa. But those Western governments were also under increasing pressure for their 'support of the evil apartheid regime', which over time became too onerous for them to continue to resist. This had a direct bearing on the decision on both sides, the financial and political cost to South Africa also steadily becoming prohibitive, to move to a negotiated settlement of the perennial South West Africa question.

In a private conversation during an interlude in the World Trade Centre negotiations at Kempton Park in 1992, I asked the leading communist in the negotiations, Joe Slovo, what he thought the effect, if any, of the South African armed action in South West Africa and Angola had been on the Soviet Union's thinking at the time. He responded obliquely in typically Marxist terms to the effect that the balance of forces were predicated upon objective realities, which invariably affected the strategy and tactics of any organisation or undertaking, and that the South African military had probably established some new objective realities there. He declined to comment on what the effect on Soviet thinking was, saying he didn't know. Joe Slovo had been slavishly loyal to his masters in Moscow all his life, even through the era of Joseph Stalin's most unspeakable atrocities.

Clausewitz on winning

In view of the SADF's winning culture, the question arises of what the concept of 'winning' actually means in military terms. Classically, the purpose of war is to destroy the enemy forces in a decisive battle, thereby winning the war. However, this is no longer a realistic option in modern warfare, where forces are virtually never concentrated to an extent that their destruction may end a war and deliver victory. Wars today require a more subtle approach, and in this respect one can do no better than refer to the views of the great Prussian soldier and theoretician of war, Carl von Clausewitz.

Writing in the early nineteenth century, his basic analytical framework is as useful now as it was then, and still provides a point of departure for strategic theorising and application in armed forces and military training institutions worldwide. One can, of course, write theses on Clausewitz, as many scholars have done, but for present purposes only two of his fundamental tenets are pertinent: the purpose of war is to impose one's will on the enemy by achieving own objectives and preventing the enemy from achieving theirs, neither of these necessarily implying military victory in every engagement; and, war is the conduct of politics by other means.

17

Cuito Cuanavale

The so-called Battle of Cuito Cuanavale in the late 1980s, more properly a series of battles along the Lomba and Quito rivers in Angola between South African forces and ostensibly FAPLA, provides an excellent case study in considering the basics of Clausewitzian theory. The 'Angolan' forces, with large numbers of Cuban combat troops and Cuban commanders, were heavily supported by Russians and a wide variety of other East European advisors and combatants. This sequence of events has been most imaginatively held up by South Africa's adversaries as their 'glorious victory', but no reputable observer believes this. So what really was the final result of the battles of the Lomba River? I refrain from any comment on specific engagements as I wasn't there, but the overarching outcome is crystal clear to anyone looking at it objectively.

In September 1985, the MPLA/FAPLA and their communist sponsors decided on a final conventional offensive to excise the bleeding ulcer called UNITA. At the time there were an estimated 50 000-plus Cuban troops in Angola, backed by military and technical personnel from the Soviet Union and East Germany, about 1 000 and 2 000 respectively. The aim of the offensive was to occupy the sparsely populated areas of southern Angola, with the headquarters of UNITA at Jamba in the south-east as the ultimate objective. The assault force, according to official records, consisted of some twenty Cuban army brigades, supported by about 100 helicopters of various types, thirty modern MiG-23 fighter aircraft and fifty MiG-21s, and later even a few state-of-the-art MiG-29s. Heavy transport aircraft were also available in large numbers.

During 1984 and 1985, the FAPLA forces were modernised and equipped with brand-new armaments for this operation, including approximately 300 T-55, 175 T-34 and later even some T-62 tanks, as well as fifty amphibious PT-76 armoured fighting vehicles. The Soviet Union was rendering comprehensive, large-scale assistance to the communist forces, and equipment lost on the battlefield was immediately replaced. The renowned Comandante Arnaldo Ochoa Sánchez was put in command of Cuban forces, while the Soviet general Konstantin Shaganovitch was in overall command of the entire theatre of operations. Their intent was clear.

The result was failure. This huge, well-equipped force was stopped dead in its tracks scarcely halfway to its stated end objective. Never more than 3 000 South African soldiers in support of about 8 000 UNITA troops confronted the communist coalition. The South Africans and their allies succeeded through their expert use of excellent self-developed and self-produced artillery, good command and innovative tactics, including imaginative use of exceptionally brave Special Forces, and an obsolescent but cleverly employed air force. In particular, the subsonic Aermacchi MB-326 'Impala' ground-attack jets proved a thorn in the side of the potent Soviet Mi-24 'Hind' assault helicopters, which were withdrawn from battle after suffering heavy losses to the Impala.

In the final analysis, South African forces prevailed by effective application of limited resources. Some authoritative international commentators have pointed out that the defeat of the communist coalition at and around Cuito Cuanavale, and subsequent resistance to their further provocations in the south-west of Angola in 1987/88, was a contributing factor to the demise of the communist edifice in the USSR and Eastern Europe from November 1989, when the Berlin Wall was breached. The huge losses suffered by their forces in the South West Africa/Angola conflict lends credence to this view.

General Jannie Geldenhuys, former Chief of the SADF, provides the following selected comparative figures of losses on both sides:

SADF:

Tanks	3
Armoured fighting vehicles	8
Other vehicles	3
Mirage F1 aircraft	2 (1 in an accident; 1 in enemy action)
Bosbok reconnaissance aircraft	1
Personnel	34

Communist coalition:

Tanks	94
Armoured fighting vehicles	134
Logistics vehicles	389
MiG-21/23	9
Helicopters	9
Artillery systems	15
Personnel	2 000 plus (est.)

So, the South Africans imposed their will on the opposition in preventing them from achieving their objective of annihilating UNITA and their HQ at Jamba, thereby achieving their own objective, which had been to do exactly that. The simple logic of the outcome in Clausewitzian or any other terms is irrefutable, irrespective of the endless agonising analyses, assessments, opinions and propaganda that Cuito Cuanavale has engendered. The eventual political outcome was that, together with other domestic and international factors, the USSR recognised the futility of the military efforts of its surrogates in southern Africa, cut its losses and withdrew from Angola. Had the South Africans really failed at Cuito Cuanavale, the outcome would surely have been quite different.

It is still averred in propaganda by the communist forces and their sycophants in South Africa and elsewhere that they were victorious in preventing the South Africans from occupying Cuito Cuanavale. It needs to be emphasised that occupying Cuito Cuanavale was never a primary objective of the South African forces. It was thought a good idea to try to do so in order to consolidate the destruction of the last vestiges of the communist force there, but this was then realistically considered unnecessary in light of the already achieved strategic objective. In any event, the enemy forces had been seriously hurt and were on the run, and in view of the prospect of further casualties, the idea was abandoned.

In the aftermath, the CO of the 'victorious' Cuban forces, the respected Comandante Ochoa Sánchez, was relieved of his command and Fidel Castro took over the Cuban forces personally, mainly by telephone from Havana (according to General Malan). Ochoa Sánchez was shortly afterwards tried on trumped-up charges, sentenced to death and executed, a strange outcome indeed for the commander who achieved such a glorious victory. An even more absurd result must surely be the continued annual commemoration of that victory by so-called progressive forces in South Africa, including placing the names of fallen Cuban soldiers on the Roll of Honour at Freedom Park in the shadow of the Voortrekker Monument outside Pretoria (which, incidentally, more or less confirms the figure of Cuban personnel losses stated above). The truth was that all they achieved was to deliver to the South Africans a solid platform for negotiation, which resulted in constitutional dispensations in South West Africa and later in South Africa that epitomised the opposite of what they and their masters in Moscow had sought but failed to achieve, and forced them to withdraw all their forces from Angola.

The headline to one respected South African newspaper's report on the battles reads: 'Why Cuba's scapegoat general died at dawn – Fidel's fight not to lose face – Castro explains why Angola lost battle against SADF' (*Business Day*, 27 July 1989). Back in Cuba, Ochoa Sánchez declared: 'I was sent to a war which had already been lost, so that I could carry the blame for the defeat.'

Nothing further has since been heard of General Shaganovitch. A Russian officer who had been involved in the fighting but whose name escapes me, told the media of the respect the Russians involved in the conflict had developed for the South Africans' fighting prowess, and their disdain for that of some of their 'heroic' comrades, of which the ANC and MK claim to have been a part.

I have for this chapter relied on much media reporting, the internet, discussions with people who were there and books by two esteemed South African generals, both former Chiefs of the SADF and most intimately involved with the war, General Jannie Geldenhuys, *Dié wat gewen het*, and General Magnus Malan, *My Lewe Saam met die SA Weermag*. The facts that both provide are on record and verifiable, but I have approached their assessments and opinions with caution, given their unshakeable commitment to the SADF and its achievements. I wanted to convey my own views on the outcome and this caveat is in no way intended to cast aspersions on the integrity of these two exceptional soldiers and South Africans.

18

Fallout at Home

And yet, after all that had transpired in the war in South West Africa and Angola, and with much historical hindsight and taking into account the objectives of the Soviet Union in the region and in the Cold War, so-called learned analysts, including some highly regarded lawyers such as Professor Lourens du Plessis of Stellenbosch University, still maintain that South Africa's military action in the region had been 'illegal and unnecessary'. After hearing Du Plessis divest himself of this opinion in an SABC radio interview (in 2008, I think), I phoned him asking whether he could refer me to any specific research he or anyone else had done that objectively came to such a conclusion as regards the 'unnecessary' part of his statement. He rather brusquely said no, and declined to respond to further questions on the subject before ending the conversation. Of course, he was under no obligation to respond to an unknown small-fry phoning him out of the blue, especially cursorily in a telephone conversation. But his reaction did not speak much for his confidence in his casually delivered opinion, broadcast on a public radio station nationally and, in view of his standing as an academic lawyer, probably also resonating internationally.

At its simplest, Article 51 of the UN Charter confers the right to self-defence on states, which has never been challenged by any member state. Ample precedent and opinion exist that this also necessarily implies justification for pre-emptive strikes across international borders in cases of immediately imminent attack from across such a border, with provisos such as proportionality to the threat, lapse of time from becoming aware of the threat, etc. In the case of South West Africa, attack was not imminent, but had already started.

In the case of the war in Vietnam, the USA argued in the UN Security Council that although South Vietnam was not a sovereign country, it had the right to self-defence in terms of Article 51 and America was therefore entitled to assist it on request. South Vietnamese and American actions included massive pre-emptive strikes into North Vietnam, Laos and Cambodia, setting a resounding precedent. Although there was much agitation and protest in civil society and from states worldwide in opposition to this view, there was no formal countermanding of it by the Security Council. South Africa's involvement in South West Africa closely approximated that of the USA in Vietnam.

Of course, South Africa had nowhere near the political clout of the USA, and came under increasing global pressure, especially from the UN and the International Court of Justice. With costs escalating alarmingly, South Africa eventually accepted the termination of its League of Nations mandate to administer South West Africa and consequently had to withdraw from that country. The whole process had been so overwhelmingly politically inspired and legally tenuous that South Africa was surely justified in having regarded the matter as one of realpolitik rather than legal nicety, and acting accordingly. After all, vital national interests were at stake. This led eventually to a negotiated settlement and the installation of a democratically elected government based on a liberal-democratic constitution, instead of one to the taste of the Soviet Union being imposed on the country from outside. This was later replicated in South Africa. The settlement in South West Africa also engineered the total withdrawal of all outside communist forces from Angola.

Many more 'expert analysts' have vented their opinions in line with Du Plessis', including complete military, legal and political ignoramuses. Having deprived themselves of any role in the shaping of our recent history of democratisation, draft-dodgers are a case in point. Many objectors were, to my mind, simply too self-centred or afraid to do their bit in the contestation between the forces of freedom (in the longer term) and those of the enslaving, already failed Marxist/Leninist persuasion. A senior ANC negotiator at Kempton Park, since deceased, was once quoted in the media as saying that if these draft-dodgers had really had the courage of their convictions and the necessary moral fibre, they would have left the country and joined the armed struggle against the racist regime in the field.

However, there were also many principled objectors to combat service who offered themselves for equally essential clerical and other non-combat duties in the military, especially those very brave young men who volunteered as combat medics. Others refused compulsory military service for a wide variety of reasons. I am now of the opinion that more care could have been taken by the authorities in handling cases, for instance, of people clearly psychologically unsuited to withstand the ravages of war, instead of regarding them simply as mommy's boys or homosexuals. With hindsight, the efforts that were apparently made to 'cure' the latter were especially horrifying.

I have a high regard for the many principled members and supporters of the End Conscription Campaign who, abhorring apartheid, could not in good conscience fight for its survival, as they saw the purpose of the war. Although to my mind they were blindsided on the communist menace, apart from those who were themselves Marxist, one cannot but have respect for people who are prepared to stand by their moral convictions and sacrifice much in order to uphold them. Some of these have also become equally principled and respected commentators on the shortcomings of the post-apartheid administration in power in South Africa since 1994, although mostly somewhat understated.

But I have nothing but contempt for those draft-dodgers who refused their services out of pure self-interest and cowardice, or simply to be fashionable under peer pressure. Quite often they were from affluent English-speaking homes and had never inconvenienced themselves out of love for country and society, or in the service of anything but themselves. To their shame, some of the most successful fighting units in Angola were formally English-speaking and consisted mostly of English-speaking South African patriots.

As regards the draft-dodgers in general, Shakespeare's Henry V's celebrated exhortation to his troops before the Battle of Agincourt in France early in the sixteenth century, seems apposite:

> We few, we happy few, we band of brothers;
> For he to-day that sheds his blood with me
> Shall be my brother; be he ne'er so vile,
> This day shall gentle his condition;
> And gentlemen in England now-a-bed
> Shall think themselves accurs'd they were not here,
> And hold their manhoods cheap whilst any speaks
> That fought with us upon Saint Crispin's day.

I am proud that both my sons did their bit and need never 'hold their manhoods cheap'. How those who did not do so feel today is a personal matter purely for them.

19

Honouring the Living and the Dead

From time to time items appear in the printed media and on television on soldiers who fought in South West Africa and Angola, now in or approaching middle age, reminiscing about their experiences and their condition in the aftermath, some of them obviously in need of professional care. But they should be assured that they did themselves, their country and the universal brotherhood of soldiers very proud indeed. They may bask in the knowledge that their brave and effective efforts made it possible for the dire political log-jam that had built up in our country over centuries, to be breached by peaceful negotiation. They forced our adversaries into such a settlement, saving us all from the latter's stated objective of revolutionary conquest.

Had our armed forces not been as successful as they were, the consequences could truly have been too ghastly to contemplate: a settlement in the form of an enforced one-party, Stalinist government with all that would have entailed in terms of the destruction of personal freedom and a command economy doomed to failure. With the irreplaceable support of global communist inter-ests in such a case, it would not have mattered much what a new government's ideological orientation would have been, although our current government's upper echelon is at the time of writing heavily staffed with leading commu-nists. Instead, the eventual outcome for South Africa was a truly democratic constitution with a capitalist-based, free-enterprise market economy, a Bill of Rights that guarantees personal freedom and individual rights, a free media, and an independent judicial system with a constitutional court as supreme arbiter. As Clausewitzian 'politics by other means', the war therefore achieved a historic political victory for South African arms in both Namibia and South Africa. The only thing that we had begun to lose was the awesome burden of the stigma of apartheid.

Yet even now some prominent commentators, like professor of philosophy Anton van Niekerk at the University of Stellenbosch, still characterise those who justify our successful military challenge to the Soviets as seeking to jus-tify apartheid. To those of us who hailed the end of apartheid and worked extremely hard over decades to replace it with our exemplary democratic system, this imputation, devoid as it is of any factual basis or logic, is simply mind-boggling. Of course, many commentators and currently empowered politicians and others in South Africa and elsewhere would have welcomed the advent of a Stalinist 'workers' paradise' under the leadership no doubt of people like the arch-Stalinists Joe Slovo, Gwede Mantashe and general secretary of the SACP Blade Nzimande. They and their cohorts will forever resent the role the SADF played in preventing this, as will the many Marxist scholars in their much-vaunted objectivity. The current 'national democratic revolution' in South Africa constitutes a frantic unconstitutional, anti-democratic and racist effort to achieve their aims by means other than those that were thwarted, in no small measure, by the SADF.

Freedom Park on Salvokop outside Pretoria is a project flowing from the findings of the TRC to promote reconciliation between participants in the various wars in which South Africans have been involved through the ages. These are said to include pre-colonial wars, genocide, slavery, the First and Second World Wars, the two South African Wars of Liberation against the British Empire (the First and Second Anglo-Boer Wars) and the liberation struggle. There has been only disdainful rejection by Freedom Park authorities in the person of its director, Dr Wally Serote, of suggestions to also honour the role of the South African soldiers who stemmed the communist bid to establish their hegemony in our country.

Some crucial questions remain, begging answers from those who contend that the SADF's military confrontation of communist and communist-backed incursions in South West Africa and Angola was unnecessary, illegal, even a tragically wasteful loss of life: Why would the Soviet Union have allowed their surrogates to negotiate Western-style, capitalist and democratic constitutional states in Namibia and South Africa if they had prevailed militarily? For those opposed to war in principle: Should Hitler not have been confronted militarily to prevent his domination of the world, and was the loss of the thousands upon thousands of eighteen- and nineteen-year-old lives in that endeavour unnecessary? They should also in the context of South West Africa/ Angola bear in mind that the Soviet Union under Lenin and Stalin forcibly subjugated, tortured and killed millions more people before, during and after the Second World War than even the heinous Nazis did.

An offer to Freedom Park of cooperation and mutual support from the dynamic management of the Voortrekker Monument and Heritage Foundation just across the road has been brusquely declined. So much, then, for their professed objective to promote reconciliation between the former combatants. But the Voortrekker Monument and museum have ensured that the legacy of those brave soldiers of the SADF will be honoured by generations to come. An impressive Wall of Remembrance has been erected there with the names of, among others, the South African soldiers who fell in the South West Africa/Angola war.

In January 2011, Chris Kantewa, a former detachment commander of PLAN, visited the Voortrekker Monument to pay his respects at the Wall of Remembrance to the fallen South African soldiers, against whom he had fought some fierce battles on the border. He laid a wreath at the wall and expressed his respect and high regard for the fighting prowess of the South African soldiers. I've heard it said by South African soldiers who were there that this respect was mutual. May Freedom Park take note of the real meaning of reconciliation.

20

Change of Tack and Destination

By the end of the 1970s it had become clear that the time for finding a peaceful settlement between the peoples of South Africa was running out. Making war was becoming unaffordable and international isolation and pressure, especially economic sanctions, were throttling the country. Internally, mass protests were succeeding to a worrying extent in making the country ungovernable. This included crass intimidation of the masses of law-abiding black citizens by the most barbaric of methods imaginable, such as murder by way of the infamous 'necklace' method of burning people to death, and killing large numbers of black policemen and elected black members and officials of local governing bodies in townships by beating, burning or shooting them to death. The horrific methods of enforcing consumer boycotts by, for example, force-feeding even elderly women with soap powder they had bought, are an abiding image of the time.

However abhorrent, new 'objective realities' were created by these cruel methods inside the country. The capacity of the existing structures of authority to contain the situation by forceful means had been dissipating over a period of years. There was no sharing of responsibility for what had gone wrong in the country, the mostly Afrikaners in government having to bear the full burden. And it had become increasingly clear that the human resources the power structures could muster in the security forces and services were being seriously overstretched. Such resources, drawn from such a small white population base, could simply not indefinitely carry the enormous workload of trying to contain the threatening insurgency from the overwhelmingly larger black population whose support the ANC had largely secured.

The political logjam seemed increasingly insurmountable to more and more fine, motivated people, their stamina bludgeoned by quite inhuman demands. I saw hard men cry from sheer exhaustion, and become depressive. This inordinate strain on human physical, mental and spiritual endurance has not yet been properly investigated and accounted for, except to a limited extent regarding soldiers who fought in the field. In one late-night meeting on South West Africa at CSI, the very senior presiding officer said something like: 'Boys, can't we just give the bloody place to SWAPO so that they can have the hassle for a bit?' We all laughed heartily, but it was only a half-joke.

The homelands policy started off as an honest attempt at shared responsibility, which held the seeds of a solution had it been done more equitably, with white taxpayers prepared to be more indulgent towards its financing, traditional leaders more accommodating to the rapidly modernising youth and prepared to give up some of their despotic prerogatives and authority, and true democracy instituted with regular free elections and accountable government. But black people were no longer prepared to accept regulation of their lives foisted on them without consultation, and the conservative traditional leaders no longer enjoyed much purchase with the urbanised masses. It can only be speculated what the outcome may have been if accommodation instead of coercion had been initiated between the 1930s and 1950s, when the anti-violence Albert Luthuli was president of the ANC.

The deprivation of dignity and opportunity had become too much for the black population to bear. In 1976 in Soweto, they discovered they could do something about it. The control of the situation by the authorities had become decidedly tenuous. I was by now on pragmatic and moral grounds convinced that the insurgency could not be stemmed by forcible means and that it was time to break the logjam of racial confrontation in the country by negotiation, with all the risks that would entail. We had to change tack for a new destination where all citizens would share the responsibility of governing a democratic country. I had no doubt that this would have to lead to a black-dominated government under a truly democratic constitution that would uphold the rule of law with the usual checks and balances that save governments and the populace from their own folly.

I had never shaken off the moral and ethical admonishments of *Woord en Daad* and was convinced that South Africans, and especially Afrikaners, although probably not on account of the limited reach of *Woord en Daad*, had also come to other insights on the morality of apartheid. I do not agree with the view put forward by some highly respected South Africans, like Dr Niel Barnard, that the movement towards negotiation was motivated by purely pragmatic considerations, although that was, of course, a compelling component. But without the deep moral sense of wrong that had developed over many years in the Afrikaner psyche in particular, pragmatism would probably not have been enough. Mainstream Afrikaners were regaining their capacity for empathy, which had become dissipated through their struggle over centuries for self-preservation.

Negotiation was surely the only way of achieving a peaceful democratising revolution, and the sooner the better while the government's instruments of power were still largely intact, with the proviso that such instruments be applied strictly towards maintaining order while pursuing agreed ends. I was sure that the SADF would fulfil that role admirably, as it later confirmed through its overall responsible conduct over the transition period. But I did not think that the military, apart from its role in preserving stability, should be a main political player in this inevitable process, with which I out of conviction wanted to be associated. I was also completely at one with the views being expressed by NIS on the real internal sources of instability in the country. In 1980 I was promoted to full colonel but, being neither a fighting soldier nor a *Broeder*, as a secondary consideration I thought my chances of further progress career-wise in the SADF were slim.

I knew, respected and liked a number of people at NIS from having initially served with them in the old DMI from 1968 to 1970. Towards the end of 1980 I became aware that they had a vacant position that they were having difficulty filling, and to which my background and seniority seemed suited. I was worried about my negotiation position if I should simply up and apply for the job, and so thought I would rather try to get them to offer it to me.

One Saturday night at a dinner party at mutual friends, I met an NIS man called Johan Mostert who worked as a researcher under Mike Louw, the then head of one of the directorates of research there. I gave Mostert, a perceptive man, to understand that I had decided to leave the military and was looking for something else to do. On the way home I said to my wife that I knew Louw, a reflective man, well enough to know that he would not phone me on Monday, but on Tuesday. On Tuesday he phoned to invite me to lunch, where he offered me a job. Mostert, who had in fact recruited me to become his direct superior, has remained a highly valued and trusted friend, and has attained high rank in the intelligence world. He has been one of my main sounding boards on the past in writing this book.

I formally requested a transfer to NIS, which was refused by CSI General Wessie van der Westhuizen. So I resigned and, in terms of military protocol, asked for permission to see him to take my leave formally. Again he refused. He also refused to allow me the usual official farewell, but the admirable Rear Admiral Dries Putter (later Vice Admiral and Chief of the Navy), my immediate boss, arranged an informal drinks function to say goodbye, which I greatly appreciated. It was quite interesting to see who of my colleagues attended and who didn't. I was told that Wessie's pique at my leaving was that I could be so thankless as to leave so soon after he had prematurely promoted me to the rank of colonel – shades of my mother, I thought. But I had little doubt that Wessie's visceral contempt for NIS was his main motivation.

I was making a new but not unfamiliar beginning. I was sure I had found the right tree.

My grandparents: Ouma and Oupa Maritz, 1946

My parents: Dr Pieter and Mollie (née Maritz) Spaarwater, 1954

With my friends Bruno, 1947 (collies and sister incidental), and Japie, 1951

Siblings Pieter, Ina-Marié and Maritz in 1948 …

…and, a bit later, in 1998

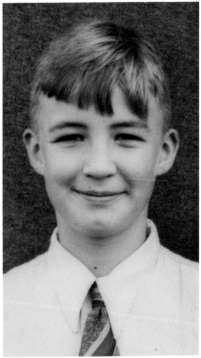

Off to boarding school, 1952

With my mother, 1958

Flip Kruger, Steyn Verster and me
after a parade at the Rand Easter
Show, 1958

Mentors *extraordinaire*: Major General Fritz Loots and Colonel (later Brigadier General) Dirk Greyling

Chinese military delegation, Grootfontein Air Force Base, South West Africa, 1976 (me adjusting my cap in the background)

Receiving an award from Lieutenant General 'Wessie' van der Westhuizen, CSI, 1979

Promoted to colonel, 1980. The red band at last!

On the fortified island of Kinmen north of Taiwan facing the Chinese mainland, 1987. Back row: Tonie van der Merwe far left; Daan Opperman second from left; me far right. Front row: Dr Niel Barnard, DG of NIS, second from left; Ms Pitout, Taipei office, second from right

Luxury accommodation in Freetown, Sierra Leone, 1987. Left to right: me, Daan Opperman, André Barnard, Pierre Fourie

'Recruiting' a fellow passenger on an Air Jordan flight from London to Freetown, 1978. Unkind unauthorised photo courtesy of Daan Opperman

With a Chinese delegation, 1990. President F.W. de Klerk and Dr Niel Barnard in front with guests, me at the back

Dr Barnard decorating the head of the Chinese intelligence service, 1990. Mrs Engela Barnard far left, me far right

Proud moment *en famille* at NIS awards ceremony, 1988. Left to right: Bosman, Anna, me, Suzanne, Cobus, Lisa

Greatest source of pride: my grandsons, offspring of daughters Suzanne Schubert and Lisa Spaarwater-Muller. Left and right: Christiaan and Michael Muller; centre: Mika and Everaad Schubert, 2011

BEGINNING III

National Intelligence

21

'Welcome' to NIS

I arrived in my airy and sparkling clean corner office (yes!) in NIS on 1 May 1981 as a divisional head in political research, at a rank somewhat lower than my former one in the military. There was a small pot of lovely little yellow flowers on the conference table at the front of my desk, and the place reeked of welcome and good cheer. My two deputy heads of division, Pieter (Rassie) Erasmus and Johan Mostert, were there to receive me and had arranged a welcoming tea. All members of the division were there for me to meet, including the sweet and pretty secretary assigned to me, Naomi Swanepoel, daughter of a later chief director of research, Pieter Swanepoel ('Oom Swanie'), whom I learnt to respect as my superior and later to highly appreciate as a dear friend. He was an ex-security policeman from the Van den Bergh era of the Security Branch of the SAP and of the Bureau for State Security (BOSS), and a man of acute intellect and a delightful sense of humour. I thought Naomi would be a good listening post for this almost top boss of mine – after all, the new man in their midst needed to be appraised, especially coming as he did from military intelligence, in some NIS quarters at about the same level on the adversarial scale as the ANC.

I welcomed the early opportunity to tell something about myself and how I envisaged the participatory management style we would follow, emphasising that the only way forward was with an open-door approach and mutual trust, together with ongoing honest communication while always maintaining respect for the opinions and dignity of others in differences which were sure to arise by the very nature of our job, and which I would welcome. I emphasised that this type of approach could not be one-sided, and that we would get to know each other better in this regard as we went along. My 'maiden speech' seemed to be fairly well received, but some vacuous and bored 'I've heard all of this before' types of expressions under furrowed brows were also in evidence. I had expected scepticism at this outsider, whom they did not know except by his dubious background, coming in as their immediate boss.

My two deputies were both clever and well informed on their areas of responsibility. For the rest they were chalk and cheese. Johan was extrovert and gregarious, a well-spoken ideas man, healthily ambitious, an organiser and something of a wheeler-dealer, although I never thought him to be self-interested, and brimming with contained self-confidence. Rassie was about the exact opposite. From a more robust background and more or less unspoken, he was a shy introvert with brittle self-confidence and he was seemingly unambitious. He was extremely reluctant to speak before any audience. Part of his job required him to brief higher authority as well as outsiders from time to time, which sometimes required considerable encouragement.

In the first week or two I was there, I went to Rassie's office two doors away from mine to speak to him about some work-related matter. It was at about 2 p.m. on a Friday afternoon and I found him with two or three chums from outside the division gathered around his desk, on which was arrayed bottles of liquor and glasses, the party starting to warm up for the weekend. I made it clear that this was unacceptable during working hours and instructed them to put away the bottles and glasses and carry on with their work.

The Monday after, Rassie came to my office to ask for an appointment. He had something serious to discuss with me. I said that he did not need an appointment and invited him to take a seat. He said he wasn't ready and would come some other time. A few days later he turned up and told me that two things worried him. He said he wanted to apologise for this bullshit of the stupid little yellow flowers someone had put on my table. He didn't know who was responsible, but added, more or less: 'It was probably Mostert, again.' And on the question of the drinking in his office: 'If that is your attitude, you're not going to make it in this place.'

I developed tremendous appreciation for both of my deputies for the unwavering support and loyalty they gave me, although Rassie first needed a bit of time for reflection. He came to me again some time later merely to tell me, without being specific, that he now realised I had meant what I said on my first day in the job. It was quite endearing and I thought Rassie had handed me a reprieve, conceding to me at least the potential to perhaps make it in this place. I have an enduring soft spot for him.

22

Research

I had over time heard hair-raising tales of the harrowing experiences re-searchers had to endure for many years at BOSS under General Van den Bergh. Mike Louw had initially nominally been the head of research, at the time a position with no defined responsibilities and no influence – in fact it wasn't really a job at all, it seemed. Van den Bergh once said to him he did not know why they (the researchers) were there and that they should keep themselves occupied as best they could with whatever they wished. This was a discouraging and demoralising period for people like Louw, Piet Coetzee and others whom I knew to be excellent researchers and analysts, and who had opted for BOSS when it was established in 1969 and we in the old DMI had been given the choice of joining either of the two. Graduates were referred to in derogatory terms as '*die mense met graadjies*' (the people with little [academic] degrees). Van den Bergh, known as Lang Hendrik (Tall Hendrik) because of his height, apparently did have a remarkable intuition for the baddies and their nefarious ways, saying that he had this little man on his shoulder who told him things. He apparently did not need researchers to do so.

BOSS under Van den Bergh had been strongly executive-orientated and influenced by ideology and the politics of the day. He had been close to Prime Minister John Vorster since they were incarcerated together in the Koffiefontein internment camp for activities in opposition to South Africa's participation in the Second World War on the side of Britain. After the demise of Vorster in 1979 and consequently that of Van den Bergh, Alec van Wyk became the DG, to be succeeded by Niel Barnard in 1980. This brought radical change in approach and atmosphere, including a change of name from the Department of State Security, as BOSS had later become, to the National Intelligence Service (NIS). NIS reported to political authority first through Roelf Meyer, then a deputy minister in the office of the state president, and later through the minister of justice, Kobie Coetsee. Tertiary academic qualifications became a requirement for most research jobs. Between Barnard and Louw the place was intellectualised and transformed into the nearest thing the state had to an objective think-tank. It had no executive functions to confuse wishful thinking with reality, or to be concerned with extraneous aspects like potential budgetary consequences of their assessments.

In early 1970 I had applied for a job at BOSS, mainly because rumour had it that they were paying far better salaries than the SADF. I was then a really poorly paid lieutenant with four mouths to feed at home. I appeared before a selection committee consisting of mainly ex-SADF officers who had joined BOSS in 1969. It was chaired by Brigadier Renier van Vuuren and included Colonel Mike Wilson, with whom I had had a clash when we were previously both at DMI. They asked me why I had been disloyal when I had the chance to join the organisation in 1969 but elected to remain in the SADF, but would not respond to my question of what they meant by disloyalty.

They merely rejected my application, obviously doing their best to ingratiate themselves with their new boss, the Tall Man, who was then the main protagonist in the new organisation's quite vicious battle for turf with the SADF. General Rudolph Hiemstra was then commandant general (as Chief of the SADF was then designated) but in this contention fronted by Brigadier Fritz Loots, the head of DMI. The full story of this confrontation, led at a political level by Prime Minister Vorster and minister of defence P.W. Botha, will probably never fully be told as all the main players are now dead. To the best of my knowledge none of them ever wrote anything in this regard.

I was livid and told the committee I would speak to General Van den Bergh myself. I phoned him at home early that very evening, introduced myself by my military rank and asked to see him as soon as possible on an urgent personal matter. He told me I could come to his house straight away if I wished, without any further ado or questions asked. Van den Bergh had a fearsome reputation as Vorster's hatchet man, even literally, according to some, but I found him to be a pleasant and gracious man when I turned up at his home in Waterkloof Ridge, Pretoria at about 7 p.m. There was a large lawn and no fencing around the property. At my ringing he opened the front door himself, with a huge, pitch-black Alsatian by his side, looking menacing but, more chillingly, I sensed, silently and unmovingly staring me straight in the face. I assumed that it had been police-trained and could probably have turned into something quite different at an appropriate command. But I found the lack of security measures amazing, considering that the general at the time must have been the most hated man in South Africa in certain quarters. I surmised that the premises were probably fitted with CCTV surveillance.

Equally amazing was his willingness to see me immediately, utter small-fry that I was and in the service of his main antagonist at the time. The thought, however, also crossed my mind that he might only have been a good intelligence operator, intent on finding out as much as possible about the 'enemy', but he asked and said nothing in that regard. He offered me tea and cookies and listened to my story, which I told with no punches pulled at the selection committee and its ex-military members. He empathised and said he would see what he could do. I got no feedback, but was later told that he did in fact speak to the committee about me, urged them to be fair and told them it was their responsibility to do the right thing, but did not interfere in their decision.

When I arrived at NIS, I had from CSI already had quite a bit of professional contact and cooperation with researchers there. I was particularly impressed with the people now in senior leadership positions in Research. Among these were Cor Bekker, Pieter (PC) Swanepoel, George Grewar and Mike Louw, as well as some outstanding subordinate managers and researchers, my deputy divisional heads included, all independent-minded and free-thinking people. I don't mention more names as it could still be embarrassing to some of them. The effect of the appointment of Niel Barnard as DG a year earlier was evident in the reorientation the organisation had been undergoing since.

An atmosphere of honest enquiry and discourse prevailed, with no apparent fear of what any 'big brother' outside of normal supervisory structures might say or think. Everyone seemed intent on being everyone else's devil's advocate, sometimes exaggeratedly so and sometimes merely mischievous. The indiscipline it projected was irritating. An overarching editorial committee of wiser heads saw to it that some of the more extremely innovative, even imaginative, thinking did not enter wider formal circulation in the security community, sometimes giving rise to quite vehement disputation within the committee. From the start I found it a stimulating and enjoyable environment to work in.

With all the good things I heard and read NIS saying when I was still with CSI, I was sometimes amused and even irritated by a tendency towards long-winded, rhetorical pretty writing, with flowery colloquialisms, idiomatic expressions and rare 'high Afrikaans' vocabulary that tended to obfuscate rather than enlighten. Mike Louw himself was surprisingly susceptible to such stylisation, often a hallmark of products of the University of the Orange Free State, his alma mater. It also, perhaps understandably, sometimes came from excellent analysts from the world of journalism, who had been schooled in writing for other purposes, with adjectives abounding.

But I was surprised by the really bad writing of some Afrikaans-speakers in their home language. This applied especially to some university graduates, even post-graduates, in disciplines such as history, political science and economics. This in particular afflicted products of my own alma mater, the University of Pretoria. I once asked a bright young political science honours graduate from there why he was unable to write properly in Afrikaans. He explained that they were encouraged to write cryptically, particularly in the political science department, even in long essays. This was to save them and their lecturers time and trouble, as long as the latter could understand what they meant. They ended up only half literate in expressing themselves in writing in their own home language.

In many cases of written English, grammar, syntax and vocabulary were often primordial and barely sufficient to convey meaning. I found it disturbing coming from graduates of Afrikaans universities – had they been reading only spoon-fed notes in Afrikaans and no textbooks or academic articles by international experts? This also provided some lighter moments such as when one of our top economics researchers had to brief outsiders in English and at question time had serious problems expressing himself off the cuff. After battling through one or two questions, he refused to take any more, saying 'My English is up' (directly from the Afrikaans: '*My Engels is op*' – exhausted).

Concerted efforts to recruit researchers from English universities were less successful than hoped, understandably for the time, due to politically influenced security considerations. The lack of a nuanced command of English by Afrikaans-speakers in government service created wider problems, for instance in the negotiations for a new constitution in the early 1990s and beyond. I was once accused of writing dictionary English, to which I retorted it was only that if you needed a dictionary to understand what you were reading, adding that that was precisely the function of a dictionary. I later got permission for some selected researchers to be sent to England for short periods of targeted research and exposure to an English environment.

Mike Louw was Director of International Political Research and my immediate superior when I arrived at NIS. I knew him well from our younger *jolling* days at DMI. Over time we had some serious differences of opinion, but I developed huge respect for his incisively analytical mind and unshakeable intellectual integrity.

Under Barnard, NIS rapidly gained credibility and the respect of the highest authorities in the land, including P.W. Botha, who had succeeded John Vorster as prime minister and later became president of the country. Restructuring of NIS brought about the rationalisation and expansion of its research component. This included the creation of a properly structured chief directorate for research, together with its personnel establishment. Not all former members of BOSS, who had been drawn mostly from the Security Branch of the police, were suited or inclined to research work, although there were some outstanding exceptions. Apart from Pieter Swanepoel, an excellent analytical brain and equally excellent writer, a man by the name of Edwin Barkhuizen comes to mind. He was a temperamental and sometimes difficult-to-handle former security policeman, but had superb qualities as a researcher and writer.

Owing no doubt to General Van den Bergh's influence on the initial struc- turing of BOSS, salaries were one notch above those for similar positions in the broader civil service. This meant that a chief director at NIS carried the civil service rank of deputy DG and was remunerated on that salary scale, equalling that of lieutenant general in the military. Good salaries at entry level together with other attractive service conditions drew well-qualified candi- dates, not all of whom would, of course, pass the stringent psychometric and security vetting processes, sometimes regrettably so. There was a range of sports facilities at 'the Farm' recreation and training facility in the south-east of Pretoria, and a well-equipped in-house gymnasium replete with a sports kineticist. Members were encouraged to make use of these also during office hours, further creating a positive and pleasant work environment.

After I had been at NIS for about eighteen months, Louw was promoted to Chief Director Research and I took his place as Director of International Political Research. This was a satisfying appointment, and I worked with mostly able and dedicated people over a broader spectrum of substantive matter, with more scope and challenges from a management perspective as well.

One aspect that I found strange in NIS was that researchers and opera- tional agent handlers ('controllers') were strictly forbidden to have any contact with one another. At CSI there had been reasonably free intercourse between the two. The rationale was that contact between them could lead to cross- contamination of mindsets and carried the danger of compromising agents.

If researchers should not be careful in their analyses and writing, for instance, to not inadvertently divulge the access of a particular agent to his/her subject of interest, it could be a dead giveaway. I argued that for a researcher not to have insight into the positioning of a source heightened this risk, and that not to trust people, carefully selected as those at NIS were, was more dangerous than trusting them. Experience in general later proved this to be correct, giving a boost to morale and assisting me greatly in leading and managing people. But at the time I was barking at the moon.

Such contact could be valuable as agent handlers quite often have peripheral information around a subject that they don't regard as pertinent and therefore don't formally report on, but which a researcher with a broader background in the subject matter could immediately recognise as something of value. One result of this separation was that researchers and their operational counterparts, both often feeling the need for scrutinising information together and jointly reaching some analytical insights, took to arranging clandestine meetings outside of the office, replete with counter-surveillance and other security measures. Agent handlers in general appreciated the guidance they got from research analysts in planning and fulfilling collection requirements put to them.

After some changes in management later, mutually profitable relations developed between researchers and agent handlers, to the extent even that researchers were put in direct contact with agents by their handlers in appropriate cases. This enabled researchers to better evaluate specific reports in the context of the fuller picture they already had on record. But the decision as to whether such contact could take place was always the sole prerogative of the handler.

Research output from NIS from the mid-1970s, usually supported by the Department of Foreign Affairs (DFA), which was nominally also a member of the security community and who had in some instances been a front-runner, gradually inspired a rethink in the higher echelons of government about the South African security situation. This prepared the way for the realisation that the only way out was to proceed to a negotiated settlement. No one in the intelligence community had a greater influence on bringing this about than Mike Louw, with the strong leadership and support of Niel Barnard, in gaining the confidence of the highest decision-makers. NIS had, under Louw's research leadership, for instance, warned that the Tricameral Parliament, established in 1983, would be disastrous for retaining ultimate white control and leaving out any constitutional accommodation of black people.

They were right; black people were incensed and their resolve strengthened. In direct reaction to the new parliamentary structure, which was again organised along racial lines, the United Democratic Front (UDF) was established and became the most effective mobilising agent of grassroots agitation against the government. It also brought about the consolidation in one movement of just about all the disparate anti-government civil society organisations in the country, thus constituting a formidable internal arm of the then still-banned ANC. This greatly facilitated one of the four pillars of the total strategy of their struggle, namely mass protest action inside the country.

NIS also warned that the states of emergency instituted in certain hotspot magistrates' districts in June 1985 when civil disobedience was getting out of hand, and which were extended to cover the whole country in 1986, would not solve any problems, although in the latter instance even more draconian security action did in fact manage to suppress the unrest to a temporarily manageable level. I suspect this might also have had to do with the fact that discussions had by then already started with Nelson Mandela in prison. But repressive measures became harsher, including the detention without trial at one stage of some 16 000 agitators, and sustained allegations of illegal and inhuman methods employed by the police increased further. Later, through the TRC and criminal prosecution, some of these were proven to be true.

Mike Louw was a sensitive, moral man without the ruthless streak that is often assumed to be a prerequisite for senior managers, especially the heads of intelligence organisations, to survive in these highly stressful jobs. He was a rational intellectual devoid of any bombast, but whose acute mind and moral courage enabled him to exert the compelling influence he gained with the former government, as well as with its successor that came to power in 1994. He had the unshakeable courage of his convictions and uncompromisingly told truth to power as he saw it. But he was consistently and fiercely opposed and vilified by his colleagues in the police and the military, the former because they never got their heads around what strategic intelligence was all about, and the latter because his truth didn't suit theirs.

Louw successively became DG of NIS after Niel Barnard, and later of the South African Secret Service (SASS). I can't help but think that with this mild-mannered and soft-spoken man's personality profile, the enormous stress of these jobs later on sometimes affected his judgement in interpersonal relationships, and made him irascible with people who disappointed him. It must also have contributed to hastening his sudden death of a massive heart attack at the end of 2009, after his retirement from government service. For me it was an intensely sad personal loss.

Towards the end of 1985, Louw was promoted to deputy DG and I took his place as Chief Director Research. Having served for about a year in this job, I was appointed Chief Director Operations. This came as quite a surprise as I had for some time been asking the DG for a lesser job in Operations, but had been consistently refused, usually being fobbed off with a standard 'perhaps later'. He seemed a bit exasperated when I now again said that I would still prefer the lesser job I had been agitating for. I was reluctant to leave the stimulating intellectual environment of Research and would miss the close friendships I had made there. But I was gratified and excited at the challenges of the prickly and slippery new tree.

23

Politics Almost Intervenes

At about this time my disillusion with traditional politics, the paucity of new ideas and the lack of moral and political courage among the powers that be, became something of a crisis of conscience for me. I had spent most of my productive life working myself to a standstill in defence of systems and policies that over the years I had become convinced were no longer tenable, practically but especially morally. Could I go on? Because of the thought processes prevailing in NIS, which I knew were permeating the upper echelons of government, I thought yes, I could, and indeed had to keep going. But I also felt an urge to become more active in pursuit of my convictions. I became involved with the Democratic Party (DP), formally becoming a member on 26 July 1989. Membership was allowed by civil service rules, but I was soon elected chairman of a branch of the party in the east of Pretoria, which was not allowed. Shortly after that, I got nominated to the federal council of the party, which was even worse. But I had become determined to 'do something' and carried on flouting what I knew to be the rules.

An even greater risk for a civil servant was to follow. The DP had been formed in early 1989 out of the former Progressive Federal Party and some other liberal elements. The new party was led by the so-called triumvirate of Dr Zach de Beer, Dr Denis Worrall and Mr Wynand Malan. I got a message from someone, I think it was Martin Brink, an attorney and then leading light in the DP in Pretoria, that De Beer wanted to see me about a party position that needed filling. My wife and I visited De Beer on an appointment at his home in Parktown, Johannesburg one Sunday afternoon, where Malan was also present, but not Worrall. They said they were looking for someone to appoint to the position of chief executive of the DP, and that I had been recommended for the job by colleagues in Pretoria. Would I be interested?

I said certainly, very much indeed, in principle, but that I would have to think very carefully about it. They proceeded to interview me and at the end offered me the job. I undertook to give my answer as soon as possible and spent the better part of that evening soul-searching and agonising. It was a huge opportunity, considering the frame of mind I was in. But in the end my answer was not too difficult to reach. It would be a full-time job and they could not make me a really acceptable financial offer in relation to what I was then earning at NIS. In consideration of my impending pensioning from the civil service within a few years, and the fact that I still had children at school, I phoned De Beer the following morning and on these practical grounds, with real regret, declined the very tempting offer.

A day or two later, at the conclusion of a top management meeting at NIS, the DG announced that he had something serious to discuss with us ex-agenda. One of our senior members was conniving with the DP, he said. I rather sheepishly, I suppose, put up my hand to acknowledge my 'guilt'. He adjourned the meeting, asking me to remain behind. I told him I had received but declined an offer of an appointment with the DP. He merely said he was glad I had done so, and had no recriminations or questions concerning my loyalty or security status, as he might well have had. It was a gratifying demonstration of trust, and my appreciation for Barnard rose a further few notches. It was fairly clear how he had found out about the connivance but not my identity. Unless he knew it was me, and had put me to the test. I also assumed that our counterintelligence people would in future probably be having a closer look at me.

It was the end of what could almost have been a political career. A further chapter in politics in a different context was to follow some years later.

24

Niel Barnard and the Afrikaner Broederbond

Niel Barnard

Lukas Daniel (Niel) Barnard was raised in the conservative environment of Otjiwarongo, in Namibia. He was schooled there, at Windhoek High School and at the University of the Orange Free State in Bloemfontein, along which axis of experience his world view was shaped. In Bloemfontein he was no doubt steeped in Afrikaner philosophy and culture as expounded by especially the Dutch Calvinist philosophers Herman Dooyeweerd, a legal scholar and political philosopher, and Abraham Kuyper, a politician and journalist and one-time prime minister of the Netherlands. Their influence stretched deep into the academic, theological and philosophical spheres of Afrikaner intellectual and political tradition. Together these two great scholars, in particular Dooyeweerd, can be said to have established the rationalised philosophical framework for the strongly Christian-national, conservative Protestantism of the Afrikaner community. At the time, I am told, the more pragmatic and less ideological behaviourist and systems analysis approaches to political studies had not yet found purchase in Bloemfontein.

With a scintillating academic record, Barnard was a very young professor of political science at the University of the Orange Free State when he was appointed DG of NIS in 1980 at the age of thirty-one. He was first afforded a study visit to the USA, I think in New York, which he would no doubt have utilised to the full, enriching his view of life and the world in general. At NIS he amply demonstrated his immense capacity for learning and gaining understanding of the worldly realities of the intelligence industry. His appointment initially met with derision from the hard men in CSI and NIS, but they soon learnt that Barnard was not to be trifled with. He quickly gained the respect of those very same hard men. He was always perfectly courteous and respectful towards them in the true conservative Afrikaner, even biblical, tradition of respecting your elders – they were generally much older than he – while still getting his way. He was loyally supported by two other powerful men at NIS in particular, the excellent former teacher and academic, Cor Bekker, who was Chief Director Research when I got there, and Gert Rothmann, a former security policeman and then the able and experienced Chief Director Operations. I developed the greatest admiration and respect for both these impressive men.

Another of Barnard's sterling qualities was his refusal to pass the buck, of which I delivered him a few from Operations. He took punches himself, which required considerable courage as he reported to the irascible P.W. Botha. But he was not averse to delivering a few punches himself, and his moral courage was recognised by even senior cabinet ministers who would ask him to raise sensitive matters with 'the boss', which they did not have the stomach for. It was said at the time that an increasingly irrational Botha conducted a reign of terror in the cabinet, with even the venerable Minister Gerrit Viljoen saying what a relief it was that the atmosphere of fear in the cabinet had departed with Botha when he left in 1989 to be succeeded by F.W. de Klerk. Courage also underlay Barnard's capacity to take immediate decisions as soon as he had familiarised himself with the content of a particular matter.

It was a fulfilling pleasure working under Niel Barnard. He was concise in his views and instructions, and I always felt assured that he would back me should things go awry when I sensibly and accountably did my job. But I never developed a personal relationship with him. He was the sort of man who gave the impression that he did not relish people getting too close to him, which I did not resent in the least. My overall impression of him was one of a basically shy, introverted man, but with an outstanding mind and powerful personality, upon whom responsibilities were thrust that few men of his age and background would have survived. He once told me that he had not received a single briefing or any orientation whatsoever regarding NIS before stepping into that cauldron.

Barnard's interpersonal skills were sometimes awkward and, for such a courteous and perceptive man, strangely lacking in sensitivity. But it would serve no purpose to elaborate on this, save to say that it caused the deep, abiding resentment of some people who felt insulted and humiliated by him, and in one particularly painful incident by me as well for remaining silent when I should have spoken up. These residual resentments are a great pity, in view of the good job Barnard did overall. But another of his attractive traits was his willingness to acknowledge his mistakes, as I experienced on more than one occasion. Once, in an emotionally charged incident, he unjustifiably accused me and another senior man of disloyalty. When I objected to this, he retracted and unreservedly apologised.

Stirrings in the AB

I have always thought that there was more behind Barnard's appointment than merely his own sterling qualities. The political gestation in Afrikaner circles since the late 1960s had also manifested in the AB. Never having been part of this secret Afrikaner cabal and resenting the holier-than-thou implication of its very existence, I recognise that their cadre deployment and affirmative action were very different in quality from the similar later processes adopted by the ANC government from 1994 onwards. From its inception in 1918, the AB promoted Afrikaner identity and interests in the face of the vicious onslaught against them, indeed also 'total', initiated by Lord Alfred Milner after the Anglo-Boer War and perpetuated by his only slightly less imperialistic Afrikaner successors, Louis Botha and Jan Smuts.

In the earliest stages of Afrikaner rule from 1948, the anointed were by and large able and effective people fit for the purpose of their assignments. The early NP (read AB) cabinets were successful in promoting Afrikaner interests without destroying the country. Up to at least the 1960s, when the country experienced its highest economic growth rate ever, government was effective and efficient. Only in respect of the race and ethnicity question were they disastrously at a loss, as is now apparent with hindsight. I fully supported even this aspect of governance at the time, and developed my later views only gradually as the South Africa of the changing times unfolded and reality brought the *Woord en Daad* chickens home to roost for me.

A 'vicious and dangerous liberal onslaught'

During the late 1970s, a momentous, nicely illustrative, even amusing reflection of the ideological battles within the Afrikaner community as manifested in the AB occurred by way of three little books authored by prominent figures in the organisation.

In 1977, a group of Afrikaner and Broederbond conservatives published the first of these under the title *Afrikaner Liberalism* (112 pages). It was compiled by Professor P.S. (Piet) Dreyer, a professor of theology in the Nederduitsch Hervormde Kerk, politically the most conservative of the Afrikaans denominations in the theology faculty at Tukkies. Dreyer was a leading conservative, theologically and politically, and the book was a compendium of contributions by some conservative church, academic, political and other influential thought leaders. These included Dr Andries Treurnicht, once moderator of the Nederduitse Gereformeerde (NG) Kerk and at the time of publication of Dreyer's book the immediate past chairman of the AB, former editor of *Die Vaderland* newspaper in the Transvaal and later main founder and leader of the Conservative Party (CP); Dr G.D. Scholtz, a conservative journalist whom I thought to be honest and incisive and the editor of *Die Transvaler* newspaper, the mouthpiece of the Northern NP (I credit him with making me a lifelong avid reader of Afrikaans and, ironically because of his criticism of the English press, English newspapers); and Dr J.D. (Koot) Vorster, brother of Prime Minister John Vorster, an ultra-conservative theologian and one-time moderator of the NG Kerk. There were seven chapters by seven members of the AB in the fields of religion, politics, the media, economy, education and sport, all decrying the insidious infiltration of liberalism into all facets of Afrikaner life. The book postulated the thesis that liberalism had 'always been the fundamental threat to the Afrikaner people' and still was, especially as 'the most vicious and dangerous liberal onslaught' was then emanating from within Afrikaner ranks.

The book was published during Gerrit Viljoen's term as an enlightened and reformist chairman of the AB. He succeeded Treurnicht to that position in 1974. Viljoen was a pre-eminent classical scholar and lawyer, an activist for Afrikaner interests and the Afrikaans language, and founding rector of the Rand Afrikaans University in Johannesburg. In 1978, Viljoen himself, while still serving as chairman of the AB, published the second book in the trilogy, *Ideaal en Werklikheid* (*Ideal and Reality*, 103 pages), in which he described the failure of apartheid to address the problem of relations between peoples and decried the unwarranted indignities and deprivation it was causing black citizens. He postulated that the ideal of apartheid did not match the realities on which it was being superimposed, and that a rethink had become necessary.

The third book, *Afskeid van Apartheid* (*Farewell to Apartheid*, 104 pages), by Willie Esterhuyse, a professor of philosophy at the University of Stellenbosch and a highly regarded member of the AB at the time (he later resigned, I understand), was published in 1979 while Viljoen was still chairing the organisation. In it, Esterhuyse identifies apartheid as a function of the racist superiority complex the Afrikaner had inherited from Western culture, warns against the 'destructive explosive power of racial discrimination', calling it scripturally unjustifiable, and exhorting Christians to join the struggle for justice. It seems that the conservatives were justified in their assertion that the main liberal threat was coming from within Afrikaner circles.

This contention for supremacy between conservative and liberal forces in the inner circles of Afrikanerdom took a bizarre turn when the late Professor Carel Boshoff, ultra-conservative theologian at Tukkies, son-in-law of Dr Hendrik Verwoerd and founder of the Orania Afrikaner enclave in the Northern Cape, succeeded Gerrit Viljoen as chairman of the AB in 1980. He was replaced in 1983 by Professor Pieter de Lange, rector of the Rand Afrikaans University. De Lange's appointment was a portent of things to come, as he was said to be one of the influential reformist voices in the organisation. The election of Boshoff in 1980 seems to have been an aberration of the true balance of forces in the AB, as the conservatives, led by Treurnicht, resigned from both the AB and the NP and established the CP in 1982.

De Lange visited the USA in 1986 where he met with Thabo Mbeki in New York. According to Patti Waldmeir (*Anatomy of a Miracle: The End of Apartheid and the Birth of the New South Africa*), De Lange undertook to promote the ideas of reconciliation and a peaceful settlement between the peoples of South Africa. I know of no further information that came out of this meeting, but the substance was not really relevant as the mere fact that it took place held huge significance. It also appeared to confirm that the long-standing domination of the AB by conservative forces had come to an end, in spite of Carel Boshoff's incongruous election to chair it.

The AB and reform according to O'Malley

The speculation and assumptions regarding the role of the AB in initiating the reform process have largely been overtaken by the work of the Irish journalist and author Padraig O'Malley. He spent about ten years, between 1989 and 1999, researching in-depth South Africa's process of transition to democracy, including interviewing a large number of participants. In 2004 he established a website about this period titled *Heart of Hope*. The full corpus of this exhaustive work is cached as *The O'Malley Archives* in the care of the Nelson Mandela Centre of Memory and Dialogue in Johannesburg, and is accessible on the internet. From these archives it appears that O'Malley had access not only to senior people in the AB, but also to at least some of its documentation. Its authenticity at face value is compelling, even down to the spin some of his subjects tried to put on their telling. On the website www.nelsonmandela.org/omalley, the following sequence of events is described:

In 1986 a working document entitled 'Basic political conditions for the continuing survival of the Afrikaner' was circulated among members [of the AB]. Important statements for discussion included:

- All political groups must be included in drawing up a new constitution, which by implication includes the ANC.
- Blacks must be admitted to the highest level of government.
- The cabinet must be able to have a black majority.
- A black must be able to become President.
- Although an attempt would be made to protect minority rights, no guarantees could be built into a new constitution. The document put it as follows: 'The above participation, and therefore power-sharing, must be such that there is no domination of one group over another ... it means that there can no longer be a white-entrenched government. But neither can there be a black-entrenched or Zulu-entrenched government, for example.

In 1989 the 'Basic conditions' document was followed by a document titled 'Concept guidelines for political dialogue'. The purpose of this was to build on its predecessor and to formulate specific constitutional guidelines. It was discussed in depth at branch and regional level. Experts in the field of political studies in the organisation were invited to explain the different dispensations. In some cases ministers and even the present State President were called upon to answer critical questions relating to the document.

During 1990 a further document, ''n Moontlike staatkundige model vir Suid-Afrika' (A possible constitutional model for South Africa), was released.... It contained proposals for a possible constitutional model for South Africa and was presented to the Ministerial Committee on Negotiations of the Cabinet.

Niel Barnard, with his particular qualities of heart and mind, seems to have been chosen to front this project in the security establishment from the influential position of head of NIS. Mike Louw filled the role of point man in the work-level discourse with the other intelligence agencies. There was talk that Barnard had been appointed secretary of the AB, but I am unable to confirm this. NIS would, of course, have been a perfect place to safely store Broederbond records, from which embarrassing leaks had over time been plaguing the organisation.

The late Chris Hani, former leader of the SACP once said to O'Malley: 'Never apologise for taking my time, you are a historian. I am only sorry that it is left to an Irishman to record – it is something we are at fault for not doing ourselves.'

I am fully at one with Hani's sentiment. It irks me no end and further stokes my resentment that the so-called elite Afrikaner leadership should have chosen to divulge the foregoing historical information to an Irish (or any other) journalist, but had not bothered to inform us Afrikaner 'plebs' what they were 'leading' us to at the time. I am now even less part of that 'us' than I have ever been.

It would be a great boon to Afrikaner, South African and universal historiography if the AB in its new, ostensibly reformed guise as the Afrikanerbond, with its professed stance of greater openness and candid engagement with national affairs, were to fully address what O'Malley conveys in his *Heart of Hope*. Why not come out now with a full explanation and motivation, either confirming or refuting, or even expanding these archives? Who better than Niel Barnard, Pieter de Lange and F.W. de Klerk to record the backroom political tendencies and sequence of events that have so profoundly influenced the history of our country?

If we should leave our contemporary history uninterrogated and therefore uncertain and susceptible to misinterpretation, historical distortion will be the inevitable result. And time is of the essence, as such distortion, if not countered now, will become false history written by propagandists, especially the masterful communist ones, and will confound the understanding of generations to come of the rediscovery of their future during the latter decades of the twentieth century. And the justified pride in the courage of their forebears to grant them this precious gift, surely the apotheosis of what one generation can bequeath to those that follow will be lost to posterity.

A final remark about Barnard as DG and as a member in good standing of the AB: this affiliation clearly never influenced his appointments of senior personnel. Gert Rothmann, kept on by Barnard as Chief Director Operations after the demise of BOSS, and later promoted by him to deputy DG, was outspokenly derisive of the AB. Mike Louw, to the best of my knowledge never a member of the AB, successively became DG of both NIS and the SASS, mainly on Barnard's recommendation. He also promoted me to successively more senior positions and once consulted me in confidence on an appointment he had to make to a senior position. Of the two candidates, both of whom I knew well, the one was a Broederbond member and the other not. I had no hesitation to, on merit, recommend the one I knew to be a member. This again illustrated Barnard's determination to be even-handed, knowing full well that I was not a member of the AB.

An amusing incident occurred when a man called asking to speak to Dr Barnard. He was not available and his secretary, not knowing what it was about, put the caller through to me, as sometimes happened. I asked his name and introduced myself, and he then asked me what my position was. When I merely said I was in a senior position and offered to help him, he immediately started prattling on about meetings and other things I hadn't the foggiest idea about. I realised that he was assuming that being in a senior position at NIS I had to be 'one of us'. I interrupted him, told him I didn't know what he was talking about but would tell Dr Barnard that he had called. When I did so, Barnard, angry and embarrassed, said something like *'die onnosel donner'* (the stupid bugger), the only time I recall ever hearing an even mildly strong word from him.

I had become aware, thanks to Messrs Wilkins and Strydom, that almost the whole of the high command in CSI and the SADF were *Broeders*. My not being one, as well as the drawback I had of not having been a fighting soldier or of the inner circles in the military, were part of my reason for leaving the latter. Career prospects were of lesser concern to me, but, apart from the children I had to feed and educate, I did not want to remain stuck in a rut for the rest of my career until the top brass no longer knew what to do with me. On the available information, I decided to take my chances with NIS.

25

Operations

When I arrived in Operations on 1 November 1996, I found a huge backlog of files in a large safe awaiting decision by the chief director. Some had already been delayed for months, apparently for no other reason than a fear of making mistakes. This is one of the most frustrating and demoralising management failures for people at the coalface, especially those in a fast-moving operational intelligence environment, and carries many risks. I don't for a moment propose over-hasty decision-making, but unwarranted delay when all salient facts are available, is debilitating to the people who are doing the work, and stifles initiative. A decision responsibly taken but proven wrong or ineffective can in most cases and within bounds be changed and a new start made, with damage control or cutting of losses occurring as needs be.

I embarked on a gruelling night-and-day project to work through the backlog together with the relevant directors and sub-managers. Not only was this a great educational opportunity to get up to speed with my new chief directorate, but it also provided an early opportunity for me and my new colleagues to get to know one another better. Again, there was some scepticism about my appointment from Research to the top operational job, with most of the personnel in Operations being from the BOSS era of entrants, mainly from the security police, and uncertain about the changes of structure and purpose that were occurring in the organisation.

I knew most of my new colleagues superficially from before and we got on fine. I explained to them that I was not an experienced operator but knew enough from my previous operational jobs in DMI and elsewhere to understand what they were all about and what their needs and frustrations could be. As their manager, I was there to make it possible for them to do their jobs to the best of their abilities, and to take the rap for things they might do that backfired, as things surely sometimes would, provided they acted responsibly in terms of the rules under which we functioned. I encouraged them to take properly calculated risks, without which our industry could not function to its full potential. I experienced only support and loyalty throughout my tenure, which I think back on with warm appreciation and affection.

In cases where I had promised that the buck would stop with me, it did, and

I think these feelings of appreciation became mutual. I salute the experienced old hands from the SAP and elsewhere, and also those of a later generation, who so generously accepted and supported me. I would dearly like to name them all, but unaware of what their positions at the time of writing are and whether they may be embarrassed by being named, I reluctantly refrain from doing so. For the same reason, I won't name two very capable senior people from Research who later joined me in Operations.

I came into Operations at a most interesting time, but I never regarded this from the perspective of the famous Chinese curse. I thrived on the activist environment and once again working with, for the most part, excellent and dedicated people. I thought it would be an interesting and fulfilling conclusion to my career in the high-risk business of intelligence if I could stay out of too-serious trouble.

A word on nomenclature

Terminology used in the intelligence world is sometimes confusing to out-siders and even to some insiders, like me, for instance. This is compounded by different terms being used in different countries and even by different agencies in the same country. Even the word 'nomenclature', sometimes used in the intelligence world, can be misunderstood. In South Africa and the English-speaking world in general, it conforms to the dictionary definition – a set of technical terms, or terminology, pertaining to a specific collective such as a trade, a profession, a science, an industry, a department of the civil service, etc. In the former Soviet Union, and probably in Russia today and elsewhere in Eastern Europe, *nomenklatura* referred to the cluster of top civil servants with particular influence in the state and on political life in general.

In some countries, such as the USA, an 'agent' is in the full-time employ-ment of the organisation in question. We are all aware of the ubiquitous, almost cult figure of the 'FBI agent', for instance, who is something between a super cop and an intelligence operative. The British call this figure a 'con-troller' (of agents); in South Africa it is called an 'agent handler'. They are full-time employees of the organisation for which they work. The term 'operator' is sometimes loosely used to denote anyone involved in agent handling and the collection of information.

In South Africa and most of the English-speaking world, an agent (or spy) is someone who has access to a target and reports on it to his handler. These are often referred to as 'sources' and can generally be classified into three categories: an *infiltration agent* who is recruited from outside a target area and infiltrated into such an area, be it an organisation or individual, to obtain information on requirements set by his/her handler, usually formulated by Research; a *penetration agent* who is already in an organisation and recruited to report on his/her environment, i.e. a penetration of that environment; and an *agent of influence*, who does not spy so much as act as a communications operations ('comops') specialist who can be a penetration or infiltration agent, and who plants selected information and ideas in the host environment to influence ideas and actions in desired directions, sometimes also referred to as an 'agent provocateur'. A 'sleeper' is an agent in place on or in a target but not active, awaiting developments that may require s/he be activated for whatever purpose, and can be any of the foregoing.

This attempt to clarify the subject matter of what follows is oversimplified and still somewhat confusing. But no matter, a profound knowledge of technical jargon is not required to follow the stories I have to tell.

26

Trial, Tribulation and Some Hilarity

As the backlog of files waiting for decisions seemed to indicate discrepancies regarding registered agents, we embarked on a comprehensive audit of all domestic and foreign offices and their assets, human and otherwise. It was a time-consuming project during which we also came across the perennial affliction of intelligence organisations: over-classification of documents. There are a number of good reasons for security classification, but only two main ones: to protect the identity of and access to sources (agents and others), and to prevent adversaries from finding out what we know and think about them, and how we came by our knowledge. For people everywhere there is a curious pride and jealous thrill in knowing things others don't, or supposedly don't. So when we classify, we prefer top secret to secret, and secret to confidential, sometimes even top secret to unclassified, just to be on the safe side. As an illustration, we found official UN publications put out for public consumption in pigeonholes in public spaces at its New York HQ that had been sent in by diplomatic bag and classified secret! It quickly became apparent that much work lay ahead in various respects.

Lost agents in Greece

It is established protocol worldwide between governments and intelligence agencies that declared residents, i.e. intelligence representatives placed in foreign countries with the latter's knowledge and usually under diplomatic or private sector cover, do not spy on their host country or against the host country's interests. Quite often, of course, this is reaffirmed in its disregard rather than its observance, as regularly witnessed by expulsions of both real and so-called diplomats from countries, sometimes tit-for-tat. Such expellees are usually declared *persona non grata*, i.e. no longer welcome in the former host country. This often causes diplomatic embarrassment and political crises between even ostensibly friendly countries. Many more such incidents than those aired in public are handled discreetly between intelligence agencies, sometimes with the approval of governments and sometimes without, depending on whether in a particular case there are reasons, political or otherwise, for either creating or avoiding embarrassment and confrontation.

Greece had never featured in any meaningful way in the international isolation of South Africa, or in the context of insurgency movements against us. Productive relations with host services there were based on the fact that they had good access to expatriate Greek communities worldwide, some of whose members regularly featured in the ranks of revolutionary movements, including those acting against South Africa. There was also a large Greek community in South Africa in which the Greeks had an interest and on which we could reciprocate, a sound basis for such a relationship.

From our audit of the records it appeared that at one stage we had three registered agents in Greece, all of whom had been dormant for some time, had submitted very few reports and had been paid fairly well for a number of years, but whose payments had inexplicably ceased about two years before. There were no records to explain the whys and the wherefores, and there did not seem to be any protest from the agents in this regard. It also appeared that our resident in Athens had for close on three years not submitted a single report to head office, and had not seen or spoken to his liaison agencies for about two years. Apart from the standard jobs of maintaining sound professional liaison with the local intelligence services and doing background clearance checks on prospective immigrants and tourists to South Africa, residents were also expected to report where they could on South African exiles in their host countries.

We replaced him with an experienced and conscientious man who was instructed to trace the agents and confirm their usefulness (access, etc.) or otherwise, and make recommendations on whether they should be reactivated or their services dispensed with in a fair and equitable manner. Few things are as dangerous to intelligence operations as disgruntled agents. For our non-Greek-speaking new resident, the task of tracing the three disappeared agents was daunting. Eventually, after about two years, all three were traced: one had died of an alcohol-related illness some years before, the second was in prison serving a long-term sentence and the third, who had been an academic at the University of Macedonia in Thessaloniki in that province, had immigrated to South Africa.

Astonishingly, it had been one of the latter's briefs from our former resident in Athens to report on Soviet troop movements in Bulgaria and movements of the Soviet navy through the Dardanelles. The answer to the question of how an academic in that part of the country could fulfil such a brief apart from reading newspapers, which was in any event done at home with areas of real interest later thoroughly Googled, was unclear. CSI also did not think such input could have helped them too much in the counter-insurgency war being waged at the time in South West Africa and Angola. The shipping tracking facility at Silvermine near Simon's Town in the Cape in any event monitored all shipping relevant to South Africa globally, including and especially that of the Soviet navy.

A useful banking system

A prominent 'diplomatic' representative of the ANC, I shall call him 'D', approached a bank in a lesser European country for a substantial loan. He only needed the money to sustain himself for a year or two, but had no collateral security to offer. He was, however, quite certain that the ANC was going to win and become the government of South Africa, and would then generously compensate the bank for its assistance to one of their cadres in his time of need. The bank, unfortunately, could not help him. The bank official, 'A', who interviewed him, however, was serendipitously a valued cooperative of NIS. Of course he felt compelled to help the poor man. Fortune can sometimes frown and smile upon humanity at the same time.

'A' invited 'D' for a drink after hours, which was readily accepted. The company was convivial and through that night and many nights to follow, it became apparent that 'D' was in dire straits. The important and demanding job of representing his organisation with the European capitalists, who expected him to maintain certain standards, was being jeopardised by his being paid a pittance and that only intermittently. He was quite sure that the responsible treasurer was stealing money owed to him, but he could not complain as the treasurer had a direct line to Lusaka and he did not. He was a senior man in the field and was being treated with disdain by his bosses, whom he hardly ever saw or heard from. So he had to suffer in silence for the cause, which he was in all honesty not even sure was ultimately going to prevail. Judging by the way he was being treated, he sometimes doubted it very much.

It was soon clear that 'D', living alone as a bachelor, was hopelessly addicted to sex, which cost him large amounts of money in brothels and pornography, as well as to alcohol, which cost him at least as much. With these albatrosses to bear, and strongly resentful of the treatment meted out to him by his superiors and thoroughly demoralised, he was a gift on a platter to any half-decent intelligence operative; a classic case study on how not to handle your agents in whatever industry or guise. Deprivation, whether real or perceived, and isolation in a foreign country, especially for a fairly un-sophisticated African in Europe, is a works-every-time recipe for disaster or success, depending on one's point of view.

Of course 'A' thought the way 'D' was being treated was deplorable, and of course he would do his level best to help him. He plied 'D' with the where-withal to indulge his needs, which was much appreciated. The sponsors (and especially their head office!) were amazed at the costs such activities could run up in a very short period of time. Rationing was introduced, which increased the panic-induced urgency of 'D's desire to please. 'A' could not really help (neither could he compromise his career), but he knew someone who would know what to do. A conference of operatives was held in Europe to devise a plan. At the request of the people on the ground, I was there to give my approval – and, of course, to take the rap if so required. Knowing the capabilities of the excellent people involved, I hardly looked at the planning before giving my approval.

Just around various corners in Europe, in a manner of speaking, we had available some of the brightest and most experienced operators on earth. 'A' handed the ANC man to someone who could help him with his financial woes. This man, 'B', was one of ours who had been cultivating the bank official, 'A', but who was also a declared resident and could not take the risk in such a politically fraught endeavour in his host country, which was more or less pro-ANC at the time. So he summoned two or three colleagues from other European countries to the planning session. It was decided that one of these would be an affluent French banker, 'C', with business interests in Africa. The man was perfectly suited to the role.

[For ease of unravelling the somewhat complex plot:

A – the friendly bank clerk;

B – our resident in D's country;

C – our affluent French banker from another country; and

D – the ANC diplomat.]

'C' was introduced to 'D' and offered him assistance as promised. All he asked for in return was for 'D' to keep him informed of developments in Africa, especially in South Africa, where 'C' had extensive investments and one never knew what the evil apartheid regime would get up to next regard-ing foreign business interests on its soil, especially those of ANC supporters like 'C'. 'D' would keep his first benefactor, 'A', informed of his relationship with 'C' by way of regular written reports. 'C' personally lent 'D' some money to tide him over in the interim when the bank couldn't help, for which amounts 'D' signed receipts and which he would repay to 'C' as and when possible. Arrangements were made for the secure delivery of 'D's reports and remuneration, and 'C's requirements. It was in the best interests of 'D' and 'C' that others did not know of their relationship of trust. 'C' did not like his good deeds advertised. The trap was firmly sprung, but the seasoned operators were not too thrilled. It was too much like taking candy from a kid.

The operation was a complete success and a classic example of how human weakness is sometimes the essential, some would say shameful, stuff of intelligence work. It is also conventional to keep operations as simple as possible, which was on the face of it not so in this case. But our people involved were nothing if not innovative and unconventional, and somewhat playful at that. 'D' eventually became a senior ANC representative overseas, in international organisations and high councils of the party. An added bonus was the entertainment value of the impressions and assessments 'D' conveyed of 'C', his French benefactor, which were regularly considered and analysed together by 'A', 'B' and 'C'. The latter bore the brunt of the hilarity when his colleagues fully agreed with 'D's opinion that 'C' was shifty-eyed, too fat, a typical capitalist pig who couldn't be trusted, and who was only interested in his own riches and not really in human suffering, 'D's included.

'C' was probably the most outstanding operator and agent handler we had, and a wonderful human being. The others involved in this episode were not far behind. I did not personally follow the further course of this operation, but was given to understand that 'D' delivered valuable information over a number of years. He died some time later from the effects of some or other of his various overindulgences. We were sad to lose him.

27

Outward Movement

From the late 1960s Prime Minister John Vorster's NP government embarked on a so-called 'outward moving' foreign-policy initiative in an effort to counter international economic and diplomatic sanctions that had been instituted from the early 1960s by the UN and a large number of individual countries, especially in Africa. The objective of this policy was to overcome the tightening isolation of the country by establishing new commercial and diplomatic relations. The effort was concentrated on Africa, where chances of courting favour by offering generous assistance and terms of trade had the best potential. Improved relations with black Africa could blunt the animosity and solidarity of the African group of nations in the Organisation of African Unity, the Non-Aligned Movement (as President Julius Nyerere of Tanzania said at the time, 'less non-aligned against the West') and the UN. There was an immediate energising of efforts by NIS, CSI and the DFA to occupy turf as securely and quickly as possible in the interests of the country, but also to enhance relative pecking orders at the highest levels of government.

In this contention between the various agencies, the SADF, through the then DMI, was a clear leader. In as early as the mid-1960s they had succeeded in gaining access to French-speaking West African countries. As a declared resident in Paris, then Captain Neels van Tonder had established a remarkable rapport with his French counterparts in the era of President Charles de Gaulle and his influential Africa advisor, Jacques Foccart. Years of fruitful cooperation with positive political results followed. The SADF also had the advantage of having the executive capacity to provide highly desirable commodities like armaments, expertise and other material to destinations with potentially productive political gain. It had the further advantage of reporting to minister of defence P.W. Botha, then already a strongman in the cabinet.

The DFA had the drawback in these endeavours of being captive to its own protocols and ethics in aiming to establish open diplomatic relations with target countries, as was its primary job. Of course this would be first prize, but few governments in Africa were then prepared to accept the political consequences of such relations with the apartheid state. I was more than once exasperated by the lack of understanding of the demands of covert political action of this nature by top officials of the DFA. I once provided the then DG of the DFA, Brand Fourie, that otherwise outstanding servant of the country, with clear documentary evidence of covert spying in South Africa on South African interests by a declared resident of the West German intelligence service, the Bundesnachrichtendienst, which was a strict no-no in intelligence protocol terms. These efforts were focussed in particular on the DFA. I offered him assistance in countering this threat and he undertook to look into the matter. When I enquired a week or two later, he told me that he had submitted the 'allegation' for comment to his German counterpart, who categorically denied it. Leaning over to the open safe next to his chair, he took out the cable with the German reply to convince me. And that was that.

Fourie was an old-school diplomat who seems never to have got on board regarding covert action. When a new breed of outstanding younger people like Neil van Heerden, Rusty Evans, Dave Steward, Derek Auret, Herbert Beukes, Sean Cleary and Tom Wheeler reached the upper echelons of the DFA, we enjoyed only excellent cooperation, and we always tried to tread carefully in respecting their diplomatic constraints. Declared NIS residents stationed in diplomatic missions across the world generally received excellent cooperation and support from most of the DFA ambassadors and other personnel. However, there were exceptions, one being our ambassador to one country who forbade our man to use embassy cups and cutlery in the tearoom. If I could remember his name and station, I would mention them.

At NIS it was standard procedure that where we had consolidated a contact with a government in Africa or elsewhere, we would, in consultation with the contact, involve the DFA if that should be the potentially fruitful way to go in a particular instance. But we very often found resistance to the DFA being involved. A common attitude was that the DFA was not to be trusted with keeping matters confidential. One African president, the late Gnassingbé Eyadéma of Togo, in declining our suggestion that the DFA should become involved, said to me that the moment the DFA became aware of a particular contact, 'Pik Botha would the next day make a statement to the press'. Of course this was exaggerated and unfair, but the DFA's negative image in this respect was not entirely undeserved.

Furthermore, in at least one case an African leader kept us in the dark about contact he had with other South African agencies, obviously for manipulative purposes. Scandalously, some of our colleagues encouraged such duplicity by themselves not keeping us informed, leaving an extremely negative impression of South Africa and its operatives. It was later intimated to me that this could have been the case with Eyadéma. Such cross purposes were certainly not conducive to furthering our efforts in Africa.

There was considerable animosity in CSI towards the DFA since the early African contacts made by Neels van Tonder in the time of CSI's forerunner, DMI. This had elicited the ire of the minister of foreign affairs at the time, Hilgard Muller, who regarded it as an intrusion on the DFA's domain. Fortunately, DMI prevailed in that confrontation, and much mileage was gained in Africa. But the SADF was always disinclined to keep the DFA or NIS informed of their operations, leading on at least two occasions to the deaths of valued NIS sources in neighbouring countries. It was also adept at using its access and information for manipulative purposes. A good example was CSI's compromising of the DFA and thereby the South African government by taking Louis Nel, the deputy minister of foreign affairs, on a visit to the RENAMO HQ in Mozambique, thereby breaching the Nkomati Accord that had been signed in 1984, but which the SADF officers involved hadn't wanted in the first place.

In 1986 foreign minister Pik Botha was engaged in negotiations with the Eminent Persons Group of the Commonwealth, which was then visiting southern Africa in an effort to engage the parties contributing to the instability in the region in seeking a way forward out of the confrontational situation. While these discussions were going on in Pretoria, the SADF launched cross-border raids on targets in Lusaka, Gaborone and Harare, all three Commonwealth capital cities, 'to forestall terrorist attacks against South Africa' from base areas of the ANC and PAC. Naturally this phase in the negotiations came to an abrupt end.

Before the TRC in 1997, Minister Botha denied having authorised Nel's trip to RENAMO in Mozambique, a statement that the facts seemed to contradict. On the same occasion Botha described the relationship between the DFA and the SADF as follows: 'In these matters ... a clear divergence of views existed between the Security Forces and Foreign Affairs.' It is astonishing how the political authorities could for so long have allowed such distrust and strife between two departments fighting on the frontlines for ostensibly the same cause, to so clearly jeopardise the interests of South Africa in crucial times. But to my mind the abovementioned raids were also a timely lesson to those neighbouring states as well as to SWAPO and the ANC that the impending negotiations would not provide the latter with a free pass to carry on their violent incursions into South West Africa and South Africa. It was the timing and the lack of coordination that were the concerns.

Also in this context, in about 1983, I was assigned to an interdepartmental team attempting to reach agreement with the Mozambique government on a non-aggression pact to end the tension between that country and South Africa, and which culminated in the Nkomati Accord of 1984. The president of Mozambique, Samora Machel, had indicated his willingness to facilitate such an accommodation by restricting the freedom of movement and action of the ANC in and from his country. Many visits took place to the Mozambique capital of Maputo, mainly to confer with Sérgio Vieira, Machel's chief interlocutor at the time, and progress was being made. The DFA was represented at work level in these discussions by the amusing Boet Malan, and from NIS I was accompanied by Piet Coetzee, our divisional head of research for the area. Both parties had an interest in ending the tension – South Africa to curtail ANC incursions from Mozambique, and Mozambique to limit the risk of SADF retaliatory raids on their soil, which were causing them considerable damage and embarrassment.

In these exchanges I got to know the delightful head of the Mozambican intelligence service, Fernando Honwana. He once told me that he had lost the keys to his safe and had no one who knew how to open it. He didn't want to ask the Russians. I generously offered our people, who would gladly have opened it for him in a jiffy, but he laughingly declined. A graduate of the University of York in England and speaking perfect English, I teased him for being the epitome of the Black Englishman, to which he responded by calling me a Russian Boer. Puzzled, I asked him how on earth he came to that analogy. He said the Russians and the Boers had much in common: both were secretive and never let on what they were really thinking, both spoke little, took a long time to make decisions and liked crayfish. And neither liked black people. He offered the one redeeming feature of both: once they gave an undertaking they stuck to it. This sentiment must have dissipated for him regarding the Boers because of the cross purposes between the SADF and the rest of the South African establishment that played out in subsequent events concerning RENAMO. Sadly, Honwana died in the aeroplane crash in South Africa in 1986 that also killed President Samora Machel.

After one meeting with the RENAMO leadership under the chairmanship of Deputy Minister Louis Nel at the state guesthouse in Waterkloof

Ridge in Pretoria, I was relaxing with two of the top generals in CSI. The chief spokesperson of RENAMO, Evo Fernandes, had submitted a very good memorandum for discussion, which left the South Africans little room for manoeuvre. As a consequence, little or no progress was made. I remarked on the excellence of this document to the generals and they more or less simultaneously said something like, 'But of course, who do you think drafted it?'

Some time later I was at another meeting, this time in Nel's office at the Union Buildings and again with some top CSI generals. Out of the blue Boet Malan launched into a veritable diatribe against the SADF for the role they were playing in 'deliberately sabotaging' the efforts being made to reach an accommodation with Mozambique. Nel found a way of proceeding with the meeting without the CSI officers reacting in any way, and I thought it amiss of him not to ask the latter for their comment on such a serious allegation. It was a surreal and embarrassing situation for everyone, but my respect for Boet Malan rose a few notches for telling it like it was. I wondered whether Nel had perhaps put him up to it.

Kaunda

It was under these circumstances that my telephone at NIS rang one morning early in 1987. It was a Dr M calling from State House in Lusaka, asking to speak to Brigadier Daan Hamman. I knew Hamman well from CSI, a competent and thoroughly professional officer with little taste for the political intrigues in the intelligence community, and a salt-of-the-earth human being. It was an unfortunate irony that he should later in his career fall foul of exactly such intrigue. Hamman had been the director of foreign relations at CSI, but I happened to know that he had shortly before been transferred to another post in Army HQ.

I told Dr M that Hamman was no longer available but that I was in a position to assist him and would be pleased to do so. Without hesitation or any further questions, he said he was the political advisor to Zambian president Kenneth Kaunda and that he was calling on instruction of the latter. President Kaunda wanted to see me as soon as possible as he had a message for President Botha. Of course I said 'Of course'. He said they would be in touch again for an appointment. He took my private number and contacted me a few days later to arrange a meeting with Kaunda in Lusaka. I am still puzzled as to how Dr M got through to me at NIS while looking for Hamman at CSI.

When I reported this initial contact to the DG, he was amused but also gratified at my opportunistic initiative, especially as I hadn't lied to the man. A few days later I was at State House in Lusaka accompanied by my trusted and highly valued friend and colleague, the invariably high-spirited Dr Daan Opperman, our director of foreign liaison, a go-getting organiser of men and affairs who accompanied me on many such flights into Africa and elsewhere. We chartered a Learjet because the SAAF, whom we sometimes used on such trips, could not be trusted not to alert CSI to this development, no doubt having previously shuttled Hamman to and fro. Soon after our evening take-off from Lanseria Airport, a hostess approached us with snacks and to take our drinks orders. We had neither expected nor ordered this, but she assured us it was part of the package. As we took off, Daan leant back comfortably in his seat and sighed, 'A-a-a-h, may we never be poor again!'

In Lusaka we spent the night at Roan House and were fetched the following morning in good time for our appointment at State House at 10 a.m. Roan House, an old but perfectly maintained guesthouse built by mining interests, was an elegant place. Staffed by a rotund, caring Mozambican housekeeper who craved South African periodicals with which we provided her from time to time, and a pleasant and skilful chef-cum-butler, it made for unsurpassable comfort and service in the best possible taste. Together with the friendly host at State House, we always looked forward to our visits there.

At State House we were received in a small ante-room by a male secretary and immediately ushered in to see the president. The simplicity of the small office was impressive, the only ornament a small bust of US president John F. Kennedy on a shelf against the wall, certainly not quarters speaking of a self-important man. The furnishings included a modest writing desk, a few simple but comfortable chairs for visitors and a small table covered with a red cloth in a corner. KK, as his own people and others respectfully referred to him, rose from behind his desk and walked over to greet us. He then proceeded to give us a comprehensive briefing on his credo of 'humanism', which, he said, required that we in southern Africa must now start talking to each other. He gave me a letter for President Botha and said he would like to maintain this contact. He asked that henceforth I be the only conduit for confidential messages between the two of them.

Other visits followed, in the course of which I developed respect and even affection for Kaunda's genuine warmth and humanity, while fully aware of his consistent efforts over many years to isolate South Africa and extend succour to the ANC and MK. But listening patiently to his regular, lengthy introductory remarks on humanism at every single meeting later became quite a chore. I never doubted the sincerity of his concern for the state Africa was in, especially the instability then prevailing in southern Africa. The ANC was still using Zambia as a safe haven and the country was suffering the consequences by way of raids on their facilities and personnel by South African forces on land and from the air. With Mozambique, Angola and Zimbabwe gaining independence in the 1970s and early 1980s, another concern was that SWAPO in South West Africa and Angola on the Zambian border, was being pursued by South African and UNITA forces into Zambia, posing an ongoing threat to the latter's stability. The large-scale presence of Cuban combat units in Angola compounded this threat.

It was clear from the start that KK was anxious to carry on his self-assumed role as an interlocutor between the ANC and SWAPO on the one hand, and the South African authorities on the other. He had over time been in contact with South African business and political interests, including holding a meeting some time before with President Botha, facilitated by CSI and Hamman, I assumed. Although he had a record of strong anti–South African sentiments, I felt that he could out of self-interest be an effective broker in the talks that I was sure were to follow between the antagonists in the region.

On one visit we took along some of our researchers and met KK at a bush lodge on the banks of a river in the east of the country, where he had us flown from Lusaka. It was a modest place and our small group with the president and his secretary were the only people there. Outside on the river bank, the president sat with his back to the river with us seated in a semi-circle in front of him, and proceeded with his now customary exposition on humanism. While he was at it, a herd of about seventy elephants of all sizes and ages came ambling along the opposite bank of the river. Having heard about the marvels of humanism before, my attention inevitably strayed to the captivating sight of these magnificent beasts just across the fairly narrow river. Counting them required concentration and I was a bit dozy, although I was still vaguely aware of the droning in the background. I was startled when a different sound disturbed the flow: 'You're not listening to me. Let's first watch the elephants and have some tea.' The gentle, fatherly reprimand was quite endearing.

We used to take along a little gift for the president on our visits, of which he was always appreciative. He was especially fond of South African boxed fruit juices, which he called 'presidential wine'. On one occasion we took along a gift from President Botha, some or other commemorative medallion in a wooden presentation box. On arrival at State House, the secretary in the ante-room very politely asked whether we would mind if the security people had a look at the package, which of course we didn't. When we had finished the session with the president and were preparing to take our leave, we told him about the present we had brought along and asked for it to be fetched from security to be presented to him. He instructed his secretary accordingly. When we had waited for quite a while making small talk, the secretary returned and said that the package seemed somehow to have been mislaid, but would surely be found shortly.

KK then asked: 'Have I played for you?' I said no, wondering what he meant. He rose and removed the cloth from the 'table' in the corner next to his desk. It was in fact a small house organ. He sat down at it with his back to us, and started playing and rather plaintively singing spiritual songs. It was entrancing. Here was the small, elderly scourge of British imperialism and apartheid, with thinning hair but still with his trademark spiky tuft, looking and sounding so vulnerable from behind. I cherish this poignant memory. The medallion was eventually found, but its temporary loss had afforded us this priceless experience.

In keeping with the standing approach of NIS not to assume roles that did not fit our basic mandate, we cleared it with KK and started taking selected diplomats from the DFA along to see him. On one occasion we asked a very senior man to accompany us. In the discussion with KK, this man proceeded to set out the South African approach to Africa and more or less demanded that 'Africa' do certain things. I was disturbed by his arrogant and condescending tone. As he carried on I cringed and knew trouble was at hand. KK took serious offence, justifiably, I thought. He angrily berated our colleague, saying, among other things: 'I will not have you trying to teach me, young man.' I intervened by saying that I was sure nothing was further from the diplomat's mind (which I wasn't) than wanting to teach him, but that we were all frustrated that eminent African leaders like him were not reacting as positively as we had hoped to the government's efforts to facilitate peacefully negotiated, internationally acceptable settlements for the various disputes in the region, which they had been demanding. He calmed down and we knew who not to bring along in future. Some diplomat.

In contrast, on a later visit, the pleasant company and steady composure of the then DG of the DFA, Neil van Heerden, was a singular pleasure. I had the privilege that evening on our flight back of listening to him expose the architect at the core of his soul in explaining the plans he was drafting for a new building for the DFA that was then in prospect in Pretoria. But, as so often happens, history sadly intervened between the man and his dreams and it was never built. However, Van Heerden played a significant role in the process that eventually consummated the independence of Namibia in 1990. He did his profession and country proud in working tirelessly to create an unarguably greater historical monument than a building of bricks and mortar. It is still a matter of puzzlement to me that Van Heerden was not used more meaningfully in the later CODESA negotiations.

Late one Sunday evening early in 1987, my telephone at home rang. On the line was President Kaunda himself, asking me to be at State House at 10 a.m. the following morning on an urgent matter. I was not to worry about getting permission from my bosses; he would 'fix it with P.W.' After getting authorisation from the DG, my trusty factotum, Daan Opperman, master networker and friendly persuader, overnight arranged a charter flight that saw us reporting to State House in good time the following morning. Unusually, when we got there KK was waiting in the ante-room. He said there was a man in his office he wanted us to meet. I asked who it was, but he merely said 'see for yourself'. I protested that I was not a free agent and couldn't in an official capacity speak to just anyone off my own bat. After his insistence and by now standard assurance that he would fix it, I agreed to hear what the man had to say and report back to my principals. He ushered us into his office, closing the door behind us, with him remaining outside.

It was Sam Nujoma, the president of SWAPO and one of the umpteen Public Enemies No. 1 of South Africa at the time, together with a sidekick. After exchanging pleasantries (in Afrikaans), I explained that I would have nothing to say to him, but would listen and report to my superiors. He was surprisingly brief and to the point: in essence, we had been making war for too long and it was time we started talking to each other about making peace. Something was obviously hurting him and SWAPO, and I had a sneaking suspicion that the SADF might feature in that something.

NIS handed the project over to the DFA to take further, which as far as I know was the beginning of the tortuous formal negotiation process that resulted in Namibia's independence three years later. I think Kaunda played a bigger role as mediator in the settlement of that vexed dispute than he is given credit for. Separate from but intertwined with the signing of the Nkomati Accord between South Africa and Mozambique in 1984 and the latter placing meaningful restrictions on the presence and freedom of movement of the ANC in that country, Kaunda was known to have put pressure on the ANC regarding its presence in his own country. What influence his mediation might have had on the eventual negotiated settlement between the South African government and the ANC has not yet been fully described, but my feeling is that as the chairman of the so-called 'Frontline States', it could have been more substantial than it appears to be on the surface. I had no further direct role in the matter.

Many years before, in the early 1960s I think, my one-time Chief Director Research at NIS and later dear friend, Pieter Swanepoel ('Oom Swanie'), had been the head of the security police in South West Africa. He told how information once came to hand that the exiled Sam Nujoma was flying back to Windhoek from Zambia by light aircraft to demonstratively 'take back his country'. In a late-night telephone call, Prime Minister Hendrik Verwoerd personally instructed Swanie to put Nujoma straight back on the aircraft the moment he landed and send him back whence he had come. When Mrs Swanepoel, Tannie Marina, heard about this, she was upset that the man would not even have anything to eat. So she prepared some sandwiches and a flask of coffee, which she gave to Swanie for Nujoma. The latter gratefully accepted the food and drink and took it on board with him, leaving Tannie Marina, a no-nonsense woman, highly upset at the loss of her flask. Almost thirty years later, when Nujoma legitimately returned to Namibia to lead the country to independence, she saw her chance and insisted that Swanie get her flask back from him. I'm not sure that he did. Such can be the high drama that plays itself out in the ruthless world of international politics.

Oompie

At Cambridge in the early 1970s I got to know two Sierra Leonean fellow students who impressed me as thorough gentlemen and good company. One went on to become his country's foreign minister and later attorney general (he was also to become an Olympic hurdler in Munich in 1972), and the other, I was told, a high court judge. They were surprisingly apolitical and not knee-jerk condemnatory of apartheid as most people there were, but enquired rationally why we thought apartheid necessary. We had many discussions and they had sympathy with the white peoples' and especially the Afrikaners' cultural and existential dilemmas, but could not accept that legislation on things such as influx control, job reservation and the prohibition of sex and marriage across the colour line could solve our problems. As usual, it was difficult to explain. It was much easier to be rudely attacked, as happened on occasion, because then one could merely be aggressive and fight back. I appreciated anew how unenviable the task of our embattled diplomats was in having to defend the indefensible.

Years later, when I was working in research at NIS in the early 1980s, when conditions in Sierra Leone had become of international concern and the 'outward' foreign policy of our government a priority, an operational colleague showed me a talent-spotting report on the Sierra Leoneans I had done years before for the BOSS man then in the embassy in London. I had completely forgotten about this and so, apparently, had they. When my report resurfaced they made discreet contact with the foreign minister, using my name for the purpose. I was asked to meet the man in London to develop the contact.

It was a pleasant reunion, where I met Oompie for the first time. He was an influential regional chieftain in Sierra Leone whose president, who had come to power by military coup, had grown up in his village and therefore was his traditional son. This made Oompie the pre-eminent kingmaker and distributor of largesse in the country. It also meant that the president owed him deference and depended on his wise counsel. Oompie was to be our host on our visits to his country.

Diminutive in stature, Oompie strode the streets of Freetown like a colossus, handing out fistfuls of banknotes from his packed briefcase to selected passers-by, who greeted him with reverence and for most of whom he had a word either of approval or disapproval, speaking in the quaint and not easily understandable Pidgin English of the streets. Moving along the street in Oompie's wake gave one a marvellous feeling of royalty, and we seemed to be held in awe by the populace for being so close to the little great man. After a block or two it became natural to wave a dignified royal hand in greeting the masses, but our rate of progress was somewhat retarded.

As usual, I was accompanied and flawlessly supported in this project by Daan Opperman, who organised the whole effort, and two other colleagues: a technical man, Pierre Fourie, who was to assess the needs we had been briefed on in the London meeting with the minister, and a political analyst, André Barnard. There were few flights to Freetown's Lungi Airport at the time, even from Europe. Air Afrique, supposedly serving West Africa, was at its last gasp before its final demise and was to be avoided. The only reasonable option for getting to Freetown was by Air Jordan from London. This airline was 'dry', but our little group was nothing if not resourceful and we were surreptitiously quite comfortable on the flight, later even a bit jolly. I had a seat next to a very pleasant and dignified older Sierra Leonean man, who let on that he was a senior official in the government there. In discussions in our cluster on board, I announced with some bravado that I was now going to recruit my neighbour to our cause. Unfortunately for my dignity and repute, the ever-alert Daan took a photo of me fast asleep in my seat next to my 'target subject', of which he gleefully gave me a print when we were back at home.

Oompie put us up in 'his' (state) guest house with linoleum floors, threadbare furniture, no hot water, occasional electricity and a resident housekeeper with immense concern for our well-being. He prepared us delectable dinners on a grill over an open fire outside the back door, rather than on the spanking new Aga anthracite stove in the kitchen. It was later confirmed that the country had run out of almost all domestic fuels – paraffin, gas, coal and anthracite – because of foreign-exchange problems, in spite of it being a significant diamond producer.

We found that the diamond industry, centred in the north-eastern region of the country, was under the control of an international syndicate run by Lebanese expatriates in areas that police could not even reach. The syndicate had built their own landing strip in the mining area for export purposes, had brought in heavy machinery such as huge draglines and bulldozers, maintained their own security services, employed local people from the remote area at a more or less nil wage, and paid no taxes. The only other expense the producers had were goodwill gestures towards a few selected officials, the Diamond Commissioner among them, we were given to understand. I have since had the sneaking suspicion that Oompie may also have been a beneficiary – the mines were situated in and near his fiefdom – but I would not like to be uncharitable to our gracious host.

Our main interest was the fact that the president of Sierra Leone had undergone military training at Sandhurst in Britain where he befriended the president of Nigeria, General Ibrahim Babangida, the dominant figure and country in the region. They had remained close personal friends. To gain access to Babangida would have been first prize as Nigeria was targeted as a high priority of the outward policy. We had to assume that the Brits would have a strong finger in both those pies.

Oompie suffered from a serious but curable eye disease, treatment for which was not available in his own country. Arrangements were made for him to see a world-renowned ophthalmologist specialising in Third World eye diseases at the Kalafong Hospital near Pretoria. As a bonus, treatment would be protracted and Oompie would need to visit South Africa from time to time for that purpose.

The specialist was sympathetic to our cause, on which he was briefed as far as was deemed necessary. However, he declined our suggestion that he keep Oompie slightly ill for as long as possible to facilitate our continued access to him, confessing that he only knew how to cure people and not how to keep them ill. Oompie would, however, require regular replenishment of his medication and we would need to visit him for that purpose. He undertook to introduce us to his president when we did so.

On our first visit to Freetown, Oompie's driver was to have collected us from our guest house at 9 a.m. on the day after our arrival for a first audience with the president. The driver arrived on foot at 5 p.m. a day later, carrying a bottle of Johnnie Walker Black Label whisky as a peace offering. Someone else had taken the car. Even with tepid water we thought the Black Label was generous compensation for such a slight inconvenience. Thanks to the muezzin's daybreak call to prayer from the minaret right next door, in which Daan joined with gusto, we managed to be on time for our appointment at State House the next morning. We followed Oompie a regulation two steps behind into the room where the cabinet was in session, walking straight past the armed guards, who saluted as we passed, neither knocking on the door nor being announced. As we entered, the ministers and the president silently rose as one, paying their respects to Oompie with deep bows. The ministers then left the room as if on cue.

The president was a powerfully built, pleasant man whose attention span spoke of the many distracting matters of state on his mind. He had been advised of the purpose of our visit and would do his best to facilitate the contact we sought with the president of Nigeria. It would, however, take time and would carry certain costs, which we could discuss later. He would only be seeing his friend and brother again at the Organisation of African Unity meeting in about six months' time and no, he could not discuss such an important matter with him on their secure telephone line or visit him by chartered aeroplane paid for by us (in any event, we soon realised, there were none to be had).

In the meantime, we were most welcome in his country and he appreciated very much what we were doing to help his father the chief. We might wish to consider assisting him with the rehabilitation of the more or less defunct – because of 'various factors' – diamond industry and broadcasting system. The latter would enable him to address his people directly throughout the country to announce their fine relations with South Africa, when the time was ripe. The people would react even more favourably if we could, together with Oompie, find a way of providing certain essentials like bicycles, gas, three-legged pots and tin buckets to ease their daily existence.

We already had some preliminary suggestions for what might be a fruitful course of action, pending the assessments of our technical expert. We might be able to involve the De Beers Diamond Corporation and the South African Broadcasting Corporation. From preliminary studies it seemed to us that the riches of the diamond industry, with improved management and adequate security measures, could go a long way towards solving the country's balance of payments and other economic problems. We understood, however, that there were some rough types involved and we suggested that a small South African security, even military, presence might be necessary to manage this aspect. We gave assurances that this would be done efficiently and discreetly to ensure absolute confidentiality and avoid any embarrassment to the country or its president. Such a discreet military capability could perhaps also assist the president in other ways.

Naturally we would do our level best to assist our dear friend the chief with his requirements. To manage this involvement properly, we would need a resident from our organisation to be placed in the country for liaison purposes. The chief had generously offered to arrange accommodation and support for such a representative. The president appreciated and agreed with everything we said and 'as a military man' urged us to get on with it and not waste time.

Surveys were done, our resident was put in place, recommendations for large and small works were made and Oompie's imports were procured through South African business friends. But our rehabilitative recommendations were rejected for lack of funds. Payment for the imports was guaranteed from official NIS sources, motivated to the effect that the amount might eventually prove to be irrecoverable but that the potential benefit justified the risk under the circumstances.

A first delivery to fill the specified requirements was received by Oompie's personal agent at the dockside in Freetown and consigned to an unbonded warehouse that he controlled. Shortly afterwards, Oompie informed us that that was the last he had seen of the goods and also the last time he would use that agent, who had on previous occasions disappointed him. In our future dealings he would ensure that a reliable agent handled his business with us. I gave him a categorical assurance that that would not be necessary. I accepted Oompie's word that he would try until his dying day to recover every lost item and pay us what was our due. I assume that he is still doing so, if that day has not already arrived.

Sierra Leone finally started to implode in the late 1980s. Tales of the most horrific factional and ethnic slaughter flooded the world media, initially with almost equally horrific international disinterest. Our resident has long since been recalled. The last time our people visited the country to wrap up our withdrawal, evacuate the resident's household and deliver a last consignment of medicines for Oompie's eyes and other ailments, they were held at gunpoint at Lungi Airport until Oompie belatedly arrived to rescue them. The 'sanitised' SAAF C-130 Hercules was ordered to depart immediately.

The consignment we delivered to Oompie did nothing for the president's political salvation. He was deposed by military coup and lived in exile in neighbouring Guinea, where he died in 2003. He never managed to speak to his brother, President Babangida of Nigeria, whom we never got to see and who was in any event also deposed by force of arms shortly afterwards. The president might well have found some solace in the fact that his country, insofar as it still existed, was then in an immeasurably worse state than when under his rule of benign incompetence. My two learned friends, the justice minister and the judge, as I understand it, are both practising law somewhere in Europe. Oompie, I hope, is still ruling his rural fiefdom, in spite of the dire tribulations of his country. His region was among the areas of the fiercest fighting in the civil war, and no doubt also in the battle for control of the diamond fields there.

I will never forget how touched Oompie was when, at the end of our first and my only visit there, he was at the airport to see us off and we explained that our nickname for him was a term of respect and endearment in our

Afrikaans culture. He had obviously been suspecting the opposite from the racists. I hope his eyes are doing well and that he is getting full value from the large suitcase full of size-four shoes he bought on his last visit to South Africa. I hope his briefcase remains stuffed.

I still do not know what happened to the consignment. What use is idle speculation? I do know that Mike Louw, then DG of NIS, in 1992, I think it was, after an apparently quite hectic time before the parliamentary standing committee on public accounts, succeeded in persuading them to write off an amount of R1.9 million as authorised but irrecoverable expenditure.

28

A Word on Travel

My operational job entailed much travel, both domestic and international, a desirable fringe benefit in the eyes of many. Travel indeed broadens the mind, but in excess it can also dumb-down that self-same mind, numb the senses, harass the soul and punish the bum no end. I started off really loving flying (in airliners, not in small vomit comets), but ended up hating it with a passion. I developed an aversion to flying that lasts to this day. But in the brief halcyon days when senior people were allowed to fly first class on long overseas trips, it was a pleasure. Because of international sanctions and boycotts, we had no landing rights in Africa and in most other countries, and had to fly non-stop to Europe, the Americas and the Far East.

The Blues Labelled

The first educational travelling experience Mike Louw and I had together when both still in Research, was an overnight flight to Japan in first class with British Airways. We were babes in the wood regarding the luxuries this offered, and at cocktail time ordered Johnnie Walker Black. Neither of us had tasted it before, but had been told it was something to be relished, especially if you could get it free, as supposedly was the case in first class. It would also be, we thought, the stylish thing to do. The hostess was seriously apologetic that they didn't have the Black, but could she let us have the Blue instead? We had been looking forward to the Black so much that we were really upset and berated her and her airline in no uncertain terms. We condescended to take the Blue, but made her understand that we thought it a jolly poor show of the much-vaunted airline. We only later learnt from the cognoscenti on such things that the Blue, which we had never heard of before, was quite a few cuts above the Black, in taste and in price. We laughed at each other and our collective naivety and pretentiousness. How educational travel can be.

Lecturing at Harvard

Another privilege afforded by travelling was a rare opportunity of two days free on the east coast of the USA with two colleagues. Our business had been in Washington and New York and we were waiting for a suitable flight back home, so we decided to visit Boston. Walking around the campus of Harvard University in Cambridge, Massachusetts near Boston, we came across an open lecture room in the law school. I thought my two senior companions from operations, Basjan Rothmann and one other, could do with a bit of polishing up on their knowledge of the law and sat them down for a lecture on the South African Law of Things. I made notes on the blackboard that I instructed them to take down, but when they refused I was left embarrassed without disciplinary powers.

I have since wondered what the janitor must have thought of this strange language; sub-headings like 'Die Romeinse Reg', 'Die Romeins-Hollandse Reg' and 'Die Engelse Reg', under the main heading 'SAKEREG'. He or she would probably have left it for the next law lecturer to puzzle over, rather than risk destroying a great pearl of wisdom from some foreign expert. I know my lecturer in the subject at Tukkies, the late Judge of Appeal Pierre Olivier, would have been horrified at having done such a bad job of teaching me, but I am confident that they of the glazed eyes in front of me didn't have a clue. I am still considering whether I should put 'Lectured at Harvard Law School' on my CV.

The UN ambassador

On the same trip I wanted very much to meet the American ambassador to the UN, Jean Kirkpatrick, a woman for whom I had great admiration. I mentioned this to an official in our mission there and she agreed to try to facilitate a meeting. After waiting a while, at my insistence we simply walked into the General Assembly during a break in the session, went to Kirkpatrick at her seat and introduced ourselves to her as diplomats, of course. I was confirmed in my admiration for her by her friendly reception and kind, albeit guarded, words about South Africa. We had a brief chat, and left. Our UN ambassador, Dave Steward, was clearly livid but constrained in pointing out to me the dire diplomatic embarrassment that could have resulted if ill-disposed people on the crowded floor should have recognised this 'spy' (which I wasn't, then still being in Research) from NIS talking to the American ambassador. I took Dave's admonishment to heart and apologised to him. It was a thoughtless caper. On that visit he also invited me to a pleasant dinner at his home in Manhattan and took me to a wonderful Irish pub near the UN on 2nd Avenue, I think it was.

Compensation

Travelling presented all sorts of opportunities to view some of the world's great natural scenery and magnificent art and historical treasures, but mostly there was never time to appreciate these bonuses. In an overwhelming number of cases, I would arrive in one of the greatest cities in the world for a meeting that very evening or the following morning, and depart again straight after, either for home or another city for another appointment. Crossing time zones, getting little or no sleep, attending meetings in a daze, reading off hardly decipherable notes the next morning, hastily reporting back home in urgent cases over sometimes bad communications, nursing a sore back, bum and neck, and swallowing nasty food on countless flights – it could be sheer hell at times.

But certainly there were sometimes great compensations. Watching a concert at the Kennedy Center in Washington featuring the oldest symphony orchestra in the world, the East German Gewandhaus zu Leipzig under the baton of Kurt Mazur; seeing the original Broadway show *Cats*; jogging in Central Park, New York; walking through the Englischer Garten in Munich; and witnessing the glories of the Louvre in Paris, the Rijksmuseum in Amsterdam, the Prado in Madrid and the Metropolitan Museum of Art in New York, where Jean-Baptiste Carpeaux's sculpture depicting the myth of Ugolino and his Sons particularly captivated me. With his two sons looking up at him in adoration and complete trust, the father looks to Hades in sheer terror at the tragedy about to befall them dying from hunger. With two small sons of my own at the time, I was deeply touched by this stunning allegory. As Dante Alighieri wrote of Ugolino in the *Divine Comedy*, I also 'discerned in [his] face the aspect of my own'. There were over the years other memorable experiences, in England in particular, where we lived for two years before I started my professional travelling.

These glittering interludes were unfortunately very few and far between. I came to fully appreciate the old ditty: 'I joined the navy to see the world, but what did I see? I saw the sea.' It perfectly encapsulates my experience, except that I saw the inside of an aeroplane far more than I saw the sea or anything else.

The Dutchman

During the sanctions years we were only able to travel in Europe to Switzerland and the UK without a visa, and so we had to resort to other means to get about in the world. We had a good capacity to produce all sorts of documentation, including South African passports in other names, but which had limited use outside the aforementioned two countries. We could also manufacture passports of foreign countries, but these carried a higher risk of international confrontation and embarrassment if discovered, and we avoided them as far as possible. The first prize was always a legally issued passport of a foreign country of good international standing. These were extremely difficult to obtain unless one had some official assistance from inside the security establishment of the country in question. And if you did obtain such a passport, you needed a story to justify your being in possession of it. Such stories are referred to as 'legends'.

Through Nico Fourie, our effective resident in The Hague, we had established good relations with a well-disposed senior man in the Dutch intelligence service, who offered to get us a genuinely issued Dutch passport in a name of our choosing. Through research, we found the name of a Dutch immigrant who had died in South Africa and who had been about my age. According to my legend, I was born in Edam in the Netherlands but as a youngster had moved through Australia and Rhodesia to South Africa, where I eventually settled. Confused about what sort of accent I should have after such meandering, I accepted that it would also confuse even a serious enquirer and that my normal South African one would do.

To authenticate my legend, I had to visit my home town, Edam, to get the lay of the land. I stayed in the boardinghouse of Mrs Bos under my new name for a week. My orientation was plain sailing. Apart from a medieval cheese weighbridge, some interesting old buildings, a few street names and plenty of water, there was not much else for me to memorise. The town reminded me of the Afrikaans humorist and radio personality, Fanus Rautenbach, who once announced the prizes for a radio quiz he was promoting as first prize two weeks' holiday in Bronkhorstspruit, and second prize three weeks.

Had it been a real operation, my downfall could have come quite early when dear Mrs Bos recognised my surname and told me of my relatives still living in the town, some of them about my age. When she said she would tell them I was there and invite them over for coffee to meet me, I had quite a time convincing her not to do so. I preferred to spend the week at her lovely establishment in quiet rest and recuperation, which I badly needed (that part was true). The next time I visited would be better. She was a sympathetic lady and said I did look worn out, and couldn't she call me a doctor? I again had to decline her caring generosity.

I did not stay the full week but did have my Dutch passport, of which I was as proud as I am of my Dutch heritage. The only proviso for its future use was that I did not enter the country through Amsterdam's Schiphol Airport; all the other ports of entry whether by land, sea or air were, somewhat surprisingly, fine. But this was almost forty years ago. Things changed drastically with the later implementation of the Schengen Agreement that enforced external border control for entry into Europe, for better or worse. And, of course, the passport afforded me access to every other country in the world.

29

Outward Movement Inward

I had over time been advocating an own NIS 'outward movement', arguing for greater openness in intelligence work, including getting rid of the classification (and over-classification) of just about everything as 'Secret' or higher, and being more accessible and publicly visible as an organisation. I basically argued that this could only enhance the security of real secrets and do much to dispel the negative image of intelligence, in particular of NIS as the inheritor of the legacy of BOSS as a dark force hanging over the heads of innocent citizens going about their legitimate pursuits. I had some discussions with the DG and deputy DG regarding this matter. I once even argued for overtly sending some of our mature researchers and operators to an open international conference in the USA that the CIA was advertising in the media. We could have discreetly arranged this through the local CIA people.

The suggestion was summarily rejected as too dangerous. I could never fathom our consistent collective assumption that in talking to the 'enemy' we would necessarily lose out. Of course there were risks involved in such an approach generally, and in this case the CIA would certainly have eavesdropped and talent-spotted for possible recruits among the conferees. They would without a doubt have tried to establish what their guests knew and how they found out about international players and their relations, which was to be the theme of the conference. But surely there would also have been the same risks for them?

On the same theme, I once had to meet an agent of the Soviet KGB in Vienna to give him a message from his regular contact in NIS, who was unavailable at the time. He was a taciturn but not unfriendly man, and we had a pleasant dinner. The conversation unfortunately was not very stimulating, covering mostly inane topics, including a bit about the condition of Africa, about which he was either non-committal or uninformed. On parting, I suggested that he visit South Africa to see for himself what the real conditions there were. He was taken aback and got somewhat tongue-tied, but said he would suggest it to his bosses. But this man was no longer young and clearly not a heavyweight in his job. I got the impression that he had more or less been parked in Vienna, maybe to divert attention from the many very active KGB spies in that city, a favoured haunt of such at the time.

I reported this home and was severely reprimanded by the DG. What would the president say if he should hear about this communist being invited to our country, he asked, and seriously questioned my judgement. I was amused by how the ĶGB man had been caught off guard and wondered at how much mileage we could get from adversarial counterparts by being a bit innovative at times. But the fear of being contaminated by the 'other' is a traditional bugbear of especially the Afrikaner. Shortly after I left NIS, I heard that senior people from there were visiting the KGB in Moscow, and were even received in the Kremlin.

It was disappointing that we so often lacked the confidence that we were well able to assert ourselves and exploit opportunities, especially with the very able people we had on call. I regularly raised my conviction that it was more dangerous to distrust our people than to trust them. Nobody can be policed for twenty-four hours of every day. I was not irresponsibly advocating throwing things open, but merely asking to rationalise and improve the functioning of our industry.

It was in this context that I asked permission to openly and formally make contact as NIS with journalists in the alternative media and even with hostile organisations in South Africa, a request that was also initially peremptorily denied. Of course, our people on the ground had many fruitful covert relations with both, but I was intent on reaching such people of integrity at senior levels who wouldn't spy for us but whose insights, especially those concerning internal conditions, about which they often knew more than we did, could benefit us. I also thought that conveying a better image of NIS than the stereotypical one to such quarters could produce useful results. We were already benefiting from the insights of top editors and journalists of mainstream Afrikaans and English publications, without their ever being asked to spy or compromise themselves, but they were as ill-informed as we were in some areas.

Allan Boesak

As talks and rumours of talks with adversaries were already in the air in 1987, attitudes in the top management of NIS began to soften and I eventually got permission to speak to the Reverend Allan Boesak, one of the founding leaders of the UDF. The UDF was a wide-ranging and effective mass-protest movement established in reaction to the 1983 legislation for the Tricameral Parliament. It was in effect the domestic arm of the then still banned ANC and the prime mover in mobilising internal resistance to the regime. I was given to understand that the outcome would be on my head. Whatever that might have meant, we met Boesak in his office in Cape Town. He and a colleague, Denzil Potgieter, a lawyer who I understood was later appointed a judge on the High Court bench in that city, received us courteously but were obviously wary of our intentions.

We put to them our need for their insights regarding what was going on at grassroots level in the Cape Town area, to enable us to more fully and reliably report to the government. They sort of agreed to engage in dialogue, but nothing came of it. This was understandable in view of the prominent role the UDF was playing in mobilising that self-same grassroots *against* the government. I sensed that they were caught a bit off guard by our direct approach. They were still some way off from considering the notion of a negotiated, peaceful settlement. But our approach broke some ice and I thought the contact could have been followed up, but I didn't have anything specifically positive to report.

Max du Preez

The next subject we spoke to was the gadfly editor of the alternative Afrikaans weekly publication *Vrye Weekblad*, Max du Preez. Daan Opperman and I met Du Preez and Jacques Pauw, a journalist colleague of his at *Vrye Weekblad*, for lunch at a place of their choosing somewhere in Johannesburg. A pleasant meal and conversation ended with the understanding that they would think about our request to obtain the benefit of their insights and that we would perhaps meet again for further discussions. We offered to pay the bill but Max understandably refused. Heaven forbid that they be accused of being bribed with a lunch to connive with the toxic forces of NIS.

As we were leaving, Max made a loud joke that could be heard by everyone present that we were spies come to recruit them. This audience of apparently mostly *Vrye Weekblad* or Du Preez sycophants seemed to be stage-managed, perhaps as a security precaution. After all, everyone knew what horrors could befall anyone tangling with these evil forces of the dark. Everybody, ourselves included, enjoyed the little joke and the acclamation of the audience, no doubt intended for the bravely defiant Max, but which we also arrogated to ourselves.

In the very next issue of *Vrye Weekblad*, Du Preez wrote how Niel Barnard had sent his 'heavies' – I have to admit that Daan was quite heavy at the time – to intimidate them. That put paid to my endeavours at outward movement inward. I again had my ears bent in an I-told-you-so session. I very much regretted this outcome as I was convinced that regular, candid discussions with people like Du Preez could have enriched and improved our reports to the government.

Years later, in 2006, Jacques Pauw had an excellent and most disturbing book published about mainly the travails of Africa, in particular Rwanda, titled *Dances with Devils*. In it he gives an imaginative version of our encounter with him and Du Preez. He recounts that they at least got a good lunch and a bottle of wine out of it at government expense, and presents Du Preez's little joke as a grand put-down. Whether his inaccurate version of the incident reflects the state of his memory or his journalistic integrity I cannot say. We were slightly flattered to think that Pauw regarded us so highly as to rate us among the devils with whom he had danced. But I've been wondering how Du Preez feels about Pauw so defeating the purpose of his careful avoidance of compromise by paying for the lunch, including the wine.

Years later in his book *Dwars* (2009), Du Preez apologised graciously, albeit cursorily, for having misjudged us. He has remained as critical of the ANC government and the condition of our country under its management since 1994 as he was of the apartheid state, and I respect him for his journalistic integrity.

30

The Fall Guy

As I have stated, I believe it to be one of the natural roles of an intelligence organisation and its officials to assume responsibility for risky projects, which, if they should come unstuck, could have dire consequences for their government, such as when diplomats, with their established protocols and rules of propriety, are involved. After all, everyone knows that spooks have a penchant for varied nefarious activities, are expendable and are the easiest to publicly repudiate when necessary. I was on more than one occasion required to fulfil such a role. Apparently it was sometimes thought I would not notice the thin ice I was treading, as I wasn't always fully briefed beforehand on the true purpose or implications of our endeavours.

Daniel Chipenda
In early November 1987 our people in Windhoek were approached by an Angolan businessman saying that one Daniel Chipenda, an expatriate former member of the ruling MPLA in Angola and then living in exile in Switzerland, wanted to speak to an authoritative South African official in Europe. He wanted discussions on the possibility of a ceasefire in the war in Angola, and to convey a message to President P.W. Botha. He was said to be acting on the authority of the Angolan government. Chipenda was a well-known Angolan pimpernel who had flitted between various liberation movements in Angola and was then said to have reconciled with the MPLA, but hadn't returned to Angola. We were wary of him by reputation, but detailed one of our experienced operational people, Louis Steyn, to first meet with him in Switzerland to try to establish his *bona fides*. Steyn's feedback was cautiously positive and he recommended that we follow up the contact. The DFA asked NIS to do the following up, as, for the reasons set out above, it would be too risky for them and the country should they do so.

On 18 November I and two colleagues, Steyn and Joe Boshoff, a director of Research, met Chipenda in his luxury suite in reputedly the most expensive hotel in Switzerland, the Geneva Hilton. He told us that he had been instructed by the Angolan government to establish a confidential line of communication with South Africa as the existing channels were not to be fully trusted. He did not elaborate on the reason, but I suspect this could have been because of the close ties South Africa had with the bane of the Angolan government, UNITA, through the SADF. Because Chipenda had asked to speak to the DFA, we went as representatives of that department, under cover names and with false travel documents. I assumed that it probably also had to do with internal tensions in Angolan politics, where the so-called Battle of Cuito Cuanavale was hotting up. He said the driver of this approach was Manuel Alexandre 'Kito' Rodrigues, at the time the Angolan minister of internal and security affairs. He said Kito would like to talk confidentially with our 'proper authorities about common interests'.

I told him that I had no way of knowing whether what he was saying in fact came from the Angolan government and that I would require some authentication such as a formal and legibly signed letter of appointment or recommendation. He had no objection and agreed to obtain something like that, but that it would take a day or two. He seemed a bit too eager to comply, flashing further red lights. He asked us to wait as it wouldn't take long. We undertook to remain readily available in Geneva for a few more days.

After two days, he phoned to invite us back to his suite, saying he now had the proof. On our arrival, he introduced us to Kito Rodrigues in person, who produced a newspaper clipping of a report carrying a photograph of him for identification purposes, as well as a letter of instruction signed by President Dos Santos of Angola. We made it clear to him that we had no mandate to negotiate but were only there to establish whether Chipenda was indeed acting on the authority of the Angolan government. We would listen to what he had to say and report back to our government. Rodrigues then proceeded to inform us broadly as follows:

- President Dos Santos had instructed Chipenda to make contact with South Africa to initiate a peace process.
- Discussions should start between Angola and South Africa at official level without outside intermediaries and, as progress is made, later shift to the political level.
- Peace had to be achieved first, after which other problems of southern Africa could be attended to.
- Chipenda should for the time being be accepted as the only channel for discussions, but that he, Rodrigues, would also be available 'when the time is ripe'.

Later that same day, we also spoke to Chipenda alone at the Hotel Le Richmond in Geneva where he elaborated further as follows:

- Although the Angolan government still stood by its known conditions for peace in that country, its point of departure was totally flexible.
- A ceasefire is the first priority.
- He (Chipenda) would like to visit South West Africa to 'speak to his people there' (the Ovimbundu people, of which Jonas Savimbi of UNITA was also a member).
- President Dos Santos is waiting anxiously to hear from the South African government.

We did not react substantively but merely undertook to convey the request to the South African government and revert to them as soon as possible. It was patently clear that the Angolan government was under serious pressure from the hostilities on its soil and quite desperate to do something about it. I had no doubt that the pressure the SADF and UNITA were putting on them and their less-than-successful communist support was a primary cause of this desperation. It seemed like a window of opportunity to be exploited in order to find a Clausewitzian 'politics by other means' way to stem the suppurating ulcer that the military situation in Angola had become to its government, as well as to the South African treasury, international political situation and national psyche.

Back in Pretoria we met with colleagues from the DFA and CSI to give feedback. We were all sceptical of the Angolan initiative, especially CSI, who were no doubt concerned about the effect it could have on their support to their proxy, UNITA, which had been extremely valuable to the SADF and South Africa for the pressure they exerted in eventually forcing the Angolan government to sue for peace. These circumstances certainly also resonated with the unexpected meeting I had with President Sam Nujoma of SWAPO through the good offices of President Kaunda of Zambia earlier in 1987, where the former for the same reason also offered peace overtures.

But the consensus between the DFA and NIS was that this initiative should be taken forward to see what could come of it. A convoluted negotiation process followed that eventually led to the end of the war, the withdrawal of all outside communist forces from Angola and the independence of Namibia. NIS supported the South African negotiators throughout by providing them with good intelligence giving them prior knowledge on crucial issues.

This successful outcome was negotiated in the Joint Commission on South Western Africa established under the auspices of the UN for that very purpose. The immediate parties to the conflict – South Africa, Angola and Cuba – were represented in this commission. NIS had a contingent led by DG Niel Barnard on the South African team, of which Joe Boshoff was also a standing member, rendering sterling service until the end. Another member of NIS in support was our director of foreign liaison, Basjan Rothmann (one of my 'students' at Harvard referred to previously), who did a great job in establishing confidential relations with the Cuban intelligence service.

Through this channel we were able to put South Africa's policy positions in perspective for those involved, on a confidential basis, when they sometimes received mixed and often confusing messages from within the military and diplomatic contingents of the South African team. The relationship was reciprocal and stood us in good stead in other respects.

I am grateful to Joe and Basjan for affording me the benefit of their notes and retentive memories in refreshing my recollection of the details of these events, which had become quite vague by the time I came to write about them. Through Basjan's good offices I clandestinely met my operational Cuban counterpart in Vienna to consolidate the contact, but had no further part in either the liaison or the 'border negotiations'.

An Arabian Knight

Towards the middle of 1988 I was instructed to meet with someone at ARMS-COR who wanted us to do something for them. The man, a senior official by the name of Peet Smith, asked me to speak to the Italian billionaire Marino Chiavelli and gave me some promotional pamphlets on their excellent G5 and G6 155-mm artillery systems, at the time widely regarded as the best of their kind in the world. Smith said Chiavelli apparently had potential clients in the Middle East for these weapons and I was to try to sell them. Why on earth should I, of all people, rather than ARMSCOR itself, try to sell these weapons, I asked. He said that apart from the acute interest of the CIA, MI6 and just about all substantial intelligence agencies in the world, ARMSCOR's association with Chiavelli was being so closely watched by international sanctions monitors that they were virtually confined to quarters. This was palpable claptrap. Both they and we at NIS routinely worked under such circumstances. All that was required was proper planning and the necessary precautions.

My suspicions of a fall-guy scenario were strengthening, but I had my orders, and tuned my antennae to the unexpected.

Chiavelli was an Italian entrepreneur living in South Africa who had done the country sterling service, and made himself a pretty packet, in procuring oil supplies through Middle Eastern contacts when all conventional channels had been cut off by international sanctions. Some people had hinted at his possible Mafia connections. I was introduced to him by SAN Captain Ters Ehlers, President Botha's military secretary, at the marvellous Chiavelli estate in Hyde Park, Johannesburg called Summer Place. He also had a comparable estate in Upper Constantia in Cape Town, and a large penthouse flat on a fashionable street in Modena, northern Italy. There he also owned a medieval monastery high up in the mountains above the city, which he had turned into a restaurant and guest house. I once had the most exquisite *antipasti* lunch there, with only the two of us present, of incredibly delicate hams, salamis and cheeses – none of which, he made a point of telling me, were from Parma – with scrumptious olives and melon from the estate. He also kept a private bottle of Napoleon brandy locked up in the cellars of the Zoo Lake restaurant in Johannesburg. Chiavelli was nothing if not stylish. He was also a most courteous and pleasant man, and a gracious host. In the initial stages of our association it was obvious that he was assessing me to see whether I would be up to the job or likely to embarrass him with his valuable contacts.

Eventually he told me that he wanted me to meet an Arabian prince in Paris. From there I was to fly to Milan and proceed onward by road to Modena for discussions on the armaments. But I was not to be seen associating with the prince outside of his country's embassy in Paris, and we were not to acknowledge each other in public until safely at Chiavelli's place in Modena. In view of the seriousness with which he regarded the security aspect, I accepted this with the proviso that I make the arrangements and that the prince submit to my guidance, or I would be out. Chiavelli undertook to inform everyone of the pecking order.

It seemed simple enough, but the prince, a very nice but surprisingly young and obviously inexperienced man, was nervous and in a state of high excitement when we sorted out our travel arrangements and security procedures at his country's lavish embassy located on one of the most fashionable streets in the centre of Paris. While we were travelling, I had as unobtrusively as possible to ward him off more than once when he seemed desperate for direct contact with me for the succour he was apparently craving. I had the distinct impression that he also thought of himself as a fall guy.

I have never been afraid of flying, but this trip started off rather frighteningly adventurous when, on a night flight from Johannesburg to Paris, I was seated next to the recently divorced ex-wife of an acquaintance in Pretoria. She was an attractive and intelligent woman whom I liked and I welcomed the company, which I usually shunned on flights. Before take-off, in between large gulps from a half-jack of Bell's whisky, she told me she was scared to death of flying. After take-off she carried on drinking apace and, together with a pleasant dinner, seemed quite relaxed. But she also took what to me looked like quite a handful of pills. When the cabin lights were dimmed for the night, she turned to me and matter-of-factly announced that she was now going to make love to me. She clambered halfway over the dividing console, snuggled up to me, drew her blanket over the two of us, and fell asleep. I had with some effort to return her to her seat. In the morning the hostess had trouble waking her up for disembarkation at Charles de Gaulle.

From Paris the prince and I travelled on the same flight to Milan, where we were fetched separately for the road trip to Modena. I almost laughed out aloud when my chauffeur turned up. He was wearing a dark blue suit, white shoes, a black shirt, a red bowtie and a broad-brimmed black Fedora with a white band. He had a drooping moustache and wore large sunglasses. I had trouble getting into the front passenger seat of the 2-litre turbo Lancia Thema because of a large piece of equipment against the front fire-wall at my feet. From time to time it emitted a loud squawk and flashing red light, at which the driver would harshly slow down from his steady 200 kilometres-plus per hour in the fast lane of the *autostrada*, his left-hand indicator lights constantly flickering. The self-evident purpose of the squawks and flashing light was confirmed by my English-challenged chauffeur in one word: 'radar'.

I was put up most comfortably in an elegant suite of the penthouse in Modena, but did not see the prince before retiring for the night. Discussions started at breakfast with general questions and remarks about the capabilities of the artillery and its range, with telling questions about whether it could from his country reach Iran, clearly his main focus of interest, and some other countries in the region. Among other things, he enquired as to the characteristics of the self-propelled G6, the capacity of the computerised control systems, and the innovative base-bleed ammunition that significantly increased the range of projectiles. I had been briefed fairly thoroughly on the technicalities by ARMSCOR personnel, but hadn't a clue about some of the aspects, such as the computer systems, a technology with which the prince seemed particularly familiar. I undertook to arrange a follow-up visit by specific experts, if required. Then came the crucial question: What about the system's capability to deliver 'special' weapons?

International speculation was then rife about South Africa's supposed nuclear weapons capability, including allegations that the G5/6 artillery system had been developed specifically to deliver tactical nuclear warheads ground to ground. I was warned that the subject might come up in discussions and was informed by ARMSCOR that I could not be told whether we had such a capability or not, and that my Arab contact should be kept guessing by my neither confirming nor denying the existence of such a capability. I thought this rather silly as I had assured them I had no knowledge whatsoever about this subject, and that neither confirming nor denying was in any event the only way I could react. But I was glad to have had forewarning that such questions might arise. The meeting and visit ended on an inconclusive but friendly note, and the experience was a remarkable one. The prince seemed impressed by my playing of my obfuscatory role, to him obviously feigned. I thought it had probably damaged ARMSCOR and South Africa's interests to have sent me instead of an expert to sell the artillery, irrespective of the nuclear question.

This incident took place in early 1988. When it was announced the following year that South Africa indeed had nuclear weapons but was relinquishing them as well as the capacity to produce them, it became clear that at the time of my visit to Modena that decision must at least have been under consideration, if not already taken. So the only purpose my involvement could have served was to save ARMSCOR some squirming – rightly so, I thought, because as the main player in the field they could not very well have credibly 'neither confirmed nor denied' to a valued client for conventional armaments.

31

Talks About Talks About Talks

Overtures to Nelson Mandela

Since the 1970s the worldwide Free Mandela campaign had been steadily gaining momentum and contact between big business and others with the exiled ANC or its interlocutors in Britain and elsewhere had been increasing. In about 1984, I was told that through minister of justice Kobie Coetsee's contact with Nelson Mandela's wife, Winnie, at the time restricted to the town of Brandfort in the Orange Free State (Coetsee's home turf), approaches were being made to establish the feasibility of discussions with Mandela in the Robben Island prison. The situation of the country was now dire, with bankruptcy staring us in the face. Things would only worsen in 1985 when Chase Manhattan Bank of New York refused to further roll over its loans to South Africa, rendering the country unable to service its international debts. The war in South West Africa/Angola was said to be costing about R1 million per day, an unsustainable amount at the time. Something clearly had to give.

In 1982, Mandela, Walter Sisulu, Ahmed Kathrada and Andrew Mlangeni were transferred from Robben Island to Pollsmoor Prison in Tokai, Cape Town to facilitate discussions, it was generally understood. Mandela had insisted that some of his senior comrades remain with him as he did not want to be accused of conducting discussions with the regime off his own bat and contrary to the interests of the ANC. For the same reason, direct telephone contact with the president of the ANC, Oliver Tambo, then living in Sweden, was facilitated for him. He was soon transferred to a more comfortable hospital suite in the prison, which gave him greater freedom of movement and allowed easier access to him. Still later he was moved to a warder's house on the grounds of Victor Verster Prison outside Paarl.

In 1987 the so-called Dakar Safari took place, in which a civil society group of high-profile Afrikaners met some of the leadership of the ANC in exile in the Senegalese capital. I was told that one of the group, Harald Pakendorf, an independent journalist and commentator, had beforehand informed NIS in the person of Mike Louw of the intended 'safari'. Louw strongly objected to the visit, fearing that it might have an adverse effect on the delicately balanced discussions with Mandela, and on the sensibilities of factions in the government opposed to talking to the ANC. He was in the invidious position of not being able to inform Pakendorf of the discussions with Mandela and the progress then already being made in that regard.

Furthermore, Mandela might view the visit as being surreptitiously sponsored by the government in an attempt to drive the wedge he feared between him and the exiles. He would have viewed it as a serious breach of trust at a stage where attempts were being made to elicit his approval of the government meeting with the exiled leadership, which he initially fiercely resisted. It could also upset the delicate applecart of steady progress being made towards the acceptance in government circles that negotiation was in fact the only remaining option.

Early in 1989 I was briefed on the discussions with Mandela under the auspices of Minister Kobie Coetsee. The main players on the government side were commissioner of prisons General Willie Willemse, the DG of NIS, Niel Barnard, Fanie van der Merwe of the Constitutional Development Service and the deputy DG of NIS, Mike Louw. Mandela was incensed when, in the face of his intransigence, he was eventually informed that discussions would be initiated with the exiles, with or without his approval. He was especially livid when told that these would be conducted with Thabo Mbeki, son of Govan Mbeki. Serious tensions had developed between Mandela and the latter, an unreconstructed communist who was opposed in principle to any talks or negotiations with the government. Thabo Mbeki was at the time the personal assistant to Oliver Tambo, who had moved to London from Sweden. Mandela was somewhat mollified when told that the younger Mbeki would keep Tambo, who had apparently given his approval for the effort, informed of all developments.

Mandela's gradual adaptation to the outside world after such a long period of incarceration has been well documented elsewhere. The sensitive handling of the matter by the government and its officials gradually eroded his scepticism, making way for the establishment of a basis of trust between them.

First meeting with the exiles

In August 1989, P.W. Botha resigned as president and was succeeded by F.W. de Klerk, initially in an acting capacity until he was elected to the position shortly thereafter. On 16 August the State Security Council (SSC), presided over for the first time by De Klerk, adopted a resolution instructing NIS to investigate the feasibility of entering into direct discussions with the still banned ANC. The resolution, crafted mainly by Barnard and Louw, probably in consultation with Coetsee and with the support of Botha before his resignation, was carefully worded so as not to further exacerbate tensions then rife in cabinet between the reformists and the conservatives, the latter at the time still widely accepted to be under the leadership of De Klerk. NIS was instructed to give effect to the resolution, which was intended to be susceptible to interpretation as a go-ahead for exploratory discussions with the ANC. The SSC resolution, translated from the Afrikaans (translator unknown), reads as follows:

> It is necessary that more information should be obtained and processed concerning the ANC, and the aims, alliances and potential approachability of its different leaders and groupings. To enable this to be done, special additional direct action will be necessary, particularly with the help of National Intelligence functionaries.

When briefed on these foregoing events, I was instructed to select and prepare a team of operational people to assist in arranging a meeting overseas with the exiled ANC leadership, and attend to security matters. I was also to get in touch with one of our covert colleagues who had contact with a 'friend' I had to meet. The friend was Willie Esterhuyse, professor of philosophy and of business ethics at the University of Stellenbosch, an honest broker of the very best kind. He was eminently suitable for such a role as he was both an insider of the Afrikaner establishment and a friend of Thabo Mbeki's. He met Mbeki overseas and a relationship of trust developed between them. Perhaps the greatest value of Esterhuyse's mediation was that, with the access he had to the Afrikaner power structures, he managed to convince Mbeki that there was a genuine desire to reach a negotiated settlement, and one that might lead to a black-dominated majority government at that.

He had to allay Mbeki and the ANC's fears of a divisive ploy by the government to mislead and drive a wedge between their varied factions, mainly between the exiles and the 'inziles', and apparently undertook to advise Mbeki should he, Esterhuyse, become aware of any government skulduggery. Without such assurances it seems unlikely that Mbeki and the ANC would at the time have agreed to enter into any discussions. It is likely that Esterhuyse also facilitated the 1986 meeting in New York between Mbeki and Professor Pieter de Lange, rector of the Rand Afrikaans University and chairman of the AB.

In conjunction with our aforementioned colleagues, Esterhuyse arranged communications with Thabo Mbeki and Jacob Zuma in Dar es Salaam and Lusaka, as well as cover names for the parties directly involved. Mbeki and Zuma were styled John and Jack Simelane (I forget who was who) and I would be John Campbell. Telephone numbers were exchanged and I was instructed to arrange a first meeting in Switzerland. Such measures might seem over-elaborate, but the danger of leaks was very real. There was strong internal resistance in both the ANC and the NP to such contact, and had news of the meeting leaked to the media, it could very well have put paid to the whole enterprise. For the same reason, we could not use our genuine passports. There were also fanatical far-right elements within South Africa who were vehemently opposed to any notion of a negotiated 'giving away of their fatherland' settlement, and who had relations with some equally fanatical organisations in Europe. Such groupings at home and abroad had over time proven themselves fully capable of ruthless armed violence to further their cause.

We also had to assume that telephone calls were being intercepted. Many people and governments the world over had crucial interests at stake and were extremely concerned about what was going on between the South African government and the ANC. But it is axiomatic that security is only as good as the people practising it, a case in point being the telephone call to my home from London asking for John Campbell, and then saying, 'Please hold for Thabo Mbeki', to the amusement of my university-student son, Cobus, who answered. I had been obliged to brief my wife and children about the possibility of such calls.

I designated our top man for the job – the 'French banker' of the 'useful banker' operation described earlier – to put together a small support team. He picked only two people, a man and a woman, to see to the logistic and security aspects with him. They arranged the venue, the Palace Hotel in Lucerne, and had to do counter-surveillance before, during and after the meeting to establish who else might be interested in the goings-on. We had to assume that our people stationed in Europe were known to intelligence services there and should therefore not be used. Although the 'useful banker' had previously been one of them, he was so professional in devising his cover, including an authentic foreign passport, that I had no qualms about his involvement.

I was to accompany Mike Louw to oversee the logistics and security, and to assist in discussions. As regards the former two aspects, I had more or less nothing to do as the matter was in the hands of the most capable people I knew. Although I was aware that the appointed leader of the little group harboured some conservative sentiments and was sceptical of the wisdom of entering into negotiations with the 'enemy', I was equally convinced of his absolute integrity and did not hesitate for a moment to give him the job. He was also fluent in French. He and his assistants were the best of the best; the sort of people who would always find a tree, were the lion snarling at their heels.

We arrived in Lucerne on 10 September 1989, a day ahead of our appointment with Thabo Mbeki – we did not know who was to accompany him, but assumed it would probably be Jacob Zuma, who at the time was the head of the ANC's Department of Intelligence and Security and already in the loop. On the eve of our meeting we got a call from our man in Harare, from where our visitors were to have departed, informing us that they would be a day late as their scheduled flight had encountered mechanical problems soon after take-off and had to return to the airport. He also confirmed that Zuma would be with Mbeki.

The next day Mbeki phoned with the same account of events. A day later, on 12 September, our man in Geneva confirmed their arrival at the airport there, advised that they were travelling by car to Lucerne and gave us an estimated time of arrival. He also informed us of their driver, an ANC exile living in Europe who later was appointed to a senior position in the post-apartheid civil service. We thought the visitors would be uncertain of what awaited them. Would the racist devils be waiting with AK-47s to blow them away and blame it on a hostile faction in the ANC? This was not far-fetched, as security forces back home were still wreaking havoc in the ANC ranks and tensions were at fever pitch. Considering their mindset at the time, I thought it quite brave of Mbeki and Zuma to attend, but it later appeared that they had also done some hedging of their own bets. We left the front door of the suite open as, hopefully, a form of reassurance.

When they entered, Mbeki's first words were: 'Well, here we are, the terrorists, and for all you know fucking communists as well.' This opening statement, together with our gift of a pack each of Rum & Maple and Boxer pipe tobacco, which we knew Mbeki favoured, broke the ice. Zuma was carrying a briefcase and I asked whether he would mind if I put it in the room next door. We all agreed that none of us wanted these initial discussions recorded. He didn't object, but neither did he notice my own briefcase next to my chair, which had slipped my mind.

Both sides expressed the sincere intentions of their principals to seek a peaceful negotiated settlement to ensure the future of the country. We agreed that neither side was authorised to negotiate and that our discussions were aimed solely at establishing whether such negotiations would be feasible. In an extended and exhausting but friendly session that lasted into the early hours, we discussed some of the most vexed nettles between the government and the ANC – Mandela's continued incarceration; the ban on the liberation movements; the involvement of the SACP with the ANC, to which our principals had serious objections; and the ongoing ANC-inspired mass protest action in South Africa with its attendant eruptions of violence. We strongly urged them to tone down their propagandist threats of violence and retribution, pointing out that the government was having difficulty in persuading its support base that peaceful negotiations would be a viable alternative to continued violent confrontation.

Mbeki especially took our admonishments in this regard seriously and voiced his own objections to slogans being bandied about. He recognised that the destructive real results of 'No education before liberation' and 'Make the country ungovernable' particularly would be difficult for any future government to reverse. In the end we fulfilled our mandate from the SSC. The ANC were clearly prepared and even eager to enter into discussions with the government. We agreed to report to our respective principals and, depending on the latter's directions, meet again to more substantively discuss devising a way forward.

On returning home, our DG was unavailable and so we had to go down to Cape Town to report directly to President De Klerk. On hearing about our meeting, he was livid. Who gave us the right to talk to the ANC? Calling us 'you people', he accused us of again doing things in our own self-willed way, accountable to no one. He really ranted on a bit, but Mike produced a copy of the SSC resolution – we had anticipated that De Klerk might not have been fully informed of the intended meeting or realised the implications of the SSC resolution adopted under his chairmanship. After all, we could not have executed our mandate to investigate the feasibility of talking directly to the ANC without talking to *some* of them. De Klerk calmed down in an instant and, as Mike put it, he 'took up the ball and ran with it'. The president later confided that he had been dealt a hand of cards that he could not exchange, but had to play. It again struck me that he was not an original reformer, although he must have been involved in the gestation within the AB described in O'Malley's papers.

This exchange took place on 16 September and, new to the hot seat, one has in fairness to take into account the tremendous pressures De Klerk must have been under in the drawn-out, tortuous demise of the Botha presidency and the advent of his own. Our appointment put us second in line to see him on his first day of taking general appointments as president, we were told. It was interesting to see who the first visitor was to emerge from the president's office. It was Alf Ries, the political guru of the more 'liberal' southern Nasionale Pers newspaper group, and of the NP in the Cape. De Klerk was representative of the more conservative views of the Northern NP, of which he was the leader, and its press. I fervently hope someone – ideally F.W. de Klerk – will one day candidly and authoritatively record the fascinating full story of the wheels within wheels inside the NP, the AB and the government at the time. The all-consuming concern of political leaders with preserving their heritage should not impose on such honest telling. Future Afrikaner and South African generations are owed the truth.

Second meeting with the exiles

I was ordered back to Europe to be available for further possible meetings there. I had also qualified for sabbatical leave, during which we were required to do something useful to the organisation. I opted to improve my primordial French, a facility NIS was short of at senior level. We had the free use of a French friend's holiday flat in the south-western French town of Perpignan near the Spanish border. I successfully applied for admission to the University of Perpignan for French studies and was admitted to an honours class that was engaged in a new translation into English of Victor Hugo's *Les Misérables*, which had been commissioned by the Académie Française and parcelled out to a number of French universities. In the seminars I had much practice in the source language, and my English was in fair demand. It was a marvellous learning experience.

Perpignan was within easy reach of Toulouse, from where I could on short notice reach any major destination in Europe by air. It was an exciting opportunity and I took my wife, Anna, and youngest daughter, Lisa, along (unfortunately not at state expense). With our dependably supportive and caring man in Rome, Ray Wilson, generously offering us the use of his private BMW 528, we were really in the pound (or franc) seats in Perpignan. My daughter and I jogged and played squash under the tutelage of a friendly Moroccan instructor, Mourad Assouad, at the Club des Sports, who asked me to teach him how to hit a backhand. Anna and Lisa also took lessons from a French tutor.

We also had the generous support of our man in Paris, Johan Russouw, and his wife Eleanor, with whom we stayed for Christmas that year and who two years later took Lisa into their home and lovingly cared for her when her year of au pairing in Paris went wrong. Eleanor sadly died of a massive brain haemorrhage in November 2011.

We were also much comforted by the interest shown by other of our people in Europe, such as our man in Germany, Wallie Krumm, who, with his wife Trix, warmly welcomed us to their home in Bonn and with whose BMW I sampled the pleasures of unlimited speed on the *autobahn*. Another was Nico Fourie in The Hague who, along with Krumm, visited us in Perpignan and presented me with a Puma sports bag, which I still use as a favoured travelling bag, albeit in a fairly tattered state, to my wife's irritation. In London, our resident Henry Stone and his wife Alet took our son, Bosman, into their home when he fell quite seriously ill with a bout of flu while backpacking in Europe, and caringly nursed him back to health. I am forever warmly grateful to these and others for their unfailingly generous support. The sojourn in Perpignan was an enjoyable and constructive life experience.

During January 1990 Mike Louw phoned and asked that I arrange a second meeting with the exiled ANC leadership at the same venue in Lucerne for 6 February 1990. It only later transpired that this meeting had already been scheduled to take place after De Klerk's seminal statement of 2 February that year, of which Mike was by then aware but I was not. Unfortunately, it cut short my time in France.

This time discussions were more substantive and even more congenial than at the first meeting. With Aziz Pahad now accompanying Mbeki, it was also more fun. We had prepared a draft of a possible way forward, suggesting four categories of matters for attention. After fairly strenuous consideration and some headbutting, the following priorities were identified:

a. The release of Nelson Mandela from prison.
b. The return of the exiles to South Africa, including members of MK in the field.

c. The release of other political prisoners and detainees and the question of indemnity against their possible prosecution in terms of still extant security legislation, including returning exiles.

d. Preparing the way for constitutional negotiations.

We agreed on these as points to be referred to our principals for consideration, and to set up working committees to consider each and make recommendations on further proceedings. From our side we again stressed that the ANC should tone down their extremist slogans and propaganda broadcasts. There was consensus that Mandela's release from prison was the overriding prerequisite for progress, and that this should not take much longer. I was not involved with the further progress of these suggestions for a way forward, but Mandela's release, CODESA and the Multi-Party Negotiation Process (MPNP) followed a similar approach to structuring the proceedings.

The atmosphere in this meeting was again pleasant and relaxed. Aziz Pahad could be a truly entertaining man. He repeatedly used the phrase 'What is to be done?' when we were indeed discussing what was to be done, but it was his invocation of the title of Lenin's philosophical work of 1902 on the situation in Russia that came across as quite hilarious under the circumstances. It was also confirmed that the ANC had been caught off guard by De Klerk's bold initiative. At the first meeting, I had a feeling that the teetotal Zuma put a bit of a damper on that occasion, although he was engagingly charming throughout. With Pahad's witticisms and his enthusiastic partaking of the fruit of the 'Scottish vine' (as long as it was halaal, which he seemed to take for granted), we 'negotiated' deep into the night. At one stage he sat on a couch with his legs stretched out and dozed off. Mbeki kicked his feet and said: 'Come on, Aziz, wake up. Don't leave me alone with these Boers.' Listening to Mbeki, I was impressed by his cogent, structured argumentation and thought it would be a mistake not to look past his seductive charm at the real man behind.

During our stay in Lucerne our team picked up that we were under surveillance while moving about the city on the few opportunities we had to do so, probably by the Swiss intelligence services. It was clearly a heel-treading operation in which they wanted us to know that they knew we were there; one of them would not have worn the garishly checked jacket he regularly popped up in along our route if he didn't want to be seen. I was determined that should we be confronted, I would tell them what we were about and that it would be on their heads if they should trip up the ground-breaking initiative. I am sure it would have worked. We obviously posed no threat to Switzerland, but it was still a serious criminal offence to use false travel documents in any country.

On the advice of our support team we thought it best to get out of Switzerland as soon as possible. Mike flew directly to South Africa, but I first had to get back to Paris on my way back to Perpignan to collect my genuine passport from the embassy. I was driven through the night over the border into France where we slept over at the first *relais* we could find, exhausted after a very long day. I heard many years later that the Swiss minister of foreign affairs had been aware of our meeting, probably informed by the ANC as a safeguard against any shenanigans we South Africans might have come up with, although this to the best of my knowledge had not been confirmed at the time of writing.*

---

* But see *Endgame*, by Willie Esterhuyse, p. 79 *et seq*, for the involvement of Richard Rosenthal and the surrounding circumstances. It may be surmised that Thabo Mbeki probably informed the Swiss authorities of our meetings there, also raising the distinct possibility that they were bugged by the Swiss.

32

Free at Last

Back in Perpignan, on 9 November 1989, I witnessed the breaching of the Berlin Wall on television, and it was immediately apparent that many an anti-communist-based edifice of power in countries the world over would soon be crumbling as surely as the Soviet monolith in Eastern Europe was. South Africa was one such country, and I thought a momentous opportunity had arisen for our government to seize the day and heave us out of the hole we South Africans had been digging ourselves into for centuries. I sat in Perpignan watching the news on French television on 2 February 1990 when F.W. de Klerk's talking head appeared on the screen from Parliament in Cape Town. In French-dubbed Afrikaans, he announced the lifting of the ban on the liberation movements and the imminent release of Nelson Mandela from prison. It was cathartic, and elation inadequately describes how I felt.

What I had believed in and had devoted most of my time, energy and conviction to over many years to the detriment of my personal life and family, had started to come to fruition. The logjam between the peoples of South Africa, which had progressively over almost two decades come to press heavily on my mind and spirit, had been irretrievably kicked apart. The immense psychological burden of white domination the Afrikaner had been carrying alone for so long was being shed for good. The clichéd new dawn was never more real for me than at that moment. I felt as liberated as any member of the ANC.

I thought with some trepidation of the daunting immediate future, but had not the slightest doubt that what De Klerk had done was unavoidable and indeed inevitable. Above all, it was the right thing to do. I was mentally and spiritually drained. Feeling cold and lonely for not being at home, I then slept for many hours as if to sleep off the hangover of the past 350 years of apartheid. I cherish the relics of the Berlin Wall that my elder son, Bosman, chipped off that rampart not long after 9 November and gave to me as a symbol of the irretrievably departed old world and a herald of the challenging new one with all its promise and excitement and menace.

Further preparatory meetings took place in Europe, at least two of which I know of in Zurich and Bern, between senior South African officials like

Niel Barnard, Fanie van der Merwe and Mike Louw, and ANC delegations that now also included Joe Nhlanhla, the future minister of intelligence. But I was no longer directly involved in this preliminary part of the process.

BEGINNING IV

Constructing Democracy

33

The Road to Democracy

There were no illusions that the road ahead would be easy. The crucial first phase of this historic enterprise started with an irreversible bang on 2 February 1990, but now much taller and thornier trees would have to be found if it were ultimately to succeed. A spate of high-level meetings and conferences took place after 2 February, the first one being the Groote Schuur conference in May 1990 at that historical building in Cape Town, where virtually the full top leaderships of the government and the ANC met to devise a way forward. A number of further high-level meetings took place, of which one in Pretoria was probably the most crucial, but more about that later.

These discussions culminated in the Declaration of Intent that enabled CODESA I to start on 21 December 1991. Later, the Record of Understanding, signed by Mandela and De Klerk in September 1992, enabled a return to negotiations in the MPNP early in 1993 after CODESA II had failed because of the Boipatong incident of June 1992, which I will return to later. Smaller meetings between representatives of the two sides took place almost constantly in search of consensus on issues for submission to the principals. These processes have been exhaustively described by people more competent than me and I will not venture too far into that phase.

One of the fundamental differences in opinion between the government and the ANC that initially caused a deadlock was that the latter demanded a quick fix by way of a relatively short amendment to the existing (1983) constitution, which contained no democratic safeguards for the protection of individual and minority rights and freedoms. The government refused to accept this as it would appear that a successful revolution had taken place, which was not the case and was politically unacceptable. They insisted on a two-phase process, with the first resulting in a comprehensive interim constitution containing agreed principles and processes as a basis for holding elections for a parliament, which would then be empowered to produce a final constitution. The existing race-based constitution could not provide the legal framework for conducting an election on a non-racial, universal franchise. Existing electoral legislation was therefore equally redundant.

Compromise was eventually reached and it was agreed (said to have been on a proposal by Joe Slovo and referred to as the 'sunset clauses', indicating that they would lapse after a fixed period of time) that an interim Government of National Unity (GNU) would jointly govern the country through a Transitional Executive Council (TEC) for five years under an interim constitution based on agreed constitutional principles, after which a constitution drafted by a democratically elected parliament sitting as a constituent assembly would come into force. All parties that would gain a certain percentage of the vote in an election to be held in terms of the interim constitution would participate in the GNU.

The Record of Understanding, signed in September 1992, incorporated the basics of this outcome and enabled the process to proceed to the final phase of negotiations and the drafting of a new constitution. It also entailed an agreement between the government and the ANC that they would first bilaterally agree on issues before submitting them to the wider negotiating forum for consideration. This in effect meant that all other parties were expected either to fall in line or be left behind. This was neither democratic nor inclusive, but was nonetheless reflective through their legitimate representatives of the will of the vast majority of the people of South Africa. Of course, it infuriated the other participating parties, but it did enable the process to proceed after the Boipatong incident had scuttled the process.

A tortuous and often acrimonious negotiation process of almost three years with much political posturing culminated in the adoption of the Interim Constitution towards the end of 1993. The first democratic general election of 1994 was held in terms of that constitution, after which the action shifted to the Constituent Assembly of the first parliament elected in the country under universal suffrage, where the final Constitution of the Republic of South Africa was produced in 1996. It has been hailed far and wide as an exemplary democratic instrument, accommodating contending interests and reflecting concessions made by all sides.

The momentous concession made by the ANC was their acceptance of a liberal-democratic constitution guaranteeing a free-market, capitalist-based economy with entrenched private property rights and a Bill of Rights to safeguard individual rights and freedoms. It is no wonder that Joe Slovo, the arch-propagandist of the SACP and the ANC, went to great lengths in proclaiming afterwards that they had got everything they wanted out of a wilting government. He would have had a tough job out of the limelight explaining this to his socialist and communist constituents and masters in Moscow, no doubt on the basis that this was only the first democratic phase of the two-phased Marxist-Leninist revolution, with the second, socialist one still to follow.

The historic concession made by the government was accepting the end of apartheid and the inevitability that whites would, at best, play a minority role in a black majority government. Formal NP policy was then still that a majority government was unacceptable, but the writing was on the wall, and eventually written into the Constitution.

Checks and balances were incorporated by way of, among other mechanisms, the Chapter 9 'watchdog' institutions designed to safeguard the Constitution. These included the Office of the Public Protector, the Human Rights Commission, the Independent Electoral Commission and the Auditor General. Together with the Bill of Rights, the separation of powers, an independent judiciary and a constitutional court to ultimately adjudicate on the constitutional compliance of any legislation passed by Parliament and lesser legislative bodies, as well as on any administrative action by official and private bodies, the people of the country had for the first time together established a firm democratic foundation for their new constitutional state.

The divisive Westminster system of the 'winner takes all' was buried for good and replaced by a so-called *rechtsstaat*, by which the law and not Parliament became the supreme authority in the land, supervised and guarded over by the Constitutional Court. In short, the rule of law was instituted in place of the rule of politics. But, as Roelf Meyer, the chief government negotiator, pointed out at the time, a constitution can only be as good or as bad as it is made by the people governed by it. It was a living instrument that had to be nurtured by the citizens of the country to take it to its full fruition.

34

Return of the Prodigals

The first priority after the announcements of 2 February 1990 and Nelson Mandela's release from prison on 11 February was to bring the exiled leadership of the ANC back into the country. They had to connect up with Mandela and the rest of the internal leadership, and be involved in the talks about talks on the way forward, which started immediately. They also had to start working in their domestic constituencies to condition their followers to the dramatically changed circumstances. There was still resistance in principle in some ANC quarters to the negotiations, which they regarded as a sell-out to the apartheid regime. With the very real rightist threats of violence as evidenced by numerous bombings, sabotage and other violent actions, it was obvious that the exiles would have to be brought in clandestinely and given security protection.

There were suggestions that elements in the SAP might pose a risk as they insisted that they still had outstanding warrants of arrest for most of the exiles, including Thabo Mbeki, and that the warrants would be executed on sight. These fears were apparently laid to rest by, among other things, discussions between Niel Barnard and the commissioner of police, General Johan van der Merwe. But the police could not be involved in the initial clandestine planning and execution of the return operation. Equally, with the security situation in the country being what it was and all sorts of rumours doing the rounds regarding the alleged activities of SADF hit squads, the SADF could clearly not be involved either. Whether this distrust of the SAP and the SADF was justified is still, in hindsight, difficult to say. But no potential threat to the process could be ignored.

Our NIS group received the vanguard contingent of the returning prodigal sons early one evening on the apron at Jan Smuts International Airport. Their group included Jacob Zuma, Penuell Maduna, a man called Gibson and a few others whose names escape me. The majority went by kombi, in the care of Daan Opperman, to an NIS safe house in the east of Pretoria. I took Zuma and a security man in the following car. He was affable but a bit nervous, making all sorts of chuckling and clucking sounds along the way. Later, over a braai we had laid on for them at the house, I asked him what his chuckling and clucking had been about. He then related his experiences after his arrest at Zeerust in the Western Transvaal in 1963. He was transferred to Pretoria where he was tried on terrorism charges, convicted, sentenced to imprisonment and incarcerated on Robben Island.

He related an encounter with one Sergeant Strydom (let's call him that) in Pretoria Central Prison. He was put in a pitch dark isolation cell without a window and with only a table and two chairs, and a standing lamp on the table that didn't work. He was left to wait, not knowing what to expect. Eventually the door opened and light streamed in, only to darken again immediately as Sergeant Strydom entered. The sergeant was enormous, as broad as he was tall. Without saying a word, he switched on the light (how is unclear, but let's not confound a good story with technicalities), started taking off his jacket and slowly and deliberately hung it neatly over the back of the chair opposite Zuma. Then he equally slowly and deliberately, still without a word, started rolling up his sleeves. Zuma's description of the size of the arm that gradually emerged from the sleeve had his audience in stitches. He had never, ever seen an arm of that size before. He immediately decided to tell the sergeant everything he wanted to know, even thinking up things he would tell him without being asked. Then, when he had finished disrobing his gargantuan arms, Sergeant Strydom, standing with his huge hands on the back of his chair, uttered his first words, staring Zuma straight in the face: '*Ja, kaffir, nou's jy in Pretoria né!*' (Yes, kaffir, so you're in Pretoria now!) This is what had so bemused him in the car voluntarily on his way back to Pretoria. His richly embellished telling of the tale brought the house down.*

As I was out of circulation on other jobs for a while, I was not aware of immediately subsequent events, but the returnees were soon transferred to an out-of-the-way hotel to the north-west of Johannesburg. Some of them were by this time venturing out to contact the local leadership of the ANC in townships on the Rand, including Alexandra and Soweto, which were more readily accessible from this location than from the north-east of Pretoria.

---

* Others have somewhat different recollections of events that evening. Patti Waldmeir (*Anatomy of a Miracle*, 1997, p. 159), an American journalist and author, records (she must have been told, as she wasn't there) that Zuma travelled to Pretoria from the airport in a car with General Basie Smit, the head of the security branch. This version has been repeated elsewhere, but is incorrect. Smit joined the party at the house later on, and with his driver, I understand, took Zuma on a sightseeing tour of Pretoria that included the Voortrekker Monument. By then I was no longer present.

After one such excursion, Penuell Maduna reported that he had been mugged in Soweto. His face showed clear indications of an assault. He offered no detailed explanation, but clearly did not regard it as a mere robust welcome home. Thabo Mbeki was mostly absent from both venues, as was Jacob Zuma. I assumed they were engaged in higher-level talks with local ANC leaders and at the Mandela/government level.

They were now mainly under the care and guidance of Colonel Beukes of the police, and I got to know some of them quite well, including Maduna, Mathews Phosa and Joe Kotane. We sometimes got together socially where they would regale us with tales of their experiences in the old South Africa, including in the Bantu Education system. They expressed appreciation for the dedication of some of their Afrikaans teachers, and I was particularly impressed by their general erudition in and regard for the Afrikaans language, especially Phosa.

Talks about negotiations now proceeded apace and a series of meetings was held between the leaderships of the ANC and the government, including between De Klerk and Mandela, as well as between smaller technical groups. During this phase, Zuma expressed a wish to meet Chief Mangosuthu Buthelezi, leader of the Inkatha Freedom Party (IFP) and chief minister of the KwaZulu homeland. A meeting was arranged and one evening I accompanied Zuma and Niel Barnard on a chartered flight to Ulundi, the seat of the KwaZulu government. En route, Zuma expressed his disgust at a member of the ANC who had recently publicly referred to Buthelezi as a 'dog'. He was clearly incensed, and added that he himself felt like 'taking up [his] sticks'. We were received at a conference facility in Ulundi by Buthelezi and what seemed to be the full governing body of the IFP and the KwaZulu government, including a contingent of traditional leaders. At the outset, the gathering started talking animatedly and at some length in isiZulu. It looked and sounded like a very happy Zulu reunion.

From the smattering of vocabulary I had learnt from my mother, a veritable white Zulu, I realised they were talking about white people, *mhlophe*, apparently referring to the presence of Barnard, Armstrong (the DG of Buthelezi's office who was also present) and me. I interrupted them, saying I thought it only fair to warn them that some of us *mhlophe* understood isiZulu (a rather gross exaggeration). They burst out in what I thought was somewhat embarrassed, raucous laughter. I had no idea what they had been saying about the *mhlophe*, but was later told they were discussing whether they should ask us to leave the meeting. They didn't, and carried on in English.

On a later occasion Buthelezi asked me where I had learnt isiZulu. I said from my mother but, out of fear that he might start talking to me in isiZulu, owned up that I had been a bit economical with the truth. When I later developed a relaxed personal relationship with him, I once found the temerity to tell him that my mother said he spoke too quickly in isiZulu and made grammatical errors. He laughed heartily and said his mother said the same.

I got to know Buthelezi well as he had previously requested NIS to establish an intelligence organisation for the KwaZulu government. I was responsible for developing the research component, providing training and regularly briefing him on the security situation in the country. In the process it became clear that he was also being briefed by military intelligence, mainly in the person of SAAF Major General Tienie Groenewald, whom I got to know well at CSI where he at one stage was my boss. Groenewald was known to have strong rightist convictions, and later became involved in rightist causes and organisations. It was perfectly obvious that he was conveying other perspectives to Buthelezi than I was, another example of the cross purposes between government agencies.

I had sympathy for Buthelezi, torn as he was between all sorts of divergent forces: his loyalty to the Zulu monarchy; his residual loyalty to the ANC, in spite of good intelligence at one time that they were planning to kill him; the exhortations by CSI that armed resistance was the only realistic option to defeat this onslaught against him, and their recruitment and training of 'security guards' for him; and the advice from NIS and others that a peaceful, negotiated solution was the only realistic option.

The KwaZulu representative and my counterpart in this joint intelligence effort was one M.Z. Nxumalo, who was later accused of alleged involvement in violent actions against the ANC in KwaZulu. As far as I am aware, this was never confirmed. When it was discovered that armaments were being stashed on the premises of our joint intelligence offices, NIS withdrew from the project. It is small wonder that Buthelezi was so hesitant and uncertain about joining the later negotiation process. Personally, I developed a liking for the man and a respect for his sincere dedication to his cause.

35

Paving the Way

The substance of the series of exploratory and preparatory meetings mentioned above has been exhaustively described and put on record by the media and others, and need not be reiterated in detail here. However, for the sake of narrative cohesion, brief recapping is in order.

Groote Schuur Minute

The historic Groote Schuur ('Big Barn') Estate in Cape Town where the first formal meeting between the government and the ANC took place was a seventeenth-century granary bought in the late nineteenth century from the Dutch East India Company by the mining magnate and arch-imperialist Cecil John Rhodes. He had it comprehensively rebuilt and refurbished by the renowned 'architect to the Empire', Sir Herbert Baker, who also designed the Houses of Parliament in India and the very similar Union Buildings in Pretoria. One can only wonder what Rhodes would have thought of the 'savages', both black and white to his way of thinking, taking over the seat of his grand vision of an Imperial British Africa to deliberate on the final destruction of his overbearing and iniquitous political heritage.

The meeting produced what is known as the Groote Schuur Minute, a brief document of two pages, the gist of which was that the government and the ANC committed themselves to resolve the 'present climate of violence and intimidation and to seek stability and a peaceful process of negotiations'. A working group was established to consider some vexing questions, such as the definition of a political prisoner, and to make recommendations regarding their release from prison and immunity from prosecution. The government reiterated its commitment to work towards lifting the state of emergency that was still in force. Effective channels of communication were established and a start was made with a process to determine the constitutional future of South Africa.

Pretoria Minute

The next major formal step was a meeting between the leaderships in early August 1990 at the Presidency in Pretoria. The parties recommitted to the

Groote Schuur Minute, and a report on the question of political offences and related aspects was compiled. The meeting produced the Pretoria Minute, a seminal document in directing the process to follow. In Paragraph 3, the ANC suspended the armed struggle to aid in bringing about a peaceful negotiated political solution as quickly as possible. A working group was established to 'resolve all questions arising out of this decision'. I was appointed as a government member to this 'Paragraph 3 working group'. The Pretoria conference was followed by a meeting at D.F. Malan Airport near Cape Town in February 1991, which considered, and in essence accepted, the report and reconfirmed what had been agreed upon before – a peaceful road towards constitutional negotiations.

The main theme of the Paragraph 3 working group's agenda was the implementation of the suspension of the armed struggle and 'related matters'. This included the return of the remaining exiles, in particular the military personnel of MK, their mustering in assembly points for demobilisation and the establishment of collection points for their weapons, including the identification and lifting of arms allegedly cached inside the country. One vexed question was the exact meaning of the 'suspension' of the armed struggle. Did it suggest that a resumption of the armed struggle would be held over the government's head like a sword of Damocles should the ANC not get its way in the negotiations? As far as I recall, it was Thabo Mbeki, who was only sometimes present, who suggested what was eventually recorded as follows:

> It is, therefore, clear that the suspension is not intended to be something of a purely arbitrary or transitory nature, but an ongoing condition meant to bring about a certain climate, viz. a peaceful solution. Since the parties have entered this agreement in good faith, it implies that from its side, the ANC has to take certain definite steps to effect the suspension of the armed struggle.

The ANC also undertook to cease related activities. The 'definite steps' to be taken towards this end included halting the recruitment, training and arming of MK members; moderating the struggle rhetoric and propaganda still emanating from the ANC; and curtailing its mass action, which tended to incite violence. Endless discussions took place on these and other points stipulated in Paragraph 3. These discussions were essentially inconsequential in practical terms, as none of the objectives was achieved – no assembly points were established, no returning MK cadres accommodated and formally demobilised, no arms caches were identified or lifted and no indemnity was granted. Phosa, one of the senior ANC negotiators in this group, told me in confidence that the ANC/MK did not know where their weapons were. Whether this was the truth or a negotiating technique is impossible to say, but given the chaotic, even non-existent, organisational and command and control structures in the ANC/MK, I tended to believe him.

An indication may be when Mac Maharaj, who was responsible for the infiltration of MK men and their arms into the country through Operation Vula even after negotiations had commenced, in a 2009 media interview evaded the question of what had happened to those weapons. The question of how many of those Kalashnikov assault rifles and Makarov and Tokarev pistols, all three regularly used in violent crimes in the country, are still in the hands of criminals and would-be revolutionaries in South Africa is politically and practically impossible for the ANC/MK to answer.

Nevertheless, the Paragraph 3 working group, like other discussion groups and contacts between the main parties, was an important confidence-building exercise in that it gave those on both sides the opportunity to get to know one another and develop a measure of mutual trust and conciliatory attitudes. Everyone started to focus on the facilitation of the process, rather than split hairs on the technicalities. Tacit agreement evolved to leave sticky, non-crucial bits aside. The report eventually submitted to the D.F. Malan Conference reflected this.

These Paragraph 3 meetings were jointly chaired by minister of law and order Adriaan Vlok and MK CO Joe Modise, who would later become minister of defence. The ANC members of the group who impressed me most were Modise and Chris Hani. Both highly intelligent and pragmatic, they contributed significantly to the group reaching agreement on some toffee aspects. Hani impressed me the most of all. His composure in even heated argument coupled with his resolve to achieve progress, moved others to begin to believe that progress could indeed be made. I suppose he had that intangible thing called charisma. But I still got the impression that he remained a relentless communist, intent on the ideological construct of 'democratic centralism'.

In contrast, Pallo Jordan, celebrated by the ANC as their in-house intellectual, impressed me the least. It was somewhat surrealistic that in one meeting he was the keynote and only speaker for the ANC side, with the rest of their contingent, including heavyweights like Mbeki, Hani and Modise, remaining silent throughout. It had obviously been arranged beforehand, but it was clear that Jordan had but a very tenuous grasp on the issues at hand and seemed far out of his depth. A personal joust I had with him across the table confirmed this impression. I could only surmise that it must have been intended to accommodate some factional interests, or to retard progress. But I later learnt to respect Jordan for retaining his independence of mind and integrity in the arcane depths of internal ANC politicking.

The NPA

In the face of increasingly violent clashes between mainly ANC and IFP supporters, and with persistent but unsubstantiated allegations of government complicity in fomenting the violence, the next important agreement was the National Peace Accord (NPA) signed in September 1991 by twenty-three parties and organisations. This emanated mainly from De Klerk's determined stance that negotiations could not progress with the continued violence hanging over the process. NPA signatories pledged to actively resist and denounce violent practices by all parties and individuals. It took place under the auspices of politically independent religious and business organisations, in particular the Consultative Business Movement represented by the able Dr Theuns Eloff, later rector and vice-chancellor of the University of Potchefstroom. Leaders of all major religions in the country also took part. Almost all political parties, leaders and interest groups bought into a countrywide network of regional and local peace committees as permanent implementation structures to monitor compliance with the Accord.

Crucially, the system created standing channels for dispute resolution, thus diverting the endless accusations and counter-accusations as to who were the perpetrators and who the victims in the continuing violence, particularly between the ANC and the IFP, away from the constitutional negotiations. Without the NPA it is unlikely that substantive negotiations would have concluded in the time they did. Although it did not stop the violence, the NPA had great value in that it promoted a culture of peaceful settlement of disputes and introduced people to mechanisms for achieving this. Its structures, under the central direction of a National Peace Committee (NPC) jointly chaired by top businessman John Hall and Methodist bishop Stanley Mogoba, through its regional and local subcommittees, established national coverage throughout the country. The Accord also introduced a new (to South

Africans) community-service approach to policing, and the conduct of the SAP and the SADF could also now be independently monitored. The transitional government later established under the Interim Constitution of 1993 utilised structures established by the NPA.

The ANC's Mo Shaik and I together managed the security subcommittee of the NPC jointly responsible for the security of the signing ceremony in a large conference room on an upper floor of the Carlton Hotel in Johannesburg. On the day of the signing, all of the VIPs were present, except for Nelson Mandela, whose slightly late arrival was of great concern to us, and, understandably, to Mo in particular. While we stood together in a staff room at the venue with a good view of the street and entrance below where Mandela was to enter, a large group of IFP members, a veritable *impi* carrying traditional weapons and chanting battle cries, or so it sounded to me, approached, dancing and prancing along in structured ranks. They filled the broad, cordoned-off street over its full breadth for a distance of about 100 metres. They were perfectly disciplined and under the effective control of marshals with whips and sticks jogging alongside. The display of discipline was impressive, but it was an intimidating and frightening sight and sound nonetheless.

Mo turned to me and said, somewhat agitatedly: 'Maritz, we must do something!' I asked him what he thought we should do and, in the absence of a response, I suggested we go down and speak to the Zulus. I turned my head to look at him to gauge his reaction, but he was no longer there. Instead, he was standing on the far side of the room as far away from me as he could get, as white as a sheet. I fully supported his unequivocally expressed rejection of my mischievous suggestion. In any event, the Zulus, maintaining perfect discipline, dispersed and there was no hindrance to Mandela's arrival or any disturbance to the proceedings.

The CDS

The Constitutional Development Service (CDS) was the prime mover of the negotiation process and I thought it would be good to get in on the action. I had already had about ten fulfilling years with NIS, and in the late 1980s my wandering spirit prompted me to start looking around for new challenges. I went to speak to the then head of CDS, Professor Andreas van Wyk, eminent legal scholar and later rector of the University of Stellenbosch. We agreed that I could well fit into that exciting environment. I did not follow it up then, but after a domestic upheaval in 1990 which saw me get divorced and marry a woman I worked with, I asked for a transfer to CDS. It was acceptable to the DG, at least partly I thought because my personal circumstances had caused him and NIS some embarrassment, although this was never said or even implied. Early in 1991, I was appointed to a post in CDS designated Chief Director Negotiations Support. Van Wyk had by then returned to academe and the new head, designated Constitutional Advisor, was Mr S.S. (Fanie) van der Merwe, who earlier had successively been DG of both the Department of Home Affairs and the Department of Justice, and had been involved in the discussions with Mandela on Robben Island.

After a month or two, I started to notice some management anomalies, which, as a presumptuous outsider, I thought needed to be brought to the attention of Deputy Minister Roelf Meyer. The head of the service was hopelessly inundated with managerial as well as substantive constitutional-development work. Fanie was a great guy with a razor-sharp legal mind and delightful wit, but I thought he did not much like managing. He was disdainful of that essential management tool, the meeting, like many people failing to distinguish between effective and ineffective meetings. In a memo to Meyer I suggested, among other things, that the job be split in two with Fanie saddled only with the constitutional work, which was increasing enormously as progress was being made in the negotiations, and that Niel Barnard be brought over from NIS as DG.

I never got any feedback and have no idea whether my input had any effect whatsoever, but the following year (1992) Barnard was brought in as DG of the former CDS, which had morphed into the Department of Constitutional Development. Van der Merwe could henceforth devote himself entirely to his constitutional and negotiation work. In this capacity he did outstanding work, supported by excellent people like Dr Henk Fourie, Professor Francois Venter, Dr Chris Maritz, Francois Beukman, Andrew Gray, Koos van der Merwe, Frans du Preez and Ando Donkers on the substantive side, and able support staff like Deon du Plooy and Johan Symington. My deputy, Dr Cobus Mostert, was indispensable to me, holding my hand in my new job in a new environment and standing in for me during my frequent job-related absences from the office. Moreover, he understood bureaucratic machinations in a civilian department, which I never did.

I was, among other things, responsible for managing the secretarial and support services of the peace process up to the signing of the NPA. In this regard I had almost nothing to do as I had an outstanding young man with me called Frans du Preez, who faultlessly did the work in this demanding job. John Hall, the co-chair of the NPC, expressed his fulsome appreciation for Frans's efficient services to the extent that I wondered whether he might be eyeing Frans for a job at the Ingwe coal-mining company, of which he was the chief executive. I was somewhat overstretched at the time and was even more thrilled with Frans's performance than Hall. It must be said that Bishop Mogoba and Hall in particular were firm but sensitive and pleasant chairpersons, successful in keeping their disparate charges on track in fulfilling the NPA's objectives.

Declaration of Intent

Numerous further meetings and discussions on the process and substance of the negotiations took place during the latter half of 1991, including between De Klerk and Mandela. With the NPA signed by almost all major political parties, business organisations, religious groups, trade unions and other non-governmental organisations, one more agreement was required to allay distrust and set the stage for substantive negotiations. In the plethora of discussions that had been taking place, the main parties had at least started to accept one another's *bona fides* in searching for a democratic solution through negotiation. A preparatory meeting for formal negotiations took place in early December 1991 under the joint chairmanship of judges Ismail Mahomed and Piet Schabort. It was here that nineteen political parties and other organisations resolved that the first plenary meeting of CODESA would be held at the World Trade Centre in Kempton Park on 20 and 21 December 1991. A Declaration of Intent, signed on 21 December by fifteen parties committed to the process, further served to allay suspicions between them. The substantive part of the Declaration reads as follows:

a. South Africa will be a united, democratic, non-racial and non-sexist state in which sovereign authority is exercised over the whole of its territory;

b. The Constitution will be the supreme law and that it will be guarded over by an independent, non-racial and impartial judiciary;

c. There will be a multi-party democracy with the right to form and join political parties and with regular elections on the basis of universal adult suffrage on a common voters roll; in general the basic electoral system shall be that of proportional representation;

d. There will be a separation of powers between the legislature, executive and judiciary with appropriate checks and balances;

e. The diversity of languages, cultures and religions of the people of South Africa will be acknowledged; and

f. All will enjoy universally accepted human rights, freedoms and civil liberties including freedom of religion, speech and assembly protected by an entrenched and justiciable Bill of Rights, and a legal system that guarantees equality of all before the law.

Sufficient consensus

The device of 'sufficient consensus' was developed, which became the basic norm in all further discussions and decision-making in the process. It implied that such sufficiency of consensus would have to include agreement by the government and the ANC, without which decisions would not be valid. This approach, to which there was bitter objection from other parties, was incorporated in the Record of Understanding signed in September the following year. Without this mechanism, majority decision would have been required in all matters to avoid disintegration of the whole process, which would have immeasurably extended if not stalled it. It is difficult to envisage what progress would then have been made between the many different parties with clashing ideologies, interests, personalities and egos.

The government and the ANC seemed to realise that they had become dependent on each other for their mutual extrication from the stalemate they had fought themselves into over many decades.

36

CODESA I

The first plenary session of CODESA took place at the World Trade Centre on 20 December 1991 under the chairmanship of Chief Justice Michael Corbett, assisted by Judge (later Chief Justice) Ismail Mahomed and Judge Petrus Schabort. The first order of the proceedings was the establishment of five working groups consisting of a total of thirty-eight delegates and thirty-eight advisors, one delegate and one advisor for each participating party per group. I was appointed advisor to government delegate Leon Wessels on working group 5 (WG5). I can't remember if I ever gave him any advice, but it was a great pleasure working with him. The government and the NP were separately represented in the negotiations, and I had on occasion to decline being appointed to any position as an NP representative. The distinction between Government and Party was very tenuous in those days, and henceforth I will from time to time refer to the government/NP.

WG5 was called something like 'Time Frames', and was charged with ensuring that all the other groups kept to deadline for their inputs to the Management Committee (MANCO) of the conference. The secretariat of MANCO consisted of the inimitable 'terrible twins' of the whole negotiation process, Fanie van der Merwe of the government/NP and Mac Maharaj of the ANC. Their job of keeping the process organisationally and procedurally on track and ensuring that the work got done still needs to be fully described, preferably by either or both of them. They developed an excellent working relationship and were a reassuring presence to all.

WG5 was something of a non-starter, as the other, more substantive groups would not be hurried in their sometimes contentious and acrimonious discussions, and rightly so. This was especially true in the case of working group 2 tasked with the development of a constitution, and whose failure to reach consensus led to the demise of CODESA. I had also been appointed as the security manager of the CODESA administrative office, and so welcomed the dysfunctionality of WG5. I was assigned to the Administrative Management Committee, where I got to work with some impressive people. A number of these were from the 'enemy', some from the SACP, others from MK and the ANC underground, whom I knew about long before there was any talk of meeting them in a work situation. This committee was chaired by Theuns Eloff from the Consultative Business Movement, who had been appointed the conference manager. Other members responsible for different portfolios included the able and affable Murphy Morobe (or Murph the Smurf), Billy Cobbett, the efficient Janet Love and Glenda Cohen, and the brilliant Andrew Feinstein. It was an enlightening and satisfying pleasure working with these and other capable people in the pleasant atmosphere maintained by Eloff from the chair, to a man and woman dedicated to the job at hand. Our work was purely managerial and I don't recall a political word uttered in meetings by anyone, except sometimes in light-hearted ribbing of one another.

An overarching technical Security Committee was also established for CODESA, comprising representatives from all involved parties, to which I was delegated by the government. This body, which carried the primary responsibility for the overall security of the convention, included a number of senior officers of the SAP, as well as representatives of the former homeland governments. To manage this committee, an overall command structure was established with Colonel Venter of the SAP and Mo Shaik of the ANC in joint overall command. There were six people under them who were responsible for devising a comprehensive security plan and arranging the procurement and deployment of security personnel, as well as the required technical security equipment. I was not part of this command structure and so could now start doing my day job at CDS.

With some provisional understandings reached and arrangements made, CODESA I, as it became known, was dissolved, and negotiations resumed in the new year as CODESA II. But seemingly irreconcilable differences remained and many matters still had to be resolved in further negotiations. Important discussions, both formal and informal, proceeded apace in the interim period.

37

Shepherd to the Elusives

My main job at CDS at the time was to liaise with parties and organisations who were known either to have rejected participation in the negotiation process, or to have shown hesitancy to join, to a large extent in reaction to the 'sufficient consensus' principle and the Record of Understanding. Such doubters were on both the right and the left of the political spectrum, ranging from fundamentalist white conservatives to black-consciousness revolutionary socialists and communists. This made for some interesting and instructive encounters. For the ultimate legitimacy of the entire negotiation process, it was important to at least make an effort to get as many organisations representing as many people as possible involved. I was to explain to these groups and individuals how important their participation would be to the future of the country, and the consequences of their exclusion.

Zeph Mothopeng

One of my early mediation errands was in mid-1990, when CODESA was still more than a year away and I was still at NIS. I was to speak to the late Zephania 'Zeph' Mothopeng, then president of the PAC. The PAC was an offshoot of the ANC that broke away in 1959 under the leadership of Robert Sobukwe. The main reasons for their defection were objections to the non-racialism of the ANC as embodied in the Freedom Charter adopted in 1955, and the related acceptance of the non-racial SACP as a partner in the struggle. As with the ANC from that very first meeting with Mbeki and Zuma in Lucerne in 1989, we had been trying to get parties and organisations to moderate their more unbridled propaganda and sloganeering, as it was making it difficult for the government to convince their support base that peaceful negotiation with the liberation movements had a reasonable prospect of success. One such slogan that particularly rankled with government supporters was the PAC's 'one settler, one bullet', 'settler' in their philosophy and nomenclature meaning a white person. It was used incessantly by both the PAC and the Azanian People's Organisation (AZAPO). I was to try to persuade Mothopeng to drop this slogan and made an appointment to see him at his home in Orlando East, Soweto. I took along a senior colleague.

A good part of Soweto was in turmoil at the time, with mobs on the streets and roads blocked with rocks, rubbish bins and burning tyres, and so we thought it prudent to go armed. What we would have done with our nine-mils in a mob situation wasn't at all clear, but such a comfortable weight under one's arm is always reassuring. In the event, Orlando East was a picture of serene calm – the locals were friendly and little ones ran next to the car in welcome. 'Uncle' Zeph was gracious and dignified, exuding gravitas in his humble and sparsely furnished yet spotlessly clean home. We were ushered in by a woman who offered us tea. He was sitting in an easy chair and apologised for not rising to greet us, but didn't explain why. He was obviously not well and indeed died about a year later.

Our host seemed quite surprised by our objection to 'one settler, one bullet', saying we were completely misunderstanding it. It was in fact intended to teach their supporters thrift in everything they did. We were so caught off guard by this explanation that both of us very impolitely burst out laughing. Zeph reacted with the widest of grins. The impact of his explanation was so overwhelming that I cannot recall whether we made any progress regarding the curtailing of the slogan or not.

APLA

The armed wing of the PAC, the Azanian People's Liberation Army (APLA), was a prominent player in the spate of atrocities being perpetrated in the country at the time. The horrific massacre in July 1993 of civilian congregants at devotions in St James Church in Kenilworth, Cape Town, by self-confessed APLA 'soldiers' – in which eleven people were killed and fifty-eight wounded – was a case in point. This virulence became more understandable to me some years later when new colleagues arrived at the National Intelligence Agency (NIA, the successor to NIS) in 1994. One of them, a personable young man from APLA, told me of his experiences in Cambodia being trained by and fighting for the heinous Khmer Rouge led by the psychopathic Pol Pot. This explained much about the excesses of which APLA was capable. The leadership of the PAC maintained that they had no control over APLA and that all enquiries should be directed to their HQ in Dar es Salaam.

After Mothopeng's death, I got to know the new leadership of the PAC. I developed respect for the sincerity of people like Barney Desai, Gora Ebrahim and Willie Seriti, who would later become a judge of the Supreme Court of Appeal. They attended the first plenary session of CODESA in

December 1991, but withdrew on the grounds that the convention had not been democratically constituted. At first they insisted that the negotiations take place in a neutral country under an independent chairman and with international oversight. However, once an agreement had been reached on an interim GNU with safeguards to their satisfaction, they relented and entered the process, eventually participating in the 1994 election.

AZAPO

My next stop was to speak to the intransigently anti-negotiation and black-power orientated AZAPO, which had contact with the radical Black Panthers movement in the USA. I spoke to one of their senior leaders, Nkosi Molala, in an effort to persuade them to moderate their polarising slogans and consider entering the process. A forbidding-looking man with a prominent scar running from over his left eye down his cheek to his chin, Molala proved to be friendly, intelligent and affable. In our discussions he asked me to call him by his first name, Nkosi, which literally means headman or chief or, in the Afrikaans vernacular of the time, the despised *baas* (boss), the mode of address of whites by blacks under apartheid. I objected to calling him Nkosi unless he called me Baas, which had him in stitches. I can't remember what he ended up calling me, but it wasn't Baas, and the good vibe that resulted moved us not one iota closer to their participation in the negotiations. Many years later, in 2010, I read a newspaper report telling of Molala's good works in uplifting youths in the black townships through his lifelong passion for soccer. Seeing the photo of him accompanying the report brought back pleasant recollections of our little encounter.

The Right

I also had the dubious privilege of having to speak to organisations to the right of the political spectrum. At the time, I counted about fifteen separate rightist groups in the country, all of which consisted overwhelmingly of Afrikaners with only a smattering of English-speakers here and there. A good number of the leaders, whom I contacted in an effort to arrange discussions, were in principle contemptuously dismissive of the negotiation process, often with the outspoken attitude that it was merely a construct of 'the communists and the anti-Christ to give our country away to the kaffirs'. A few were boorishly and personally abusive in conveying this to me. I never experienced any such abuse from even the most radical of the leftist groups, and I was not too diplomatic in dealing with it. And these didn't even include Eugène Terre'Blanche's Afrikaner Weerstandsbeweging (Afrikaner Resistance Movement). When I once reported that I was having difficulty getting in touch with them for an interview, I was told that this prickly pear was being handled 'at a different level'. I didn't think it was being handled at all.

But old-world Afrikaner gentlemen of even the far-right were a pleasure to talk to on a personal level, although sometimes it felt like we were from different planets, separated by cosmic distances. One such was Dr Walter Clark, the renowned physicist and engineer whom I understood to have been chiefly responsible for the development of South Africa's unique uranium enrichment process and nuclear arms capability. A dour but unfailingly courteous man of Scotch descent, he was shockingly honest in explaining at some length that the negotiations wouldn't be successful because blacks were incapable of producing anything of worth, whether in science or in politics. They would not be productive partners in government – the notion of a black majority government was clearly not even on the farthest horizons of his mind – as they did not have the skills and were incapable of acquiring them. Above all, they simply did not have command of the rational thought processes to contribute to governing a modern industrial state. His wrap, more or less verbatim, was that 'these dear people have the most beautiful singing voices in the world, but they're not capable of building a Mercedes Benz'.

I don't recall which group of rightists Oom Wally was part of, but he was apparently in a leadership position, certainly intellectually. They did not join the negotiation process and I don't know whether they were perhaps later subsumed into the rightist Freedom Front of General Constand Viljoen. I was, and still am, deeply saddened by these and other sincere Afrikaners in desperate distress for their crumbling world, but without a realistic thought on what to do about it. One of the saddest things I can imagine is for a human being to not have any vision of a positive future. They are, after all, also 'my people'.

COSAG

In the context of larger meetings some time later, I also became involved in discussions with the Concerned South Africans Group (COSAG) established by about twenty right-wing organisations in reaction to the Record of Understanding signed in 1992 between the government and the ANC. The founders and main players in COSAG were the remnants of the CP, led by Dr Ferdi

Hartzenberg, IFP leader Chief Mangosuthu Buthelezi and General Constand Viljoen. Viljoen had by then established the Volksfront (which later became the Freedom Front). Given the nature of his support base, I think this was perhaps the bravest act of that brave soldier Viljoen, bringing this group into the negotiations.

These leaders were certainly sincere in their concern for the future of South Africa, and took their parties into the process and the first general election in 1994, the IFP after much procrastinating and grandstanding, literally at the very last moment. The party's name and Buthelezi's picture were pasted onto the ballot paper after it had already been printed. Buthelezi protested that his photo had been 'squashed up to make me look like a monkey'.

I don't know whether I influenced any of those I spoke with to either join the negotiation process or remain outside, but it was an interesting and educational, sometimes disturbing, experience.

38

CODESA II and the MPNP

CODESA reconvened in May 1992 as CODESA II and it was clear that in spite of intensive lobbying and negotiations in the interim, fundamental and intractable differences between the parties remained. Both the government/ NP and the ANC also still had to contend with resistance from within their own ranks to aspects of what their principals were doing or not doing. The ANC was experiencing serious internal dissent from some factions against even the very fact of the negotiations taking place at all, and what was perceived by some as the ANC negotiators being on a losing tack in the process. President De Klerk also had to contend with serious internal resistance from conservatives within the NP and rightists without, but in a whites-only referendum he called early in 1992 on the question of whether he should continue with negotiations or not, he got a resounding empowering majority of 68 per cent from his constituency.

I have never understood the severe criticism levelled at De Klerk by even highly regarded Afrikaner academics and commentators that he allegedly misled his electorate on the question that was posed for the referendum. Surely the very concept of 'negotiation' necessarily implies give and take towards reaching consensus? What exactly did these objectors understand by the term? There were certainly disappointments in the final outcome, since exacerbated by a perfidious ANC government, but did his critics really expect him to get everything they demanded, which for some seemed to include a dispensation approximating the privileged status of whites and especially Afrikaners under apartheid? Did they want him to spell out such objectives in detail before even entering into negotiations? Or did they want him not to negotiate at all, and then with what foreseen and unforeseen consequences?

Boipatong

Violent clashes had been taking place in the township of Boipatong on the East Rand for some time, primarily between members of the IFP and the ANC. These centred mainly in and around large hostels for migrant workers, a relic of apartheid labour practices. These clashes came to a horrifying head on 17 June 1992, when forty-six people were killed. There were consistent rumours that so-called 'third force' elements of the SADF were involved in fomenting the violence, allegedly in support of the IFP. Nelson Mandela demonstratively took the ANC out of the talks, utilising the opportunity to regroup in the face of increasing internal resistance to the course the negotiations were taking, which some factions within the party saw as being to the detriment of the ANC. Mandela exerted huge pressure on De Klerk to do something about what he saw as the SADF running wild. This spelt the end of CODESA as the negotiating forum under that name. The ANC continued with their 'rolling mass action' which, among other things, in early September 1992 gave rise to the massacre at Bisho (now Bhisho), the capital of the former homeland of Ciskei.

Bisho

On 7 September 1992, a horde of ANC demonstrators under the leadership of that romantic communist revolutionary, Ronnie Kasrils, bravely stormed the barricades of the mighty Republic of Ciskei to liberate its citizens from oppression. But its ruler, Oupa Gqozo, hadn't read Ronnie's script and ordered his troops to open fire to protect the integrity of its borders. The battle led only to the tragic liberation of the souls of twenty-eight poor people. I was surprised to learn that Cyril Ramaphosa had been part of this assault. I simply couldn't picture him as a wild-eyed revolutionary facing fire across such a crude battlefield. His *metier* lay elsewhere in the struggle. The incident lent greater urgency to the negotiations to proceed.

Channel bilateral

Within minutes of the ANC storming out of the negotiations in reaction to Boipatong with scathing denunciations of the government, Cyril Ramaphosa phoned Roelf Meyer and said simply: 'Can we talk?' In August 1992, it was agreed between the ANC and the government that they would constitute what became known as the 'channel bilateral' for quiet continuation of dialogue out of the limelight. An exchange of documentation took place between De Klerk and Mandela and on 26 September 1992 they signed the Record of Understanding, which enabled negotiations to proceed.

The Record of Understanding caused much abiding resentment among other parties and in the country generally, giving rise to accusations that the government had 'folded' and 'given away the country' to the ANC. But the more sobering fact is that a momentous historical compromise had been reached, the fundamental objective of negotiation. It especially infuriated Buthelezi and his backers in the government and the SADF, and caused irreparable damage to his relationship with the NP, which he had unrealistically hoped, even insisted, would form an alliance with the IFP to defeat the ANC. But neither his IFP nor the NP would be of much consequence further on. The agreement opened the way for the resumption on 1 April 1993 of the stalled formal negotiations, now styled the MPNP, again to be held at the World Trade Centre in Kempton Park.

Further consequences of Boipatong

After the Boipatong incident and the aborting of CODESA II, De Klerk was determined to reassert his authority over the SADF and ward off Mandela's criticism. He instructed a senior SADF general, Pierre Steyn (SAAF), to investigate the allegations of complicity in the violence. I have not set eyes on Steyn's report, but have seen an interview with him in which he strenuously denied having recommended any action against anyone. Apparently De Klerk was not satisfied with this report, and appointed a judicial commission under Judge Richard Goldstone to further investigate the matter and make recommendations. Goldstone was provided with the services of the counterintelligence arm of NIS as an investigative capability. The commission conducted a surprise raid on a deep-cover facility of the Directorate Covert Collection (DCC) of CSI in the east of Pretoria where some unspecified irregularities were apparently discovered.

Apart from what I subsequently read in newspapers and was told piecemeal, but unconfirmed, by others, I am not sure of the exact sequence of these events and do not know what was in Goldstone's report. But I thought the raid by Goldstone on such a sensitive facility was out of order. An instruction from the president to the chief of the SADF would, with the assistance and supervision of NIS and SAP elements, have ensured full access to the facility, with measures taken beforehand to safeguard sensitive secrets from unauthorised eyes and prevent the removal or destruction of any records that might be pertinent to the investigation.

Brigadier Tolletjie Botha, CO of the DCC, reported to Deputy CSI Major General Chris Thirion. Thirion was in turn accountable to CSI Lieutenant General Joffel van der Westhuizen. De Klerk was intent on reaffirming his role as commander-in-chief of the SADF, and indicated that he wanted to dismiss some personnel, which had to include people of senior rank.

According to reports, he consulted with CSI Van der Westhuizen, Chief of the Army Lieutenant General George Meiring, and Chief of the SADF General Kat Liebenberg. The guillotine fell on Botha, Thirion and twenty-one other SADF personnel, patently on the recommendation of their superiors. Liebenberg and Van der Westhuizen were the direct line of command on whose instructions Thirion had been carrying out his high-risk job. I got sight of a report in tabulated form by Goldstone's investigating team. Next to Thirion's name, under the heading 'Transgressions' it read 'None', and under 'Recommended action' it read 'None'.

I knew Thirion and Botha well as honourable and utterly dedicated officers of unblemished integrity. Both were also sensitive human beings, and both were devastated. Botha, who was the instructor on my first training course when I started at military intelligence in 1968, fell ill shortly afterwards with cancer and died soon after. Some close to him are convinced it was psychosomatic. Thirion struggled for a long time to make peace with this cruel twist. He insisted that a general court martial be convened to try him and provide an opportunity for him to state his case. This was refused and so he sued De Klerk in a civilian high court for unfair dismissal. Before the case got to court, De Klerk offered him a self-exculpatory sort of apology which Thirion accepted to put an end to the painful ordeal.

I told Thirion, a good friend but who would not speak to me on the facts of the events,* that I thought he was wrong in directing his resentment towards De Klerk. Instead his understandable wrath should rightfully be aimed at his three military superiors. De Klerk would not have known who to fire when he decided to find scapegoats; he had scant experience of the structures and workings of the SADF, and was not very familiar with its personnel. To my mind it could only have been done on the recommendations of Van der Westhuizen and ultimately Liebenberg.

With this drastic action, De Klerk, at a crucial time, alienated his most important back-up instrument of coercive force in the negotiations, if only psychologically. I thought under the circumstances he should have told Mandela to go 'jump in the lake', and undertaken to set matters right in the SADF only if it should prove necessary. But this was not his style, and he had neither the experience nor the inclination to wield such coarse authority.

---

* But see his exposé of the full sequence of events in Hilton Hamann's *Days of the Generals* (Zebra Press, 2001).

Mandela probably sniggered up his sleeve. Of course, it is still open to De Klerk to publish the Steyn and Goldstone reports to fully explain his actions.

To me, as an outsider to these events and especially in light of Thirion's efforts to be heard publicly in a military court marshal or by way of litigation in the High Court, it boiled down to a flagrant reneging by his military superiors on their duty of loyalty to a subordinate who had been following the mandate and instructions they had given him, whether directly or by necessary implication. They must certainly have been aware of the purpose of the DCC and its facility that was raided, as well as the constant high risk it entailed. Even if *bona fide* mistakes had been made lower down, at least one of them should have fallen on his sword, rather than shafting their subordinates. Only if Thirion, Botha and the others had deliberately ignored or contravened standing instructions or direct orders, thereby acting insubordinately, which I don't for a moment believe happened, would their superiors have been absolved from taking the blame. Who else but they arbitrarily decided how far the buck should rise before it stopped?

A master's geography graduate from Stellenbosch University, Thirion, who commanded a company of the Parachute Battalion at the tender rank of lieutenant, is knowledgeable on Afrikaans literature, opened at least one exhibition of South African paintings I know of and is a raconteur and humorist of note, especially when it comes to stories of his native South West Africa and the fascinating characters one finds there. Above all, perhaps, he is a child of nature, for which he harbours a passionate love and on which he is expert over a wide field; a consummate naturalist, in fact. And all of this over and above a lifelong career as a dedicated soldier with an incisive and innovative military mind, but who did not always sit comfortably with his peers and superiors.

It was a grossly unfair ending to a marvellous career and Thirion was deeply traumatised by the events, which haunted him for a long time. I suspect that they still do to some extent. However, in the aftermath he made a great success of a widely popular restaurant he established in the east of Pretoria, Die Werf. Serving traditional South African dishes, his personal culinary skills made it popular also with overseas tourists and travel agents.

Chris Thirion is an example of that rare combination of a free-spirited Renaissance man wrapped in the uniform of a professional soldier with decorations and insignia of rank testifying to an excellent career.

39

Decent Employment

With the new overall joint security structures in place for the MPNP, my job in that regard came to an end. One of my last memories of this process is of being at the World Trade Centre very early one morning, overseeing our daily electronic sweeping of the government and NP offices for bugs that may have been planted during the night. I came across Gill Marcus of the ANC in the passage. I was surprised to see her there at that time and suspected that she could well have been on a similar mission. I had previously got to know about Gill from her activities for the ANC in London, where she was among other things involved in producing ANC publications. I had also been on some or other committee with her during the earlier negotiations. I said something like: 'Good heavens Gill! What are you doing here at this unearthly hour? You should be at home in bed.' Gill, in a flash: 'Oh, now that's the nicest invitation I've had in years.' I have always found such a ready wit immensely attractive in women, but I never saw or spoke to Gill again.

My other job of trying to shepherd standoffish organisations and individuals towards the process (who said something about herding cats?) was also almost done, and my undemanding role in the Administrative Management Committee was becoming even more so with the advent of the MPNP. The dysfunctional WG5 of CODESA had simply ceased working without being formally dissolved, as far as I knew, leaving me at something of a loose end. But I soon became involved in some other interesting activities.

The BGH

Some time towards the end of 1991 or the beginning of 1992, I was assigned to the support staff of a cabinet committee known as the Beleidsgroep vir Hervorming (BGH; Policy Group for Reform). I am uncertain whether this is the same committee referred to in some documentation as the Cabinet Committee for Negotiation, but a distinction between the two would anyway have little meaning as they were sure to have had largely overlapping purposes and membership. My job entailed regularly attending meetings of the BGH, which was the forum for cabinet members involved in the negotiations to give feedback to their colleagues and plan ways forward. It was attended on and off by pertinent senior officials involved like Fanie van der Merwe, Niel Barnard and Mike Louw. I was one of the regulars together with Marius Kleynhans, a very bright communications man, and former State Legal Advisor, Advocate Jan Heunis, then practising at the Bar in Cape Town and contracted to assist the government in the negotiation process.

When I started there, the committee was chaired by minister of constitutional development Dr Gerrit Viljoen, who was soon to be replaced by his successor, Roelf Meyer, when he fell ill. Meyer's deputy then was Dr Tertius Delport – a not-too-happy union that wouldn't last. Delport was a likeable man's man with a keen legal mind, but his vision did not stretch to the unavoidable realities of the time. Not long after Meyer's appointment, Delport was shifted to another department as a full minister, I think, and replaced by Fanus Schoeman, an engagingly unassuming reformist.

From where I and the other officials sat at the bottom of the table, the attendees arranged themselves appropriately to the left and right. The 'reformist' members in the persons of, among others, Dawie de Villiers, Sam de Beer, Leon Wessels and sometimes Kobie Coetsee, sat on the left, and the 'conservatives', Hernus Kriel, Tertius Delport and André Fourie, on the right. I don't recall who else was there, but these were the main players. Minister Pik Botha flitted in and out but was seldom there, and when he was, he seemed somewhat out of sorts. I don't recall him having a fixed seating position and he mostly stood around, although never for long, as I recall. De Klerk sometimes also chaired the meeting, especially when sticky subjects were on the agenda, which, although at times very difficult, I always thought he handled well. Conflict between the left and the right was pervasive and often acrimonious.

I never got the impression that there was a laid-down strategy with non-negotiable bottom lines and negotiables spelt out for all negotiators to adhere to, but from the *O'Malley Archives* it appears that guidelines and a model for a constitution had been circulated in the AB under the chairmanship of Professor De Lange. These were obviously not meant for the eyes of us lesser mortals. In the BGH, a seemingly pragmatic approach in the true tradition of politics as the art of the possible prevailed, with regular consideration given to what the ANC was likely to accept and what not. I am not for a moment suggesting that this was the guiding principle by which the government conducted the negotiations, but it was the process in the BGH, where the tactical situation was on the agenda on a regular basis.

Some of De Klerk's ideas seemed strange, like group rights and a permanent

GNU with a rotating presidency, dead horses that he continued to flog even though they had been buried by the Record of Understanding, and despite, I was told, his being warned that their continued raising could only discredit their promoters without any prospect of success. But it must be understood that these ideas reflected trains of thought within the AB, from which we can glean that De Klerk was probably, at least to some extent, beholden to their 'caucus'. But there were other attitudes of his that I found puzzling.

In 1996, when the new Constitution was finalised by the Constituent Assembly of Parliament, parties had to approve it for forwarding to the Constitutional Court for its assent. What to this day baffles logic is De Klerk's refusal to approve the Constitution and at the same time keep the NP in the GNU – for him it was either the one or the other, but not both. I understand that, to his chagrin, he had been subjected to much vilification by President Nelson Mandela in the joint cabinet. He certainly would have been justified in demanding at least proper respect as the former head of state and the man who had bravely taken the country into the peaceful national settlement process.

He was also under pressure from the right wing of the NP to 'preserve our traditional power base' (meaning conservative white voters), a mantra espoused by Marthinus van Schalkwyk especially. But how the juxtaposing of the two issues could help him in negotiating these dilemmas is beyond me. After Leon Wessels, the deputy chairman of the Constituent Assembly that finalised the Constitution, and Roelf Meyer, both of whom had for a number of years slaved at the tortuous construction of the Constitution, told him that they would vote for approval no matter what the party decided, De Klerk agreed to approve the Constitution, but pulled the NP out of the GNU.

From the limited personal contact I had with De Klerk, I got to like this intellectually superior and immensely engaging man very much indeed. I fully understood and sympathised with him in his well-publicised personal domestic upheaval, having experienced a similar trauma shortly before and knowing how it affected one's equilibrium. The traumatic demise of the P.W. Botha era and the advent of his own must surely also have left their mark. He has since been doing excellent work on behalf of sanity and good governance through his F.W. de Klerk Foundation and personal appearances on domestic and international platforms, including on behalf of minority rights and their protection. I also think his being awarded the Nobel Peace Prize jointly with Nelson Mandela was fully justified.

But I regretted his withdrawal of the NP from the GNU in June 1996, which had all the promise of having an ongoing influence on the government for at least another five years, as well as perhaps a longer opportunity to shape the future of the country. If his personal position in cabinet had become untenable, he could have resigned the leadership of the NP and called an election for a new party leader to continue in the GNU. He did in fact leave active politics not long after, and Marthinus van Schalkwyk became the leader of the so-called New National Party (NNP). After a brief, disingenuous alliance with the DP in the form of the Democratic Alliance (DA), Van Schalkwyk took himself and the remnants of his party into the ANC, where he garnered a cushy job for himself in the cabinet, destroying his party in the process.

I still cannot recall a single occasion when the conservatives in the BGH came up with any constructive suggestions or demands that had any realistic prospect of success. In one evening meeting, André Fourie rather viciously blamed the officials for what he saw as their leading the political decision-makers by the nose in directions he could not accept. Fanie van der Merwe, the most senior official guiding the process from the government's side, took huge offence and climbed into Fourie in no uncertain terms. During a sudden lull in the resulting cacophony, Jan Heunis, without even bothering to affect a stage whisper, asked me across the table, 'Maritz, are you going to vote for these guys again?' There was a general jerking of oversized heads in our direction, but no one said anything. Perhaps they did get a message of some sort.

Jan Heunis is a highly intelligent, principled and likeable man. As is often the case with very clever people, he tended to talk a bit over the heads of his audience in the BGH when reporting on legal perspectives emerging from the negotiations. Simply put, they did not always understand what he was saying. I have regarded Jan as a good friend ever since we first met as government officials, although we have since had very little contact. I have great respect for the man as well as the intellect.

In 2007 Jan published a readable little book, *The Inner Circle: Recollections from the Last Days of White Rule*, on his experiences close to various fires in government service. It is a rather curious mixture of a eulogy to the Heunis clan and a hatchet job on P.W. Botha. It contains photos of his father, himself as chairman of the students' branch of the NP and as a member of the students' representative council (SRC) at Stellenbosch University, and of himself, his father and his son on a fishing outing. It is, nonetheless, quite a good read that includes his telling of the thwarted AB machinations in the run-up to his election to the SRC. This was not exactly an earth-shattering event, but it is an interesting illustration of the pervasive influence of the 'Super-Afrikaners'* of the AB towards preserving its control of even lesser Afrikaner institutions. But the book also contains much of more profound interest regarding the constitution-making process.

The book recounts an unfortunate incident between his father, the late Chris Heunis, and P.W. Botha in the context of the even more unfortunate 'Rubicon speech' saga. He blames Botha for truly uncouth behaviour towards his father, and will not hear of any merit Botha may otherwise have had regarding the process leading up to the negotiations for the New South Africa. Jan is understandably disgusted at his father's treatment, who was after all a senior cabinet minister, the Cape leader of the NP and a lifelong colleague and supporter of Botha.

However, he had only his father's telling of the incident as a source, which I don't for a moment question, but, like me and everyone else, Jan wasn't there. He dismisses with thinly disguised disdain the official biography of Botha by Dr Daan Prinsloo, a researcher in Botha's presidency, which one should, of course, scrutinise with caution. Jan has clearly retained a visceral contempt for Botha, even berating me, some time before in an exchange of letters to the press in another context, for having the temerity to plead that Botha's sometimes unfortunate public persona should not obscure the fact that he was the originator of our process of reform.

Botha did in fact initiate the process through, for example, rescinding some cornerstone apartheid legislation; his 'adapt or die' speech in Upington given some time before; establishing the Tricameral Parliament that despite its dire shortcomings was at least symbolic of non-racial governance for a future South Africa; declaring the homelands policy dead; asserting that South Africa would in future be governed as a whole by all its people; and supporting and facilitating, through the SSC, the first official meetings with the exiled ANC in Europe. And all of this in the face of much right-wing opposition. At the launch of his book in Stellenbosch, Heunis stated his conviction that Botha would never have done away with apartheid because the

---

* Ivor Wilkins and Hans Strydom, *The Super-Afrikaners: Inside the Afrikaner Broederbond* (Johannesburg: Jonathan Ball, 1978).

latter had once in a private moment confessed to him that he didn't like black people. Although I also thought Botha had probably reached the limit of his elasticity as far as reform was concerned, I was surprised at such a profound prognosis from such a flimsy factual basis.

Minister of justice Kobie Coetsee was a nominal member of the BGH, but his presence there (or not) was quite enigmatic. He was charged with arranging a general amnesty for participants on both sides of the armed struggle, but seldom attended meetings and, in spite of numerous requests, never once gave feedback regarding progress. He was even absent at a special meeting called for the sole purpose of receiving a report from him on the subject. His only reaction whenever questioned on this matter was that it was in hand and progressing satisfactorily. In the event, amnesty was never agreed to or granted on his watch, giving rise to serious political complications later, including in the context of the TRC. I was surprised that he was apparently never seriously taken to task for his disgraceful conduct in this regard. To this day I have never seen or heard of any record of what he did or achieved, except that nothing came of it.

Coetsee, since deceased, was a complex personality. When Botha was asked in an interview after his retirement why he had kept Coetsee in the cabinet for so long, he replied that he wondered about that himself, unkindly referring to Coetsee as an '*eienaardige mannetjie*' (a strange little man). One evening, in the early stages of the CODESA process, I was in the foyer of the World Trade Centre talking to our security people when Coetsee literally came stumbling out of the conference hall, barely able to stay on his feet. He was blue in the face, sweating profusely and with obviously distressed breathing. I rushed up to him and he clung to me. I was convinced he was having a heart attack and told a nearby security man to urgently call the ambulance and doctor that were always on standby there.

I tried to get him to lie down on the floor so as to administer CPR, but he resisted this and appeared to regain his breath somewhat. I told him to relax, the ambulance and doctor would be there shortly. He then seemed to go into a frenzied panic and I was afraid he would have a seizure. Astonishingly, he alternately pleaded with me and ordered me to cancel the ambulance and doctor. Another man turned up who seemed to know what was going on – I think he was either Coetsee's driver or bodyguard – who said the minister would be 'all right'. I assumed that it must have been a known condition. I was once again amazed at how important image was to politicians; anything to avoid being tagged with any weakness, apparently more important than life itself.

The Roelf and Cyril Show

After the implosion of CODESA II as a result of the Boipatong incident, both sides were forced into some serious rethinking on the issues and process. After being appointed as the 'channel bilateral' in August 1992, Roelf Meyer and Cyril Ramaphosa established an excellent working and apparently personal relationship as well, and played a crucial role in keeping the substantive negotiations on track. I was appointed as a personal assistant to Meyer, and Dr Penuell Maduna, later a cabinet minister, acted in a similar capacity to Ramaphosa. There was no fixed job description, but it entailed arranging and attending meetings between the two, and general coordinating and secretarial work as required. I don't know about Penuell, but my job was varied and interesting, developing into that of a general factotum, fetcher and carrier, dogsbody, whatever else you could call it. But I was not always present at confidential discussions on substantive matters between the two principals.

It was a singular pleasure working closely with Meyer. A keen legal mind, with steady nerves and imperturbable calm, he was in the most absolute sense dedicated to the cause at hand. He worked his fingers to the bone in pursuit of what he passionately believed in: a democratic South Africa. Above all, he was a decent human being, without any of the bluster and bombastic *machismo* associated with gung-ho politicians. In traditional Afrikaner politics, this demeanour was probably a drawback. Nonetheless, Meyer rose in the estimation of the party apparatchiks to become regarded as the natural successor to F.W. de Klerk as the national leader of the NP, having already been elected as leader of the powerful Gauteng NP when Pik Botha resigned following the party's withdrawal from the GNU in 1997.

Meyer was by nature a non-confrontational reconciler who did not like conflict and preferred to avoid it. This stood him in good stead in his job as the government's top negotiator, in which much reconciliation between widely varying ideologies, world views and political ambitions was required. As one of the most junior cabinet ministers, he was appointed to succeed the venerable Dr Gerrit Viljoen as minister of constitutional development, and as such presided over the heavyweights in the BGH. Some cynics say this appointment was intended to provide a convenient fall guy for De Klerk should things go wrong, which is probably mere mischief-making. Meyer more than once told me how much he appreciated the unwavering support he got from the president.

Much opprobrium has been and still is being heaped on De Klerk and Meyer as the government's main players in the negotiations. They are alleged to have been derelict in allowing the ANC 'to get everything they wanted', such as not having achieved more for the protection of the Afrikaans language and minorities (meaning mainly Afrikaners). Much vitriol is spewed in the mainstream media and on social websites such as Facebook and others. Even highly regarded public commentators seem to think they 'sold out' Afrikaner interests. Some of these commentators, seemingly oblivious to the irony, sometimes absurdly quote as authoritative sources on Meyer's performance statements by the brilliant arch-propagandist of the SACP, Joe Slovo, Cyril Ramaphosa, Meyer's direct adversary, and Colin Eglin, former leader of the opposition in Parliament and a severe, sometimes effective, critic of the NP.

It must be borne in mind that there was strong resistance in important left-wing and delusional 'victorious' military quarters in the ANC to any negotiation at all, and they needed to be reassured of the success of their negotiators, especially in having had to accept the bane of the left: the free market economy with all its attendant property and other rights. Understandably, Slovo did his best to reassure his communist and socialist followers and masters in Moscow. But the greatest irony of all this vilification is that critics of Meyer's performance, together with many of the international world's top jurists and statesmen, almost unanimously acknowledge that the end result was an exemplary democratic instrument to underpin the new statehood of South Africa. Surely, if De Klerk and Meyer have to bear the brunt of criticism, they should also receive fulsome credit for this outcome?

Accusations are often based on allegations that Meyer 'folded' or 'caved in, giving the country away to the ANC on a platter'. It has even been said that De Klerk on one occasion supposedly said: 'God, Roelf, you have given the country away!' This is said to have resulted from Meyer's acceptance of the principle of a black majority government. The fact of the matter is that Meyer was not a free agent mandated to give anything away, least of all to Cyril Ramaphosa in the bilateral, but was accountable to the president and cabinet. The understanding developed that any agreement or accommodation reached in subordinate forums would be referred back to principals for endorsement, who could then refer it back to the groups for 'revisiting' if deemed necessary. It happened quite often that decisions were so referred back to the various smaller negotiation groups for renegotiation, adjustment or merely finessing.

Any decision by Meyer was therefore susceptible to such referral, and there has not been any instance of which I am aware where he gave anything away that could not be redeemed through this mechanism, if the president or cabinet should have so decided. Meyer and Ramaphosa between them did not conclude final agreements. I have never seen anyone offering any concrete evidence of where, when and in what way Meyer is supposed to have given the country away, and how it happened that this was not reviewed in the accepted way. The president and cabinet could have simply refused to accept any such agreement, stalled or aborted the negotiations, even fired Meyer, if it were a non-negotiable matter. Perhaps some of those ostensibly in the know could provide answers to these important questions.

One must also bear in mind that the appointment of the relatively junior Meyer as the minister responsible for the negotiations and chief negotiator engendered much small-minded jealousy and resentment from some of his colleagues, mostly of the conservative school of thought. I am convinced that much of the vitriol levelled at him originated from this. What really happened, I suspect, is that many people thought the government were up to their usual tricks when they said that they sought a truly democratic nego- tiated solution. To the surprise of such people, for once they meant what they said. Another widely held misapprehension is that the government had unlimited options. There were similar misapprehensions in ANC quarters, especially from their mythically victorious MK, giving rise to serious internal tensions in that party as well.

Constitution 1993

Early in 1993 I was assigned as a government representative on a bilateral (government and ANC) technical legal committee charged with producing a draft of the Interim Constitution which was adopted that year. My contribu- tion was negligible, but to witness great minds at work at such close quarters was an exceptional privilege. The ANC team on the committee was headed by the impressive Arthur Chaskalson and included the brilliant Mohammed Valli Moosa and Joe Slovo, Dullah Omar, Thabo Mbeki and Mathews Phosa. The government side was led by Roelf Meyer, who was supported by out- standing people like Fanie van der Merwe, Niel Barnard, Jan Heunis, Johan

Kruger and Francois Venter, the last two highly regarded professors of public law at the University of Potchefstroom contracted by the government. Francois Venter, later dean of the law faculty at North West University (formerly Potchefstroom), was a particularly impressive colleague. Soft spoken and unassuming, he was an immensely hard worker tasked primarily with drafting the results of discussions in legal format, regularly overnight writing up the day's results to be available for consideration the following day. Above all, he conducted exhaustive research into constitutions and constitutionalism worldwide, making him an unsung hero of the process of law-making for democratisation.

On one occasion, the future of the existing four provinces of the country was under discussion in the committee. I suggested that for various pragmatic reasons the provinces should remain as they were up to the conclusion of the five-year GNU period. The dissolution and reintegration of systems of governance and management, the multiplication of capacities in human resources that would be required, the distribution of assets, the devising of new borders for the mooted nine new provinces, and other aspects such as financial arrangements, would require much careful thought and time for negotiated readjustment. To my surprise, I got support from Dullah Omar, who argued the matter along the same lines. But his colleagues strongly differed, and I realised how determined the ANC was to create as many new centres of power for political control purposes as possible, and to create a whole tranche of high-level jobs for their cadres throughout the country.

During a tea break in the proceedings, Niel Barnard and I stood discussing matters in general with Thabo Mbeki and I mentioned the question of the provinces again. Astonishingly, Mbeki was instantly almost beside himself with anger, saying things with clear racist implications like 'you people still think blacks are unable to govern themselves', and much else. Barnard and I both protested that this matter was a purely technical one with no political or racial connotations, but he was unrelenting and walked away – a veritable tantrum it was. I was surprised by this irrational outburst from a man I had come to like and respect for his clear and rational thinking and pleasant demeanour. This was the first intimation I got of this intelligent man's deep-seated resentments and the huge racist chip on his shoulder. I was not surprised when these traits later came out so clearly when he led the government and country.

When I took early retirement in March 1996 from government service while with NIA, Dullah Omar, as minister of justice and constitutional development, was also responsible for the intelligence services. I wrote to him to take my leave and thank him for the pleasant professional and personal association we had had for some years. I got a gracious letter back from him thanking me and referring to the incident related above, saying that, looking at the state of the nine provinces then, it seemed to him that we had been right.

40

Reversion

I was thrilled when the draft Interim Constitution, Act 200 of 1993, was accepted by the MPNP late in 1993. Although I did not have any particular role in producing it, I had witnessed from close up how all sides had put in incredibly hard work. I was still at the Department of Constitutional Development after the advent of the new regime in 1994, but had seemingly run out of jobs there. I got a call from Mike Louw, then DG of NIS, informing me that negotiations for the integration of the various separate intelligence services into the new NIA had started, and asking that I consider returning to NIS to assist with this convoluted process. It would be a testing task, fraught with much political tension. More out of loyalty to the old firm and Louw than good sense, I agreed and was transferred back to NIS in early 1994. It was a bad judgement call that also deprived me of the opportunity to be involved in the parliamentary process of producing the final Constitution of 1996.

It was a distinctly unpleasant and unhappy time for me being involved in establishing two new civilian intelligence services, the NIA and SASS. I was appointed Chief Director Domestic Collection in NIA, a near equivalent to my former job of Chief Director Operations in NIS. Owing to insurmountable differences and tension between me and the new deputy minister of intelligence, Joe Nhlanhla, I finally, at my request, retired prematurely from government service in March 1996.

My last act was a circular to all senior subordinates and regional managers explaining that I could no longer with a clean conscience mislead them into thinking that I was still seeing to their and their work's interests by remaining in office, while no longer having either the influence or authority to do so. I was not prepared to carry responsibility for matters with which I didn't agree and could not control, and simply did not have any other moral option left. It was a sad ending for me to an immensely fulfilling career in intelligence, but also a great relief. For the first time in my life, however, it also left me with a feeling of failure and regret at a job not well done. Owing to security constraints and my continuing goodwill towards the intelligence community of South Africa, I will not elaborate on the full circumstances that brought this about. The current situation in the intelligence community, as reported in the media from time to time, adequately reflects my reasons for retiring prematurely.

BEGINNING V
End Game

41

Interregnum

After leaving NIA I was at a complete loss as to what to do with my time, of which I suddenly had bucketfuls. I applied for a total of forty-one jobs, from selling Alpha Romeos or BMWs, to many positions advertised in the civil service, from research at the National Archives in Pretoria, to positions in the South African National Defence Force (SANDF, formerly the SADF) and with firms of attorneys. It became clear that there were simply no jobs available to a retired man of fifty-eight with my 'dubious' background. Some of my friends found it strange that I was unable to relax, enjoy my new freedom and concentrate on some or other hobby, but I had none. I became quite frantic at not being able to find a way of switching off after a lifetime as a workaholic. It was a terrible blow to my self-image, and I discovered for myself how soul-destroying unemployment must be for younger people, especially those with children to feed and educate. I have no doubt that I would steal if I couldn't legitimately provide food for my children. Who wouldn't? The only success I had was in working on my wife's nerves at home. I sometimes think I was on the verge of some psychological hiccup at that stage.

I gradually took to heart the admonishments to get a hobby and got constructively involved in two things that had interested me throughout most of my life: environmental conservation and translation. I joined the Honorary Rangers of the South African National Parks and did their qualifying training, and got accredited as a translator with the South African Translators' Institute. These were important lifelines to my mental health, but did not help much to earn income for the household to supplement my somewhat meagre pension due to my premature retirement. This situation put strain on my marriage, which later spun out of control, leading to my second divorce. I was completely shattered, but it was all my own doing. I felt it was about time to start working on my bucket list.

Fortunately, some quite exciting opportunities and diversions crossed my path, to the rescue of my sanity. As a first priority I became reconciled with my first wife and mother of my children, which restored to me the family unit I had forfeited, albeit now consisting of physically dispersed adults. This provided me with a solid foundation from which to start regaining balance. I owe them all my sincerest gratitude.

Together with two fellow retirees from NIA, Dr Daan Opperman, with whom I had shared so much friendship and adventure, and Dr Cobus Scholtz, we established a security-risk assessment company. However, after about a year I resigned because of a serious clash with the latter about the future of our enterprise. Before that we had been asked by Q Data, then a leading IT company, to establish an electronic-security subsidiary, Q Tronic, but it didn't last long. Q Data had tendered for a contract put out by the Department of Transport for a new card-format driver's licence, but they 'got a message' that they would not get the contract while I was with their establishment. After two months and before I was to submit my first (positive) report to the main board (I had been made managing director of Q Tronic – I still wonder why), I was asked to leave because Q Tronic 'was not performing to expectations'. We were in fact at that stage on the verge of coming to an arrangement with the large British electronic-security company that had been responsible for that aspect at the Olympic Games in Atlanta, Georgia in 1996.

Mac Maharaj was then minister of transport, and I later read that the contract for the driver's licence was awarded to Prodiba, a subsidiary of Nkobi Holdings, a company owned and managed by Schabir Shaik. When we retired from NIA, I personally spoke to Maharaj, as we did with some other acquaintances then in senior government positions. We had a pleasant discussion in his office and I gave him a copy of our brochure, offering him and his department our services. I later understood, without confirmation, that Q Data did get a share of the contract for their IT expertise.

On invitation, I then attached myself to the successful attorneys' firm of a long-standing and highly appreciated friend, Braam van der Walt, in Pretoria. By agreement I received no income from the firm except for what I produced myself but, frankly, I can't remember doing anything that may have warranted being paid for. But I appreciated Braam's generosity in giving me a place to sit and entering me as a professional assistant on his letterhead, later even grandiosely 'consultant'. Some time later I gravitated to another attorneys' practice in Pretoria, De Wet Du Plessis, where I could concentrate on conveyancing, which I thought was the part of the law I remembered best.

The fact of the matter, however, was that I had, over the almost thirty years since having last been in practice, forgotten half of the law, while the other half had changed, leaving my competence in matters legal at only slightly above nil. And the conclusion I had reached many years before as an articled clerk that I wasn't really suited to practising law was reconfirmed. While with De Wet Du Plessis, I won an old friend and private client, Mbigi Mahlangu, a settlement of R1.2 million in a dispute with a former employer and didn't debit fees, surely the ultimate disqualifier for an attorney. I have never learnt to money-think.

Also while with De Wet Du Plessis, a thunderbolt struck our family in 1998 when our younger son, Cobus, just turned twenty-nine, was diagnosed with cancer. I left Pretoria to be with him in Cape Town. Happily, at the time of writing he has been in remission for close on twelve years. He is a pillar of support and care to his family, in particular his parents, but also to his siblings and his wide circle of friends.

During this period I became involved in politics once again.

42

The United Democratic Movement

After the adoption by Parliament of the new Constitution in 1996, both Bantu Holomisa and Roelf Meyer fell foul of internal machinations in their respective political parties.

Roelf Meyer

Meyer was still the minister of constitutional development in the GNU. The NP had been holding a series of *bosberade* (getaways) to devise ways of shedding its negative image of the past and making it more palatable to all South Africans. To this end, a new vision and mission for the party was produced, replete with a new logo and colours, which was publicly launched on the iconic date of 2 February 1996 with much fanfare by F.W. de Klerk, with Meyer by his side. De Klerk also announced that he was appointing Meyer secretary general of the party to pursue this new approach, and that the latter would resign from cabinet to devote all his time to furthering this objective.

When Pik Botha resigned from the NP in reaction to De Klerk's withdrawal of the party from the GNU in June 1996, Meyer succeeded Botha to the powerful leadership of the Gauteng NP, and seemed to be in a stronger-than-ever position in the party. He was convinced that the NP in its unaltered form would not be attractive to any potential support from other parties or individuals, but would have to disband and start afresh with like-minded partners if it was to achieve its goal of a re-aligned opposition with a realistic chance of eventually taking over the government once more. And the party would have to give a prior commitment to this approach if it hoped to attract support for such a project. He proclaimed these views in public, which were based on extensive consultations with potential partners in such an endeavour.

There was vehement internal opposition to Meyer's views on the disbandment of the NP from people like Hernus Kriel and Marthinus van Schalkwyk, the latter producing a discussion paper titled something like 'Strategic considerations', urging that preference be given to strengthening the 'traditional power base' of the party, i.e. white nationalist Afrikaners. In early 1997, De Klerk announced that he was relieving Meyer of his duties as secretary general to allow him to devote all his efforts to organising the new opposition movement envisaged in the NP's new vision and mission. At the same time, he also announced that he was appointing Van Schalkwyk as the new executive director of the NP, with a brief to build the party by strengthening its structures and ensuring that it retained and expanded its traditional support. He and Meyer's briefs would run concurrently and would complement each other.

As in the case of the approval of the Constitution and the question of whether the party should remain in the GNU or not, De Klerk once again followed an option hoping to please all factions in his party, but satisfying none. Many observers regarded this absurd arrangement of two mutually exclusive objectives as signalling that the NP was now a spent force floundering under weak and directionless leadership, and would find it difficult to play any further constructive role in shaping the future of South Africa. Then, in reaction to a question in a media interview, Meyer gave his opinion that without the drastic reorientation he was advocating, the NP would decline and could possibly become only a regional party centred largely in the Western Cape. Kriel, the leader of the party in that province, was furious and challenged De Klerk to do something about Meyer and the 'road to self-destruction' he wanted the party to follow. In effect he was demanding that De Klerk get rid of Meyer. De Klerk confronted Meyer on 6 May 1997 and told him that he was disbanding his reformative task team. He made certain proposals to Meyer, who rejected them and the next day resigned from the NP and Parliament.

Bantu Holomisa

Almost from the moment he entered the post-1994 cabinet of President Nelson Mandela as deputy minister of environment and tourism, Bantu Holomisa says he began to feel uncomfortable with certain trends he noticed in the new government. The new rulers seemed to him to be taking too enthusiastically to the ways of the previous regime, displaying huge arrogance in their newly acquired status and affluence, which he found inappropriate and offensive. As an example, he cites the fact that, early in their first term in office, cabinet voted themselves a 100 per cent salary increase. A collision course between him and the ANC was therefore charted early in the new government's tenure.

The crunch had actually come in 1992 when the military government of the Transkei, then headed by Holomisa, obtained intelligence that confirmed, among many other things, that the hotelier, Sol Kerzner, had paid Chief Kaiser Matanzima, the head of the Transkei government under apartheid, R2 million for exclusive gambling rights in that homeland. Matanzima had parcelled this out to various other beneficiaries, including R50 000 to Stella Sigcau. Sigcau had been deposed as prime minister of the Transkei in Holomisa's military coup on 31 December 1987 and was now minister of public enterprises in the Mandela cabinet and the GNU. In May 1996, with the concurrence of the ANC leadership, including Mandela, Holomisa testified about these events before the TRC. He handed in a statement on the matter that had been approved by President Mandela, together with all the confirmatory intelligence material in his possession.

An astonishing eruption followed from the ANC, astonishing because nothing of what was now being revealed had not been known since the coup nine years previously. Holomisa was vilified in vitriolic terms in public by top ANC leaders, including then Deputy President Thabo Mbeki. He was branded a liar and a cheat and an undisciplined disgrace to the party. He was ordered by the ANC to appear before an internal disciplinary committee, which he initially refused to do, branding the committee a kangaroo court and insisting on an independent tribunal. Before the hearing, several senior ANC leaders had already called for his expulsion from the party. He did eventually attend, again stating his view that it would be an unfair hearing. Mandela phoned him to say that should he apologise, he, Mandela, would square things with the now very hostile National Working Committee of the ANC. Holomisa refused. The hearing continued under the chairmanship of Zola Skweyiya, the holder of a doctorate in law from the Karl Marx University in Leipzig, East Germany, a puppet state of the Soviet Union under whose legal system trumped-up show-trials had over many years been developed to a fine art. Holomisa was expelled from the ANC.

I got to know Holomisa as a supremely confident man, even arrogant, but nonetheless a likeable man's man with no racist chips on his shoulder. I got the impression that he thought himself superior to all others, irrespective of race. He was well educated and once a decent rugby wing three-quarter in the Eastern Cape with potential for higher honours, some thought. He had also been militarily trained up to staff level by the SADF in 1984, where I understood he did well. And he had a delightful, impish sense of humour. He was my kind of guy.

Once, as we were clearing up the venue after a United Democratic Movement (UDM) conference in the civic centre of Kempton Park, a large, high-mounted television monitor in the hall was showing a cricket Test match between South Africa and the West Indies. As we watched, one of the Kirsten brothers, Gary I think it was, hooked a ball from one of those huge West Indies fast bowlers for a boundary. From behind came a growling voice: 'Take that, you black bastard!' Every head in the place jerked around in astonishment, especially in light of the culture of non-racialism we had just been carefully nurturing for a full day. We all cracked up when we realised it was Bantu.

During his military training he also picked up some choice Afrikaans expletives. As a mild example, according to Jana Warffemius, a senior official in the head office of the UDM in Pretoria, he would walk into the office in the morning and say to her: *'Goeie môre, jou bliksem.'* She then knew he was in a good mood.

The NMP and the NCF

When Meyer started publicly explaining his new role in the NP, I became interested and told him so. With De Klerk's appointment of Van Schalkwyk with an opposing brief to Meyer's, the general expectation of an implosion in the NP strengthened and rumours circulated that Meyer would leave the party. A general consensus among commentators seemed to be that the NP had now shot its bolt and could be discarded as a major force. I phoned Meyer again and told him that I would support and join him in a new endeavour if he were to leave, but not if he remained in the NP. I was convinced that his reformist efforts, in view of Van Schalkwyk's appointment and brief, would not float in his party.

When Meyer and Holomisa left their respective parties, both were determined to remain in politics and pursue their separate visions. Both embarked on wide consultation with a view to garnering support, Meyer under the style of the New Movement Process (NMP) and Holomisa under that of the National Consultative Forum (NCF). I joined the NMP and became involved in preparatory work to devise structures for a new party, and to consult other parties and individuals. I was particularly disappointed when nothing came of our discussions with the DP in the persons of mainly James Selfe, Douglas Gibson, Cobus Jordaan and Tony Leon, the leader of that party. I respected and liked them as political soulmates from my earlier involvement in the DP. I developed a special regard and liking for Leon, a battle-ready gladiator in the hardy Israel-born *Sabra* mould, although he wasn't one. *Sabra* is the Hebrew/Arabic equivalent of the Afrikaans *turksvy*, or prickly pear. His great effort to quickly learn Afrikaans up to a good standard also sat well with me.

Meanwhile in the NMP, we drafted a vision and mission, and started to produce policy papers. We had the benefit of consultations with well-disposed eminent political commentators and management specialists, as well as other defectors from the NP. These included the likes of Kobus du Plessis, Takis Christodoulou, Annalizé van Wyk, Sam de Beer and Nilo Botha, all experienced and capable people. In a stimulating and enjoyable coming together of like-minded people collectively set on creating something new, we worked furiously to give substance to some fresh ideas.

The Movement takes shape

It soon became clear to Meyer and Holomisa that they were indeed on similar missions, and so they arranged to meet at Loftus Versfeld Stadium in Pretoria in mid-1997 to discuss whether they might cooperate. They agreed to amalgamate at an appropriate time. Inputs to policy positions were solicited and received from all and sundry, which, after much discussion, contributed towards finalising policy papers. The UDM was launched on 29 September 1997 with an impressive occasion at the World Trade Centre, choreographed by the well-known South African theatre and dance impresario, Richard Loring.

A Better Future

I wrote a hagiographic little book about Meyer and Holomisa and the lead-up to the founding of the UDM, titled *A Better Future: Towards a Winning Nation in Ten Years*. For this purpose I spent much time separately interviewing the two and discussing their backgrounds, views on life and the world, political thinking and future expectations. In the process I became convinced that the two together had enough in common and in their diversity to successfully bring together support from their very different constituencies to create a new movement with great potential. Holomisa thought it politically unwise in his constituency for someone with my background to be cited as the author, and we agreed an 'editorial panel' would fill that role. I was paid fairly decently for my effort and had no objection. Unfortunately, due to secretary of the UDM Annelizé van Wyk's dereliction of duty, the book was not distributed as it should have been before the 1999 general election, for which it had been intended.

The final idealistic paragraph of my book reads as follows:

The UDM aims not only at restructuring opposition politics and gaining a role for itself in that regard, but is setting a new vision of a better quality of life for everyone in South Africa, based on common needs and values and in recognition of the common destiny which all who live in it share. It is setting new ideals towards shaping that destiny and charting a road map to becoming a world-class, winning nation in ten years; a nation that will have the means to lend succour to the most vulnerable of its citizens by empowering them to help themselves, and where everyone will be encouraged to produce the wealth needed to enable private enterprise and the state to do so; a nation where citizens will be safe in pursuing fulfilment and happiness in the way they freely choose, exercising their rights and freedoms and respecting those of others, while accepting and fulfilling the obligations which determine the content and quality of those rights and freedoms. It may well be that if the UDM does not succeed, South Africa will not succeed.

I believed in every word I wrote.

Demise

I was appointed to the support staff in the UDM's parliamentary office in Cape Town, where I did policy research and wrote speeches for members of Parliament. Early in 2000, Roelf Meyer resigned from the party to 'pursue other interests'. I was deeply disappointed and felt let down. I realised that the UDM was destined to remain a small party based largely in Holomisa's home turf of the Transkei region of the Eastern Cape. I was sure he would be able to sustain that for as long as he chose to do so, but it would lose its national reach. I was saddened at the country losing such a potential force to the good, as I was convinced it would have been. I had perhaps naively believed more passionately in the UDM than the leaders who later left it.

When Meyer told me in his office in Cape Town that he was leaving, I did not ask him why and only expressed my deep regret. To this day I do not know his reasons, but surmise that it could have been differences he may have had with his co-leader, Holomisa, who could be quite self-centred and authoritarian at times. Some close to him think that his crumbling marriage may have prompted it. It was an archaic conservative Afrikaner and NP mindset that someone with a liaison outside of wedlock, or, heaven forbid, a divorcee, could not hold public office. I have never confirmed either and have not tried to. Meyer later joined the ANC, as did a number of other UDM leaders such as Sam de Beer, Annelizé van Wyk, Cedric Frolick and Salam Abram-Mayet. Unlike the rest of these, Meyer has to the best of my knowledge not returned to active party politics.

I worked in the UDM office with a much appreciated and admired friend, Dr Johan Steenkamp. A former university lecturer in theoretical nuclear physics with a doctorate from the University of Heidelberg in Germany, Johan was also an experienced former NP parliamentarian. He had a great sense of humour, with ready repartee. Upon first meeting a rather pompous colleague, Professor Anthony Bam, Johan put out his hand and introduced himself as 'Johan Steenkamp'. Bam responded from some height with 'Hullo, I'm Professor Bam', to which Johan retorted: 'Well, in that case, I'm Doctor Steenkamp.'

When Meyer left the UDM, Johan quoted to me more or less as follows from the Book of Proverbs: 'Put not your trust in princes.' I later looked up an English translation of Robert Burns's ode 'To a Mouse'.

The best-laid plans of mice and men
Often go awry,
And leave us nothing but grief and pain,
For promised joy.

Aftermath

Later, Johan Steenkamp, Anthony Bam and I became entangled in a dispute with the UDM management on questions of our employment as a result of what we regarded as the ineptitude and incompetence of, in particular, Annelizé van Wyk and Cedric Frolick, at the time the secretary of the party and a parliamentary whip respectively. We took the matter to the Commission for Conciliation, Mediation and Arbitration on the grounds of a number of transgressions of labour legislation, where we won compensation for unfair dismissal and other grievances. It pained me to have a feeling of good riddance towards something I had believed in so strongly and worked so hard for.

43

Further Meander

Opting out?

After the demise of the UDM, I went to live in Stanford in the Western Cape, where I had built a lovely little fisherman-type cottage in a new residential area near the river for R146 000. I was looking for peace and quiet to try to do some writing. However, I hadn't anticipated that peace and quiet could be that peaceful and quiet, with only my Border collie, Catrijn, for company, a sweet and highly intelligent but not very talkative companion, which I normally appreciate within reason. After about two years I sold up for R300 000 and moved to Hermanus, chuffed at my excellent investment sense. About a year and a half later the house was on the market for R1.2 million.

Politics again, of sorts

I again became active in the DP, which after much agonising amalgamated with the NNP, led by Marthinus van Schalkwyk, to form the DA. In December 2000, I was elected as a ward councillor to the Overstrand Municipal Council centred on Hermanus. The NNP soon withdrew from the alliance and started favouring the ANC, leading to its final pathetic eclipse in 2005. But Van Schalkwyk's joining the ANC and dissolving his party was to the considerable advantage of the DA in the Western Cape.

In the council I asked for and to my satisfaction was given the portfolio of environmental management, over and above my ward responsibilities. The Overstrand municipal area stretches for about 200 kilometres along the Southern Cape coast from Cape Hangklip to Pearly Beach, and inland to Swellendam. I started consulting with civil-society conservation organisations to get my teeth into the subject and gain some idea of the concerns and needs in this crucially important aspect for the tourism and hospitality industry, which is the economic mainstay of the coastal areas in that region. I got as many different opinions as the people I spoke to – there was much bickering and very little interaction or cooperation between them. I was astonished to discover, with some difficulty, that there were sixty-one such organisations in the area, some of the one-man type and others only notional or dormant, but every one of the mostly self-appointed representatives an expert on environmental affairs with strong opinions. There was clearly much enthusiasm.

I called a meeting, to which all of them I could trace were invited, which was eventually attended by representatives of about thirty organisations. I explained that I was intent on representing their views in council as best I could, but could not do so if I did not have a consolidated approach from them as a basis from which to work. I simply could not promote sixty-one separate points of view. There was a surprisingly positive reaction considering all the egos involved, and the Overstrand Conservation Forum (OCF) was established. A strong management committee of able and dedicated people was elected, and I got a resolution passed in council that the OCF would be regarded as a structured non-governmental organisation to be consulted on all matters concerning the natural environment. I don't know whether this has been adhered to by the municipality, as I left the council not long after. I have not been involved with the OCF again but, from what I hear and read, it was at the time of writing still doing important work. The OCF is the one enduring thing that I left behind in Overstrand of which I am proud.

Back to the law

I had come to the end of my enthusiasm for working in a caucus of the governing DA with former members of the NP, with whom I had little in common politically. I hasten to add that there were some great people among my colleagues, such as the deputy mayor, Jan Kühn, and former senior security policeman Pieter Scholtz, whom I knew from our previous life, both people of integrity with whom I got on very well. With Nicolette Botha, later Overstrand Mayor Botha-Guthrie, I had a valued long-standing friendship from our having worked together previously. I had an initial tiff with the mayor, Willie Smuts of the NP and later ANC, but got to know him to be an able and experienced administrator and we got on well. I had good relations with most of my colleagues, but I began feeling crowded in the constricting caucus environment and a little bored with local politics. Apart from telephone and travel allowances, councillors were at the time not being paid, and my work was costing me money, which I didn't have. I started to think a change might be a good idea.

Late in 2001, the National Prosecuting Authority advertised a number of posts for legal advisors in the Special Investigating Unit (SIU). I applied for a fairly lowly position, was interviewed by its head, Willie Hofmeyr, the then deputy national director of public prosecutions, and got the job.

44

The National Prosecuting Authority

I at first thought it beyond ridicule for me to again seek a job in law, but it was concerned with criminal law, my only remaining legal interest, and I would be involved mostly with court procedures in terms of the exciting new 1998 Prevention of Organised Crime Act, the first of its kind in South Africa. Hofmeyr suggested my intelligence background could be useful, especially my 'contacts', by which he meant, I thought, in the underworld, of which I had none. I was looking forward to new challenges, but regrettably had to move back to Pretoria. Since leaving Stanford, I had been living in my sister's holiday home in Hermanus while she and her husband lived in Germany, and so I could up sticks without much ado.

The Special Investigating Unit
At the SIU I was mostly involved in drafting notices in terms of the Criminal Procedure Act to compel persons to testify on suspected criminal activities of which they had knowledge, and preparing proclamations for the president's signature to authorise the SIU to investigate a particular matter. The excellent system of prosecution-led investigations applied, by which investigators worked under the direction of a lawyer to obviate mistakes being made during the course of an investigation that could later sink the case in court, which very much reduces the likelihood of this happening. It was a stimulating pleasure to work in a team of experienced investigators and excellent lawyers.

The Asset Forfeiture Unit
After a short while with the SIU, I was asked to assist the AFU, located in the same building and also headed by Willie Hofmeyr, which at the time was struggling with backlogs in preparing court applications. I jumped at the chance of becoming involved with High Court matters. There were two people in the AFU, a senior sub-manager, Advocate Peter Volmink (originally from Stanford), and the excellent Advocate Richard Chinner, who were particularly supportive of and helpful to me. I was assigned to draft a full set of court documents in an action for a restraint order to prohibit the alienation of assets and their forfeiture to the state. I did a good job in a minimal amount of

time and was grateful for generous accolades from my bosses and colleagues. Hofmeyr then called me in and asked me to return to Cape Town to assist in the office there. It was the most successful of the SIU/AFU offices in the country, but they were short-handed. I agreed because I was asked, and he offered me a substantial increase in salary that he himself pencilled in on my contract of employment, which he had in front of him during our discussion.

Cape Town

Immediately on first entering the Cape Town office, an atmosphere of animosity towards me was palpable. I was assigned an incompetent investigator (perhaps calculatedly) to assist me, and between the two of us we were rather hopeless as a team. I conceded this to the highly capable head of the office, Advocate Hermione Cronje, who I later learnt had been furious with Hofmeyr for not having consulted her prior to my appointment to her office. Hofmeyr himself sort of confirmed this to me, saying that he couldn't disrupt his best office, clearly hinting it would be nice if I left. I would not do so for such an ulterior reason and suggested that he arrange for me to join the Environmental Court in Hermanus as a prosecutor, of which I knew them to be short and where I could also look after the interests of the AFU – some abalone poaching syndicates had huge assets. He agreed and arranged with the Western Cape Director of Public Prosecutions, Advocate Rodney de Kock, to appoint me there.

During my experience with the National Prosecuting Authority I gained huge respect for Hofmeyr's acute mind and absolute integrity, which was also confirmed with admiration by a hardened former security policeman with whom I had worked at NIS and who had interrogated Hofmeyr during his detention without trial some time during the stormy 1970s and 1980s. In spite of his frail appearance, Willie was a consummate workaholic with seemingly inexhaustible stamina. I thought he was overworked, but he seemed to thrive on it. I'm not sure that he was always able to fully keep his finger on the pulse of his wide-ranging management responsibilities, although he had some very capable people in support under him. I never received the excellent new salary he had offered me.

Hermanus

For about three years I enjoyed working in an environment (in more senses than one) dear to my heart, where the Marine Living Resources Act of

1998 was being applied. It was satisfying service in mostly the role of control prosecutor – managing the court roll and assisting in negotiating and drafting plea-bargain agreements. I was in my late sixties and, together with my long absence from such give and take, I was no longer competent in court work. I had two exceptionally able colleagues who became much appreciated friends as well, regional magistrate Chris Naudé and senior state prosecutor Advocate Phil Snijman. They sympathetically supported and guided me throughout my term there, but when I belatedly realised that they were in fact going out of their way to humour me, the alarm bell announcing the expiry of my shelf-life rang loud and clear.

Naudé was an excellent magistrate, according to experienced attorneys and advocates who regularly appeared before him. Snijman was no doubt one of the top environmental lawyers in the country, holding master's degrees in both environmental management and environmental law, apart from his legal qualifications as an advocate of the High Court. What set him apart from most other environmental lawyers was the fact that he had been a state advocate and a High Court prosecutor, which made him an expert in the practical nuts and bolts of applying the law. He worked tirelessly training investigators and prosecutors in environmental law and procedure. He also assisted in preparations for a projected second environmental court in Port Elizabeth, but I don't know whether that ever fully materialised.

The Environmental Court in Hermanus was established as a specialist regional magistrate's court as one arm of an effort to better curtail the poaching of marine resources, in particular abalone. All environmental cases in the Western Cape had to be referred to it for adjudication and, after the appointment of Phil Snijman, it achieved an unheard-of success rate of around 85 per cent of prosecutions. It was opened with great fanfare in 2003 with several cabinet ministers in attendance, but was closed down in 2007 despite the objections of the Division of Marine and Coastal Management of the Department of Environmental Affairs and Tourism, because the Department of Justice no longer believed in specialised courts. Environmental cases reverted to the lower district courts, where court rolls were hugely overloaded and many inexperienced prosecutors had little or no knowledge of environmental law or its application. Abalone poaching is flourishing now more than ever, with Chinese syndicates especially commanding apparently unlimited funds to pay their way with corrupt policemen and others queuing up for their largesse.

Chris Naudé was later appointed to the SIU and Phil Snijman went into private practice in his field. I have no doubt that both will be as successful there as they were in the exciting days of the Environmental Court in Hermanus.

Although I briefly tried private legal practice again, embarrassingly unsuccessfully, with the sympathetically indulgent attorney Mariki Chin in Hermanus, it was now clearly the end of the line for me in law. I rode into the sunrise in search of new opportunities, hopefully in something to do with language and writing.

45

End Game

After leaving NIA, I did practical exams and was accredited by the South African Translators' Institute as a translator in Afrikaans and English. I started out also translating from French, but this became too time-consuming and I stopped. I was admitted by the Cape High Court as a sworn translator in my two main languages, and had over time and to a limited extent been practising that craft. When I finally left the National Prosecuting Authority and the Environmental Court on 31 August 2005, I took up translation on a full-time basis. I worked mainly on legal documents like contracts and court documents, as well as a disturbing number of academic certificates and other documents for young, well-educated people emigrating. I enjoyed working with the intricacies of the two languages in juxtaposition, although translation is very time-consuming with little monetary reward.

I thought it a good idea to gain more in-depth knowledge of the discipline of translation and to interact more with knowledgeable people in the field. I had been reading a bit about the theory of translation and became interested in learning more. I enrolled for an MPhil in translation studies at the University of Stellenbosch, which I later changed to a BPhil, not having the stomach for the thesis required for the former. I graduated in 2009 having derived much pleasure and fulfilment from the course, as well as a huge appreciation for my excellent teachers. It was a stimulating and constructive experience that I was fortunate to have at a fairly advanced age. I felt reunited with my first loves that I had, through various circumstances, abandoned for such a big part of my life. I felt I was being warmly welcomed back by long-neglected friends.

During this period I translated the delightful *The No. 1 Ladies' Detective Agency* by Alexander McCall Smith, so perfectly suited to the Afrikaans language with its humour and pathos in an African setting. After being accepted with great acclamation by a publisher and with a contract signed, the deal suddenly fell through as they had ostensibly discovered some unspecified shortcomings. It later appeared that they had struck a more lucrative deal with another publisher for the publication of more works by the same author, and so relinquished their rights to publish my translation. The book appeared in Afrikaans by another translator. As far as I know nothing has come of the project to further publish this author in Afrikaans and my original publisher has gone out of business.

46

Lamentation

For a language

The one great disappointment for me in the new Constitution is that it lacks any specific protection for the Afrikaans language, the only language indigenous to our country that has developed to full utility in every sphere and at every level of human endeavour. However, having been present at some discussions during the negotiations in this regard, I don't think that realistically there was any prospect of attaining special status for Afrikaans in the context of the time. There was forceful insistence from the ANC to have English declared the only official language, but in the face of resolute resistance from mainly the government negotiators, this status was conferred on all eleven of the most spoken languages in the country, as laid down in Article 6 of the Constitution.

This article also obliges the state to 'take practical and positive measures to elevate the status and advance the use of all the indigenous languages', especially the 'historically diminished' ones. Furthermore, Article 185 established a commission to, among other things, 'promote respect for the rights of cultural, religious and linguistic communities'. Apart from the establishment of the largely toothless Pan South African Language Board (PANSALB), intended to oversee compliance with the constitutional requirements regarding languages, nothing much has happened. It is also constitutionally required to produce a so-called 'Languages Act' to formalise the abovementioned obligations.

However, through the dedication and tenacity of some outstanding activists for Afrikaans such as Wannie Carstens, Carel Prinsloo, Jacques van der Elst, Hermann Giliomee, Michael le Cordeur, and non-governmental organisations such as Afriforum and the Afrikaans Language and Cultural Association (ATKV), an Afrikaans Language Board was established under PANSALB's auspices as a statutorily recognised institution to further the interests of the Afrikaans culture and language.

At the time of writing, eighteen years after the advent of the new Constitution with its provisions for the equal treatment of all languages, a draft Act has been tabled in Parliament. If adopted in its proposed form, it will unequivocally spell the end of Afrikaans as a language for official use nationally and in most provinces. Sociolinguists are by and large agreed that this is a crucial measure of the prospects for the long-term survival of a language in its higher functions.

The English language and culture is part of my soul, but the Afrikaans language and culture is at the very core of my soul. I am an African. My language and history is African, originally derived from robust Dutch, but enriched by German, French, English, Malay-Portuguese and Khoisan influences. Afrikaans has not discarded its Germanic origins or the magnificence of its Western European history and cultural heritage, but has been moulded by our country with its harsh and entrancing semi-deserts, nurturing green valleys, expanses of high savannah and low bushveld, mountains sometimes rugged and sometimes softly rolling, bountiful seas, riches in and below its soil and, above all, the wonderful diversity of its peoples. We protected and nurtured our language through two devastating wars of liberation against the ruthless onslaught of the colonialists, and could not but name it for our continent.

(If I seem inadvertently to plagiarise the silvery tongue of Thabo Mbeki, I acknowledge and thank him anew.)

These have gelled the language into something new, something fresh and exhilarating, something fully expressive in all spheres of life, from bickering on street corners and coarsely raging at rugby matches and in shebeens, to addressing world issues in all natural and social sciences, and teaching in all disciplines in the most exalted corridors of academia; from unravelling the physical secrets of the cosmos as well as the ethereal narratives of philosophers, to arguing down-to-earth contentions in courts of law, and taking part in all political, human and humanitarian discourses. It has evolved into something elegant, expressing profound thought in the finest literature and poetry, from the most exhilarating joy to the most mournful sorrow. It is a language for all seasons and all purposes. Professor Rena Pretorius of Tukkies says: 'Afrikaners have no merit or achievement to compare with their language.' I agree.

The development of Afrikaans did not happen without sustained, prodigious effort and sacrifice by many selflessly dedicated people over more than a hundred years. They first battled the colonialist attempts to force the English language into every sphere of society at the cost of Dutch/Afrikaans, and then developed terminology to bring it to full fruition in the form that we utilise today. This process was aided enormously by the fact that an Afrikaner-dominated government ruled the country for forty-six years from 1948 to 1994, but this fact tragically also brought upon the language the opprobrium of the world as the 'language of the oppressor'. I have never heard German being blamed for Nazi atrocities, or Russian for the unspeakable injustices and profound denial of human rights by Soviet communism, both on a plane of evil elevated far above apartheid.

I often wonder with some amusement at the attitude of many black South Africans towards Afrikaans as the 'language of the oppressor', while being so enthralled by the language of one of the worst ever oppressors and exploiters of the peoples of Africa and around the world, and the originators of apartheid philosophies and practice: English. It is exalted not only for its communicative facility, but especially for the imagined social status it provides, reflecting the burning materialistic desire of previously disadvantaged people to attain middle-class status, for which they (disastrously for their own languages) strive with all their might.* This is at least partly due to the diminished traditional oral recounting of history and inadequate formal education, leading to a loss of language consciousness and pride, and indeed the languages themselves, and ignorance of the past.

And this while Afrikaner governments over decades, in keeping with apartheid policies, established separate universities for each substantial black-language group indigenous to the country. In the face of the social and commercial dominance of English, this afforded a brilliant opportunity for language development that was never realised at such institutions, with the possible exception of isiZulu. At the instigation of misguided idealists and angry political agitators, these became stigmatised as 'bush colleges' for the indoctrination of black intellectuals. In reality, many black graduates of universities like Fort Hare, Nongoma and Turfloop hold prominent positions in present-day South Africa. These institutions provided an ideal state-funded opportunity for the development of terminology and modern structures in the black languages towards full utility in all spheres of modern thought and

---

* This syndrome of 'colonised consciousness' has been described by the American negro (his term) W.E.B. du Bois and the French Caribbean writer Frantz Fanon, who both used the term 'double consciousness', the one referring to the suppressed and indigenous/original consciousness of colonised peoples and the other to that imposed by the colonialists. See in general Hermann Giliomee and Lawrence Schlemmer, 'n Vaste Plek vir Afrikaans (Stellenbosch: SUN Press, 2006).

technology, as had been done for Afrikaans. Although black resistance to political oppression rather than considerations of language is fully understood, a brilliant cultural opportunity was forfeited to politics.

With a full and constantly developing vocabulary and the simplest of grammars and phonetic pronunciation, Afrikaans is ideally suited to be the *lingua franca* of our country. It already fulfils this role in some provinces like the Western and Northern Cape, and to a lesser extent in others, as well as in Namibia. Afrikaans is spoken by about six million South Africans as their home language, is the most spoken as second and third language, and has the widest geographical distribution of all languages in the country. It can be understood in the Netherlands, Flanders, in parts of the Netherlands Antilles, and some say even in parts of the Java province of Indonesia. By the same token, Dutch, Flemish and to a lesser extent German, are accessible to Afrikaans readers.

Afrikaans is so much simpler in grammar and syntax than English, while remaining as expressive as any language. The pain of, for instance, learning the proper use of English past perfect tenses and the intricacies of subjunctive constructions, has driven many even highly educated Europeans to distraction. A Swiss fellow student of mine in England, fluent in French, German and Italian, once bemoaned his depressing frustration in trying to learn the 'diabolically inconsistent' English language.

Afrikaans pronunciation, furthermore, is strictly phonetic compared to that of English. What sense is there, for instance, in the different pronunciations of words such as 'trough', 'bough' and 'though'? Bill Bryson, in his book *The Mother Tongue*, points out many more examples and says: 'If there's one thing certain about English pronunciation it is that there is almost nothing certain about it.' He adds: 'English ... pronunciation is so ... random ... that not one of our twenty-six letters can be relied on for constancy.'* All fine for a born and bred English-speaker, but what about the poor foreigner trying to learn the language from scratch at a later age? It is notoriously difficult to learn for those who haven't taken it in with their mother's milk.

There is a concerted effort being made in South Africa to destroy Afrikaans

---

* Bill Bryson, *The Mother Tongue: English and How It Got That Way* (New York: William Morrow & Co, 1990).

in its higher functions – and no, this is not an exaggeration. In spite of the constitutionally decreed equality of the eleven official languages and the obligation placed on the government to nurture all of them, Afrikaans is no longer currency in official dealings. Telephoning government departments and expecting to be served in Afrikaans is usually futile, often eliciting offensive reactions like 'we don't speak that language here' or 'can't you even speak English?' To write a letter in Afrikaans to any official agency usually elicits no reaction at all. And this situation will be formalised if the proposed new Act should become law.

Schools and tertiary institutions are condescendingly 'allowed' to use Afrikaans, as long as they don't use it for 'exclusionist' purposes, with the practical effect that the use of Afrikaans is rapidly diminishing. Of the more than two thousand Afrikaans-only primary schools before 1994, it is said that only about three hundred remain as centres where the Afrikaans language and culture can be freely expressed and developed. Of five fully Afrikaans-language universities, none remain as such. Pretoria, Johannesburg (formerly Rand Afrikaans), Nelson Mandela Metropolitan (formerly Port Elizabeth, originally bilingual), Western Cape and Stellenbosch have either been anglicised or are implementing language policies that will inevitably lead to it. Only North West (simultaneous interpreting) and Free State (parallel teaching) are unequivocally intent on preserving Afrikaans as a language of higher learning. How sustainable these will be over time still remains to be seen.

Many Afrikaans-speakers seem readily prepared to accept their own inferiority and that of their language to English, instinctively preferring to use the latter in public, often with quite ridiculous outcomes. Sportsmen, especially Afrikaans rugby players and coaches, are particularly prone, with shining exceptions, to using atrocious English and sometimes even more atrocious Afrikaans in addressing fans and the media. This would be quite laughable if it weren't so serious. I would urge two of the best rugby coaches and speakers of pure Afrikaans at the time of writing, Paul Treu of the Springbok Sevens and Allister Coetzee of Western Province and the Stormers, to convene a national training camp to teach Afrikaans players and coaches to speak Afrikaans properly.

In the judiciary, with increasingly fewer presiding officers being appointed who have a command of Afrikaans (in keeping with transformation and the 'national democratic revolution'), the proud traditions and achievements of Afrikaans jurisprudence and legal teaching in freeing our law from colonialist precepts are being denigrated, and there is increasing pressure to remove the language as one of record in courts. A resulting absurdity is that in some cases, where prosecutors, defence attorneys and the parties before court are Afrikaans-speaking, interpreters have to be called in. Although judges president and chief magistrates are supposed to allocate presiding officers to cases taking account of such circumstances, it often does not happen. Other indigenous languages are not terminologically sufficiently developed for use in court proceedings except, again, perhaps isiZulu.

What annoys me most of all, however, is the many Afrikaners who adopt the cultural arrogance and presumption of English superiority, presuming that language to be more civilised and socially acceptable than Afrikaans. Many Afrikaners send their children to English schools 'to give them a chance in life', including leading businesspeople like the former chief executive of ABSA Bank, Steve Booysen, who, according to media reports, said so in public. One can only wonder about the pitiable German, French, Spanish, Russian, Portuguese, Arabic, Hebrew, Hindi, Gujarati, Persian, Japanese, Chinese, Korean and other millions of children the world over being deprived of a chance in life by being educated in their home language.

The superb achievements of so many completely Afrikaans-educated and trained engineers, doctors, scientists, lawyers, novelists and poets are on record. There are also proudly Afrikaans businessmen like Koos Bekker (Media24, M-Net), Johann Rupert (Rembrandt Group), Jannie Mouton (the PSG group) and Ton Vosloo (Media24) who stride the top reaches of the international business world with great success and sometimes dominance, while cherishing their Afrikaans heritage and education. But visible Afrikaans is largely disappearing from the world of commerce. I once asked twenty-two Afrikaans businesspeople in my largely Afrikaans-speaking town why their businesses had English names. To a man and woman, with a shrug of the shoulders, they said they didn't know, while conceding that their clientele was mostly Afrikaans-speaking. Colonised consciousness?

Have the minds of so many Afrikaners been enslaved by the wonderful, seductive English language and culture? To lose one's language consciousness and pride is to doom one's language to oblivion in the longer term. The attitude of English-speakers in general, however obnoxiously arrogant they can sometimes be to others, is a shining example to all of valuing one's own cultural and language heritage. Sadly though, English-speakers in South Africa and the world over suffer from an immense superiority complex, no doubt a relic of the long-departed and unlamented British imperialist global dominance, which does not seem to grant other languages a right to exist, except as inferiors. A critical mass of Afrikaans-speakers seems to agree with this and has become indifferent to the plight of Afrikaans and its future prospects. This reflects in the bad, adulterated Afrikaans (by which is certainly not meant regional or other idiolect) spoken by so many Afrikaans-speakers today.

One often gets the question from them: 'What are you worried about; we won't ever stop speaking Afrikaans?' I agree, but languages do die out, and sociolinguists and language historians are mostly agreed that this happens when they lose their higher functions, i.e. at the academic, scientific, techno-logical, literary, commercial and official level. There is a vibrant and sustained cultural celebration of Afrikaans in all its forms at the non-governmental organisation level, but these activities are driven and supported by a very small percentage of energetic and dedicated Afrikaans-speakers, white as well as black. Where will these initiatives come from in a generation or two if Afrikaans teaching at all levels continues to decline?

The vast majority of English-speakers in South Africa are oblivious to these circumstances because they never read Afrikaans newspapers or books, never attend Afrikaans cultural occasions such as plays and book-readings, never listen to or watch Afrikaans newscasts, and never make any effort to learn the language that for generations was one of only two official languages in the country. How often does one hear derogatory and hurtful statements from those quarters like 'Oh, he's quite intelligent for an Afrikaner', and this from people who are ostensibly unable to utter a word of Afrikaans in spite of having been born, bred and educated in especially the Western Cape, where Afrikaans is the dominant language and the common everyday currency. In contrast, it is significant how many black people, including foreigners, are keen to at least learn to communicate basically in Afrikaans.

I agreed with only two things that the Afrikaans-insensitive former rector of Stellenbosch University, Professor Chris Brink, said about language before he left for more congenial English climes in Newcastle, UK. He said that the English language is an unstoppable force of nature rolling over the world, and Afrikaans-speakers should address the English-speaking world in English if they wish to be understood. Both are axiomatic, which is why I have written this book in English. But surely this does not mean that we should sacrifice our language, the fullest expression of our being as a cultural entity, on the altar of English? Who could we possibly threaten by expressing ourselves through schools and universities teaching in our home language? The indifference of so many Afrikaans-speakers towards their own highest cultural heritage and achievement, the only element that makes them unique, is deeply disturbing. Perhaps Afrikaners and Afrikaans-speakers in general are not yet at the level of civilisation that inspires us to cherish our cultural assets. If we don't maintain our language, no one else will, and over time it will die. The blame will then deservedly be laid at the door of the Afrikaans-speakers themselves, and no one else.

Mahatma Gandhi's lament for the diminution of indigenous Indian languages by English is apposite:

> To give millions a knowledge of English is to enslave them. … Is it not a painful thing that, if I want to go to a court of justice, I must employ the English language as a medium, that when I become a barrister, I may not speak my mother tongue and that someone else should have to translate to me from my own language? Is this not absolutely absurd? Is it not a sign of slavery?
>
> Am I to blame the English for it or myself? It is we, the English-knowing Indians that have enslaved India. The curse of the nation will rest not on the English but upon us.[*]

Of course Gandhi did not mean that Indians or anyone else should not acquire a sound, functioning knowledge of English, as the foregoing might seem to imply. He was not a lunatic, although the overbearing English colonialists of the time thought and said so. But his frustration resonates emphatically with concerned Afrikaans-speakers in South Africa.

For a country

The first democratic general election in the country's history took place on 27 April 1994. The new dawn for South Africa arrived the following month with the inauguration at the Union Buildings in Pretoria of Nelson Mandela as the first president of the new South Africa. It was an exhilarating experience,

---

[*] Melvyn Bragg, *The Adventure of English: The Biography of a Language* (London: Sceptre, 2003), p. 263.

with the chiefs of the services lined up behind the president and deputy presidents F.W. de Klerk and Thabo Mbeki on the podium in support of the new regime but, more importantly, of the new idea of a united country that cherished the interests of all its citizens. The conciliatory presidency of Mandela was symbolised by his appearing at the final of the 1995 Rugby World Cup in Johannesburg wearing the captain's No. 6 Springbok jersey. The wily old man certainly knew which Afrikaner buttons to press, but few doubted his sincerity in seeking reconciliation between the races, which he maintained and confirmed throughout his term of office. I felt fully justified in everything I had believed in, striven for and worked for over the previous two decades and more. Mandela's vast popularity among all sections of the population signalled a bright future for the country and its entire people.

But this brilliant promise started rapidly dissipating almost immediately with Mandela's departure, and has been driving many into painful and increasing disillusionment. Deep-seated Africanist-based racist frames of reference reappeared seemingly overnight among the new governing elite, and pervasive corruption up to the highest levels in politics and government multiplied hand over fist, the infamous arms deal under President Mbeki being a case in point. This obscene 'deal' was entered into at enormous cost to the taxpayers more or less for the sole purpose of the personal enrichment and aggrandizement of those directly involved in it, including at the highest command levels of the SADF, while military planners neither needed nor wanted most of what was acquired. According to media reporting on a new book by researchers Paul Holden and Hennie van Vuuren, *The Devil in the Detail* (Jonathan Ball, 2011), the run-up to this astonishing venality and general corruption originated among the ANC leadership in exile, with some of the main perpetrators later manipulatively being shielded from any onerous consequences by President Mbeki and the top structures of the ANC.

We are constantly being bludgeoned by accounts in the still-free media of the most astonishing corruption and blatant misappropriation and theft of public funds in the highest reaches of the executive, in the dysfunctional civil service, among our guardian angels, the police, and almost everywhere else, to the extent that more and more people are, tragically, becoming bored by these litanies and would rather hear no more. And this still-free media, together with other fundamental tenets of our constitutional state, are at the time of writing under severe, determined threat from the powers that be. There is nothing secret or subtle about this assault. It is deliberate and blatant, with the head of the state proclaiming that the ANC will rule until Jesus comes, that courts up to the Constitutional Court are not gods and cannot presume to act as opposition to the government in declaring legislation to be in breach of the Constitution, and that the judiciary cannot be allowed to trump the will of the people as expressed by an ANC majority in a parliament totally subservient to the executive.

Most recently, the government announced an 'independent inquiry' into the work and powers of the Constitutional Court. On what basis does one independently inquire into the workings of the highest judicial authority in the land and to what purpose? This attitude towards the fundamentals of our constitutional state does not reflect ignorance but rather angry irritation at the limitations they place on the government in its determination to do as it pleases. Dominant factions in the ANC clearly regard the ostensibly 'grand accord' of 1994 as merely an interim stage towards later achieving their real aims through a racist, autocratic 'national democratic revolution', by which the black ANC-supporting majority of the population must dominate every facet of national life at the expense of everyone else.

And this dominance is to be asserted from the top of the heap in the relentless march to the second, socialist phase of the so-called two-phase Marxist revolution and the desired 'democratic centralist' state in a command economy. This would, of course, together with the sought-after toothless and submissive media under the control of the securocrats, greatly facilitate the concealment of maladministration and corruption throughout every facet of governance in the country, and the more equitable spreading of them through-out the land. Leading communists in government like Gwede Mantashe, the chairman of the SACP and secretary general of the ANC; Blade Nzimande, the general secretary of the SACP and the minister of higher education; and his deputy in the SACP, the deputy minister of transport, Jeremy Cronin, are in the vanguard of this assault, with their point man, the minister of justice, Jeff Radebe. Radebe is responsible for the protection of the Constitution and its 'development', a member of the central committee of the SACP and the holder of a master's degree in law from that bastion of democratic constitutional governance, the Karl Marx University in Leipzig, East Germany. He is also the head of policy of the ANC. With numerous other communists in Parliament and in senior positions in the government and civil service, it is a truly amazing edifice of influence and power for a party that has never taken part in any election in South Africa under its own name. Communism is dead for its proven failure, but there are still many diehard communists around.

Lest we shy away from what may seem an exaggerated raising of unlikely 'spectres, haunting South Africa – the spectre of communism' (paraphrased from Marx and Engels in *The Communist Manifesto*), the words of a senior member of the ANC's National Executive Committee, a deputy minister in the Zuma government and a trained lawyer, Ngoako Ramathlodi, are salutary:

> We thus have a constitution that reflects the great compromise tilted heavily in favour of forces against change. However, there is a strong body of thought arguing the view that our constitution is transformative ... the black majority enjoys empty political power while forces against change reign supreme in the economy, judiciary, public opinion and civil society. The objective of protecting white economic interests, having been achieved with the adoption of the new constitution, a grand and total strategy to entrench it for all times was rolled out. In this regard, power was systematically taken out of the legislature and the executive to curtail efforts and initiatives aimed at inducing fundamental changes.[*]

One cannot help but wonder why the 'empty political power' has remained empty in the hands of the inchoate ANC government by their failure to address the dire needs of the country in so many respects. This is also a neatly conclusive refutation of Joe Slovo's boastful assertion at Kempton Park that the government negotiators had 'folded' and the 'ANC got everything it wanted' in constructing the new Constitution of 1996. It is equally conclusive evidence of the ANC's perfidy in having ostensibly negotiated in good faith to open the future to a truly democratic and prosperous South Africa, which now appears only to have been a mere tactical ploy to grab power to gain other particularist strategic ends.

The height of the disingenuous megalomania of the ANC must surely be its most recent assertion (at the time of writing) that it is time for the 'sunset clauses' in the Constitution to be done away with, while the fact is that there is no such thing as 'sunset clauses' in the Constitution. To now hold them up as responsible for fundamental and permanent, negotiated constitutional tenets such as the protection of private property ownership

---

[*] Quoted in a column by Judith February, *Cape Times*, 30/11/2011.

and the independence of the Reserve Bank is a deliberate, unadulterated lie. Those clauses were agreed upon solely as a deadlock-breaking mechanism in the MPNP to establish the GNU and the TEC. The clauses lapsed with the election of a new government in 1999 under the new Constitution. Will true reconciliation and peace between the people of South Africa ever be possible with such a deceitful majority party and government, who have now so emphatically forfeited any moral legitimacy they may still have had?

It is chilling to reflect that the settlement of 1994 was intended to defuse the increasing instability and violence in the country, and that without it we could easily revert back to such, and worse, a situation. The signs are there in, for instance, the increasing violent protests at the lack of service delivery at local government level, which we ignore at our peril. Neither should we ignore the rising disillusionment and anger of many white people not necessarily of rightist persuasion. The government may well in the quite near future find itself unable to govern the country, even badly, while it blames everyone and everything else, including the Constitution, except its own incompetence and corrupt maladministration.

With a woefully inadequate president appointing mostly equally inadequate but often politically astute sycophants to head the commanding instruments of power in the state – including, most alarmingly of all, the judiciary – and a steadily disintegrating civil service undermining any semblance of good governance there might have been, one tends to sometimes despair at the future of our country. At the time of writing, Zuma seems set to retain the leadership of his party and the country for another five years after the expiry of his present term. And after that, what will be left of the pillars of our democracy with present trends expected to continue and intensify? With his ever-expanding estate and family at Nkandla in northern KwaZulu-Natal, according to reports now also gaining an underground bunker (so far neither explained nor disputed), and with amendments to the Constitution almost within grasp of the ANC with its subservient and obsequious majority in Parliament, which has abjectly failed to even on a single occasion fulfil its overriding mandate to hold the executive to account, the portents for our future do not seem propitious.

And the constituents are in turn to a large extent unable to hold their representatives in Parliament to account as masses of them, ill-educated, unemployed, unemployable and unable to afford television sets, radios and even newspapers, for those who are able to read, are uninformed and in any event not attuned to the niceties of democratic constitutions and governance. Who would be interested in such ethereal things if every day is a grind to find something to eat? When is the government's gross dereliction of duty towards these unfortunate masses going to explode in their faces, or are we in for another Big Man of Africa phenomenon that won't need popular support?

Such speculation is not immediately pertinent, but is not fanciful either. Don't ridicule such a dark prognosis: witness the heartfelt brotherly support of the ANC and the government for the ZANU-PF and Zimbabwe's president Robert Mugabe to remain in government after already more than thirty disastrous years in power (*Sunday Times*, 11/12/2011). Hitler came to power in Germany by legitimate democratic means. Only after that did he manipulate the German constitution and psyche to enable his wantonly murderous regime. By ignoring history, and especially African political history, we are leaving ourselves vulnerable to having it repeated.

There is a very real possibility that the embedded corruption in so many parts of the body politic and national life may well have become irreversible. The president of the republic pays lip-service to the fight against corruption, but does little or nothing practical to root it out where it clearly exists. He himself remains under a cloud for evading prosecution by political manipulation on the same set of facts that saw Schabir Shaik sentenced to fifteen years in prison. This, together with clearly compromised people in top decision-making positions, menacingly also in the police, the National Prosecuting Authority and other security services, it is difficult to see how under the current regime the country will be able to rid itself of this virulent cancer. And with repeated pathetic legal advice and inappropriate appointments causing embarrassment to and even ridicule of the inept government, prospects do not seem great for the destructive and pervasive corruption to be arrested soon, if at all. I have never enjoyed either slapstick or surrealism; the combining of the two in the ANC government is pure torture to the soul.

But at the time of writing there are also some slight glimmers of hope. The increasing disillusionment and alienation of highly regarded former stalwarts of the liberation struggle and the influential protesting voices of some of them, the apparent emergence of a more effective parliamentary opposition and the rise of a new generation of better educated and more modernist youth, all hold some promise. The resistance of various organisations, parties and individuals, including most recently the Congress of South

African Trade Unions to some extent, to the so-called Secrecy Bill to stifle the media without an exonerating clause of public interest in the case of the publication of classified information, together with an increasingly activist civil society in general, are perhaps the most encouraging developments. The integrity and bravery of the public protector, Thuli Madonsela, and the head of the Asset Forfeiture Unit, Willie Hofmeyr (although now without the primary powers to fight corruption he had at the Special Investigating Unit), are also still beacons of hope. However, how long they will last, in view of the sad example of the fate that befell the Scorpions, remains to be seen.

But a reversal of the steady decline of South African democracy before even reaching maturity will not come under the present wielders of power. We are not yet a failed state, but are certainly teetering on the brink.

Epilogue

In the preface to this book I stated my uncertainty as to what motivated its writing. In the course of it, I came to the conclusion that my overriding motivation was a wish to tell my children more about me and my doings, and to leave them something to remember me by. However, had this been my only motive I would have addressed them in Afrikaans and not English. But I also wanted to convey something of my Afrikaner and Afrikaans sentiments and thought processes to English-speakers who don't have access to the remarkable language that uniquely carries the name of our continent. It is a matter of sad regret to me that so few of my English-speaking compatriots do.

My respect for my children has led me to perhaps be more honest herein than I should have been. I have, since their early childhood, tried not to lie to them, but suspect I may have under the usual pretext of the self-serving white lie, as well as by omission, when I thought that the truth might hurt them too much or be inappropriate for other reasons, such as my own short-comings. I deeply regret the trauma I caused them by leaving their mother, but can only hope that our becoming happily reconciled in later years will soothe their pain somewhat. I have enormous gratitude and admiration for their mother, Anna, who irreproachably cared for them into adulthood, through sometimes adverse circumstances and frequently alone due to my numerous absences from home. I am sorry for often not being there when they needed me.

Children are our joy and our sorrow, the bearers of our hopes and aspirations and fears for their well-being, the objects of our sometimes smothering love and egotistical expectations, and the bearers of the often frightful burden of our own ageing and dying. Children rescue us from our own self-centred little worlds to refreshingly draw us into theirs. Above all, they are our perpetuation into the future. I am confident that all four of mine have enriched and are enriching the world through their very presence in it. I no longer presume to advise them on life's challenges for fear they may follow such advice. I simply love and enjoy them and my grandsons unreservedly, and bask in their so generous loving and caring. They certainly are what have made my journey worthwhile.

I have had a fulfilling life. I have experienced and done both good and bad, some of which I had thrust upon me, but some of my own volition. I am proud of much, particularly my service to my country; I am ashamed of much, in particular the hurt and disappointment I have sometimes brought to people close to me. There are certainly things I could have done differently, but I also find pride in things I have done that I think served the good rather than the bad. I am disappointed in myself for not making better use of what life presented me by way of talent and opportunity. But I am at realistic peace with myself and regard my experience of what life has given me as just that: life.

I am now terminally ill and quite sanguine at the prospect. I long ago, through some salutary experiences, lost my fear of that 'undiscovered country from whose bourn no traveller returns', which the Bard had his tortured Prince of Denmark agonise over. I don't fear the dreams that may come after I have shuffled off this mortal coil, because I don't expect any. I have never had my will puzzled at the prospect, or lost the name of action. I do not hanker for flights of angels to sing me to my rest, and accept that the rest will be silence. I have never been one of those people who expect to live forever, or, as lamented by Bette Midler, a soul so afraid of dying that I never learnt to live.

There is no tragedy in the dying of an old man, but there could well be in his living too long. I shun Dylan Thomas's exhortation to rage against the dying of the light, especially for his bad grammar on going 'gentle' into that good night. Death is, after all, the ironic fulfilment of life, about which we can do absolutely nothing but draw its sting by laughing at it and its attendant spook stories (no pun intended).

I never cease to be amazed at how we humans, as the supposed supremely rational creatures on earth, seem incapable of ridding ourselves of the shackle of that primordial animal instinct to preserve our lives at all costs, no matter how meaningless such a life has become, how much suffering it brings and how futile the yearning for the mythical eternal life is. I fervently hope that those I love who are to remain behind will take note, and not have their own lives soured by the passing of mine.

But, of course, neither my nor any other adequately lived ordinary life or its end should be as serious or important as may inadvertently be implied by the foregoing. At the time of writing, Fred Khumalo had a column in the *Sunday Times* subtitled 'Somewhat serious, somewhat fun', which is precisely what my life has been. I hope I got there in the telling of it.

Acronyms and Abbreviations

AB: Afrikaner Broederbond
AFU: Asset Forfeiture Unit
ANC: African National Congress
APLA: Azanian People's Liberation Army
ARMSCOR: Armaments Corporation of South Africa Ltd
AZAPO: Azanian People's Organisation
BGH: Beleidsgroep vir Hervorming
BOSS: Bureau for State Security
BSAP: British South Africa Police
CIA: Central Intelligence Agency, USA
CO: commanding officer
CDS: Constitutional Development Service
CODESA: Convention for a Democratic South Africa
COSAG: Concerned South Africans Group
CP: Conservative Party
CSI: Chief of Staff Intelligence
CSO: Chief of Staff Operations
DA: Democratic Alliance
DCC: Directorate Covert Collection
DFA: Department of Foreign Affairs
DG: director general
DGMI: Directorate General Military Intelligence
DMI: Directorate of Military Intelligence
DP: Democratic Party
DRC: Dutch Reformed Church
FAPLA: People's Armed Forces for the Liberation of Angola
FNLA: National Front for the Liberation of Angola
FRELIMO: Front for the Liberation of Mozambique
GNU: Government of National Unity
HQ: headquarters
IFP: Inkatha Freedom Party
JICC: Joint Intelligence Coordinating Committee
JSS: Joint Security Staff

MANCO: Management Committee
MI6: see SIS
MK: Umkhonto we Sizwe
MPLA: Popular Movement for the Liberation of Angola
MPNP: Multi-Party Negotiation Process
NATO: North Atlantic Treaty Organisation
NCF: National Consultative Forum
NG Kerk: Nederduitse Gereformeerde Kerk
NIA: National Intelligence Agency
NIS: National Intelligence Service
NMP: New Movement Process
NP: National Party
NPA: National Prosecuting Authority, National Peace Accord (in context)
NPC: National Peace Committee
NNP: New National Party
OCF: Overstrand Conservation Forum
PAC: Pan Africanist Congress of Azania
PANSALB: Pan South African Language Board
PLAN: People's Liberation Army of Namibia
RENAMO: Mozambican National Resistance
SAAF: South African Air Force
SACP: South African Communist Party
SADF: South African Defence Force
SAN: South African Navy
SAP: South African Police
SASS: South African Secret Service
SIGINT: signals intelligence
SIS: Secret Intelligence Service, UK (also: MI6)
SIU: Special Investigating Unit
SRC: students' representative council
SSC: State Security Council
SWAPO: South West Africa People's Organisation
SWATF: South West African Territorial Force
Soviet Union: Union of Soviet Socialist Republics (USSR)
TEC: Transitional Executive Council
TRC: Truth and Reconciliation Commission
Tukkies: University of Pretoria (also Tuks)
UDF: United Democratic Front

UDM: United Democratic Movement
UK: United Kingdom
UN: United Nations
UNISA: University of South Africa
UNITA: National Union for the Total Independence of Angola
UNTAG: UN Transitional Assistance Group
USA: United States of America
USSR: Soviet Union (Union of Soviet Socialist Republics)
WG5: Working Group 5
Wits: University of the Witwatersrand
ZANLA: Zimbabwe African National Liberation Army
ZANU: Zimbabwe African National Union party
ZAR: Zuid-Afrikaansche Republiek (Transvaal Republic)

Bibliography

Bragg, Melvyn. *The Adventure of English: The Biography of a Language.*
London: Hodder and Stoughton, 2004

Bryson, Bill. *The Mother Tongue: English and How It Got That Way.*
New York: William Morrow & Co., 1990

———. *Troublesome Words.* London: Penguin, 2002

Crocker, Chester A. *High Noon in Southern Africa: Making Peace in a Rough Neighborhood.* New York: W.W. Norton & Company, 1992

Engelenburg, F.V., and G.S. Preller. *Onze Krijgs-officieren: Portretten met Levens-schetsen der Tranvaalse Generaals en Kommandanten E.A.* Pretoria: Volkstem, 1904

Esterhuyse, Willie. *Endgame: Secret Talks and the End of Apartheid.* Cape Town: Tafelberg, 2012

Geldenhuys, Jannie. *Dié wat gewen het: Feite en fabels van die bosoorlog.* Pretoria: Litera Publikasies, 2007

Giliomee, Hermann. 'A deadly war of languages', Comment: *Mail & Guardian,* 8 October 2009

———. *The Rise and Possible Demise of Afrikaans as a Public Language.* PRAESA Occasional Papers No. 14. Cape Town: University of Cape Town, 2003

———, and Lawrence Schlemmer. *'n Vaste plek vir Afrikaans: Taaluitdagings op kampus.* Stellenbosch: Sun Press, 2006

Hamman, Hilton. *Days of the Generals.* Cape Town: Zebra Press, 2001

Heunis, Jan. *The Inner Circle: Recollections from the Last Days of White Rule.* Cape Town: Jonathan Ball, 2007

Malan, Magnus. *My Life with the SA Defence Force.* Pretoria: Protea Boekhuis, 2006

Mostert, Johan. *The National Intelligence Service and the transition to the post-1994 intelligence dispensation.* Pretoria: SANAI, 2008

Van Rensburg, F.I.J. (ed.). *Afrikaans, lewende taal van miljoene.* Pretoria: Van Schaik, 2004

Waldmeier, Patti. *Anatomy of a Miracle: The End of Apartheid and the Birth of the New South Africa.* London: Viking, 1997

Wilkens, Ivor, and Hans Strydom. *The Super-Afrikaners: Inside the Afrikaner Broederbond*. Johannesburg: Jonathan Ball, 1978

Wolfaardt, Pieter, Tom Wheeler and Werner Scholtz (comps). *From Verwoerd to Mandela. South African Diplomats Remember, Volume 3: Total Onslaught to Normalisation*. Johannesburg: Crink, 2010

Wolhuter, Harry. *Memories of a Game Ranger*. Author's own publication, 1953

Index